TM

References for the Rest of Us! ®

BESTSELLING BOOK SERIES

Are you intimidated and confused by compu~~ters~~ that traditional manuals are overloaded with ~~technical details~~ you'll never use? Do your friends and family always call you to fix simple problems on their PCs? Then the For Dummies® computer book series from Hungry Minds, Inc. is for you.

For Dummies books are written for those frustrated computer users who know they aren't really dumb but find that PC hardware, software, and indeed the unique vocabulary of computing make them feel helpless. For Dummies books use a lighthearted approach, a down-to-earth style, and even cartoons and humorous icons to dispel computer novices' fears and build their confidence. Lighthearted but not lightweight, these books are a perfect survival guide for anyone forced to use a computer.

> *"I like my copy so much I told friends; now they bought copies."*
> — *Irene C., Orwell, Ohio*

> *"Quick, concise, nontechnical, and humorous."*
> — *Jay A., Elburn, Illinois*

> *"Thanks, I needed this book. Now I can sleep at night."*
> — *Robin F., British Columbia, Canada*

Already, millions of satisfied readers agree. They have made For Dummies books the #1 introductory level computer book series and have written asking for more. So, if you're looking for the most fun and easy way to learn about computers, look to For Dummies books to give you a helping hand.

Hungry Minds™

1/01

XSLT
FOR
DUMMIES®

by Richard Wagner

Hungry Minds™

Best-Selling Books • Digital Downloads • e-Books • Answer Networks • e-Newsletters • Branded Web Sites • e-Learning

New York, NY ◆ Cleveland, OH ◆ Indianapolis, IN

XSLT For Dummies®

Published by
Hungry Minds, Inc.
909 Third Avenue
New York, NY 10022
www.hungryminds.com
www.dummies.com

Library of Congress Control Number: 2002100181

ISBN: 0-7645-3651-6

10 9 8 7 6 5 4 3 2 1

1O/RR/QT/QS/IN

Distributed in the United States by Hungry Minds, Inc.

Distributed by CDG Books Canada Inc. for Canada; by Transworld Publishers Limited in the United Kingdom; by IDG Norge Books for Norway; by IDG Sweden Books for Sweden; by IDG Books Australia Publishing Corporation Pty. Ltd. for Australia and New Zealand; by TransQuest Publishers Pte Ltd. for Singapore, Malaysia, Thailand, Indonesia, and Hong Kong; by Gotop Information Inc. for Taiwan; by ICG Muse, Inc. for Japan; by Intersoft for South Africa; by Eyrolles for France; by International Thomson Publishing for Germany, Austria and Switzerland; by Distribuidora Cuspide for Argentina; by LR International for Brazil; by Galileo Libros for Chile; by Ediciones ZETA S.C.R. Ltda. for Peru; by WS Computer Publishing Corporation, Inc., for the Philippines; by Contemporanea de Ediciones for Venezuela; by Express Computer Distributors for the Caribbean and West Indies; by Micronesia Media Distributor, Inc. for Micronesia; by Chips Computadoras S.A. de C.V. for Mexico; by Editorial Norma de Panama S.A. for Panama; by American Bookshops for Finland.

For general information on Hungry Minds' products and services please contact our Customer Care Department within the U.S. at 800-762-2974, outside the U.S. at 317-572-3993 or fax 317-572-4002.

For sales inquiries and reseller information, including discounts, premium and bulk quantity sales, and foreign-language translations, please contact our Customer Care Department at 800-434-3422, fax 317-572-4002, or write to Hungry Minds, Inc., Attn: Customer Care Department, 10475 Crosspoint Boulevard, Indianapolis, IN 46256.

For information on licensing foreign or domestic rights, please contact our Sub-Rights Customer Care Department at 212-884-5000.

For information on using Hungry Minds' products and services in the classroom or for ordering examination copies, please contact our Educational Sales Department at 800-434-2086 or fax 317-572-4005.

For press review copies, author interviews, or other publicity information, please contact our Public Relations Department at 317-572-3168 or fax 317-572-4168.

For authorization to photocopy items for corporate, personal, or educational use, please contact Copyright Clearance Center, 222 Rosewood Drive, Danvers, MA 01923, or fax 978-750-4470.

About the Author

Richard Wagner is vice president of Development Tools at Nombas, a JavaScript tools provider, and author of numerous books, including *JavaScript Unleashed*. He also invented and architected the award-winning NetObjects ScriptBuilder and served as editor for the XML-based ECMAScript Components standard. In his free time, he enjoys writing on his nontech Web site called digitalwalk.net (www.digitalwalk.net). Rich lives with his wife and three boys in Princeton, Massachusetts. He can be reached at rich@digitalwalk.net.

Dedication

To the intrepid J-boys — Jordan, Jared, and Justus. In all things, "to the hilt . . ."

Author's Acknowledgments

In writing this book, I was blessed with an unbeatable editorial team at Hungry Minds. My deepest thanks go to Christine Berman for her flawless management of this project from start to finish. Thanks to Becky Huehls for her keen editing eye and helpful suggestions, driving me to be clearer and more concise in my writing. Thanks also to Bob Dominy for his technical insights that made a strong impact on the book's overall quality and coverage. I talk about the X-Team in this book, but I'd say the book's X-Factor is Christine, Becky, and Bob. For without them, *XSLT For Dummies* would have been far less of a book.

I'd also like to express thanks to Steven Hayes at Hungry Minds for his involvement early on in the project, as well as thank my agent, Chris Van Buren.

Finally, I'd like to express earnest gratitude to my wife, Kimberly, and our three boys, the J-team, for their patience and grace throughout the entire project.

Publisher's Acknowledgments

We're proud of this book; please send us your comments through our Hungry Minds Online Registration Form located at www.dummies.com.

Some of the people who helped bring this book to market include the following:

Acquisitions, Editorial, and Media Development

Associate Project Editor: Christine Berman

Senior Acquisitions Editor: Steve Hayes

Copy Editor: Rebecca Huehls

Technical Editor: Robert Dominy

Editorial Manager: Leah Cameron

Media Development Manager: Laura VanWinkle

Media Development Supervisor: Richard Graves

Editorial Assistant: Amanda Foxworth

Production

Project Coordinator: Maridee Ennis

Layout and Graphics: Jackie Nicholas, Barry Offringa, Heather Pope, Jacque Schneider, Betty Schulte, Mary J. Virgin, Erin Zeltner

Proofreaders: John Greenough, Andy Hollandbeck, Susan Moritz, Angel Perez, TECHBOOKS Production Services

Indexer: TECHBOOKS Production Services

General and Administrative

Hungry Minds Technology Publishing Group: Richard Swadley, Vice President and Executive Group Publisher; Bob Ipsen, Vice President and Group Publisher; Joseph Wikert, Vice President and Publisher; Barry Pruett, Vice President and Publisher; Mary Bednarek, Editorial Director; Mary C. Corder, Editorial Director; Andy Cummings, Editorial Director

Hungry Minds Manufacturing: Ivor Parker, Vice President, Manufacturing

Hungry Minds Marketing: John Helmus, Assistant Vice President, Director of Marketing

Hungry Minds Production for Branded Press: Debbie Stailey, Production Director

Hungry Minds Sales: Michael Violano, Vice President, International Sales and Sub Rights

Contents at a Glance

Cartoons at a Glance

By Rich Tennant

page 211

page 119

page 29

page 293

page 5

Cartoon Information:
Fax: 978-546-7747
E-Mail: richtennant@the5thwave.com
World Wide Web: www.the5thwave.com

Table of Contents

Introduction

· ·

*E*veryone seems to be talking about Extensible Markup Language (XML) these days. You know how mothers are — I can't even visit my relatives over the holidays without my mom broaching the topic of XML at Thanksgiving dinner. Yes, XML has become quite a buzzword, but Extensible Stylesheet Language Transformations (XSLT) is the power that takes all this XML and turns it into something useful and flexible.

XSLT is a language used to transform XML documents into something new. It can take one XML document and output that document's information into a completely different structure or turn XML into an HTML document for viewing on the Web. XSLT isn't a general-purpose programming language, such as Java or Visual Basic; its focus is solely on transforming XML.

Before I get any farther along, I have to point out the "elephant in the room" — XSLT's long-winded name. Who came up with that name anyway? I think the people responsible should be forced to say, "Extensible Stylesheet Language Transformations," aloud ten times and hope their tongues don't fall off! XSLT's full name may be a mouthful, but this book carves up each piece of XSLT into manageable, chewable morsels.

XSLT can be confusing if you don't have a solid understanding of its syntax, quirky abbreviations, and the esoteric terminology it sometimes uses. But *XSLT For Dummies* can help you write XSLT stylesheets and, just as important, grasp why and how transformations work. In addition, see www.dummies.com/extras/xsltfd for code examples as well as a helpful editing tool of my own creation which I call the X-Factor.

Above all, you can use *XSLT For Dummies* as your guide for quickly developing the know-how of XSLT — without drowning in technical gobbledygook.

What I Assume About You

XSLT For Dummies starts from the bottom and works its way up: It doesn't assume that you have any previous knowledge of XSLT or XML. If you have some know-how of HTML or programming, I think you can grasp some of the concepts of XSLT quicker than a beginner, but I don't expect you to know HTML or anything about programming beforehand.

How This Book Is Organized

My aim is to help you find out how to become productive with XSLT quickly so that you can transform XML documents into virtually any kind of output imaginable. With that goal in mind, *XSLT For Dummies* is divided into five parts, each of which builds upon the previous ones.

Part I: Getting Started with XSLT

Part I kicks off your journey. You start by finding out about the core concepts of XSLT and how it fits in with HTML and all the other X technologies out there, such as XML, XSL, and XPath. You get your feet wet by writing your first XSLT stylesheet and transforming an XML document.

After you finish that, you can say *XSLT* to your buddies at work and actually have a grasp of what you're talking about when you throw around those X terms.

Part II: Becoming an XSLT Transformer

This part takes you into the belly of the beast: stylesheets, template rules, and XPath expressions. But don't worry — you won't lose your appetite. You begin by looking at stylesheets and find out, in everyday terms, the often-confusing subject of document trees and recursion. From there, you start pulling information out of XML documents and outputting it into various forms.

By the time you're done with this part, you'll be able to say, "Extensible Stylesheet Language Transformations," without stumbling over any of the twelve syllables.

Part III: Prime Time XSLT

In this part, you dive deeper into the thick of things. You find out how XSLT handles programming concepts such as if/then statements, loops, and variables, and how to include them in stylesheets. Don't worry if you've never programmed before; these concepts become clear as you read through the chapters. You also find out about how to take advantage of the more advanced capabilities of XSLT and XPath to create more powerful transformations.

I predict that after you finish this part, at least once you'll have unintentionally ordered an XSLT sandwich on rye at your local deli.

Part IV: eXtreme XSLT

As you read through Part IV, you can begin to call yourself a bona fide XSLT Transformer. You find out how to create effective XSLT stylesheets and apply them under various conditions. You find out about how to combine stylesheets and even add your own extensions. You also get the inside scoop on debugging transformations.

A word of warning: By now, all this XSLT will be swimming around in your head. You may find yourself mingling at a social event and leading with the line: "Apply any good templates lately?"

Part V: The Part Of Tens

In this part, I guide you through some practical tips and information that can make your life easier when you work with XSLT. I start out by demystifying the ten most confusing things about XSLT. Then I detail what I consider to be the ten best XSLT resources on the Web. I conclude by giving you the details on ten XSLT processors that you can download online.

Conventions Used in This Book

Snippets of XSLT code are scattered throughout the book and are often used to introduce you to a feature of the markup language. They appear in the chapters like this:

```
<xsl:stylesheet
        xmlns:xsl="http://www.w3.org/1999/XSL/Transform"
        version="1.0">
  <xsl:template match="id">
     <h1><xsl:apply-templates/></h1>
  </xsl:template>

</xsl:stylesheet>
```

If you type these stylesheets by hand, pay close attention and type the text exactly as shown to ensure that the stylesheet transforms properly. Generally, spaces don't matter much, although depending on where they are, they could change the look of the output from a transformation. However, case sensitivity is important for any XML or XSLT element. I use lowercase text in all the examples, so I recommend getting used to typing lowercase to avoid confusion or problems down the line.

If XSLT element names or instructions appear within the regular text, they look like this.

Icons Used in This Book

Tips draw attention to key points that can save you time and effort.

Pay close attention to this icon; it highlights something that's important to your understanding of XSLT or how to use it.

Heed the Warning icon because it can save you from the pitfalls of XSLT pain and agony.

Technical Stuff is the techno-mumbo-jumbo that's interesting but probably only for geeks. So, reading these sections can provide useful information, but feel free to skip them.

Part I
Getting Started with XSLT

The 5th Wave   By Rich Tennant

"Oh yeah, and try not to enter the wrong function."

In this part . . .

You watched the *X-Files* and then you saw *X-Men* on the big screen, but these were only warm-ups for the real deal — the X-Team. In this part, you find out all about the X-Team members, including XML, XSL, XSLT, and XPath, and how they work together. You also get your feet wet by transforming your first XML document using XSLT.

Chapter 1

Introducing the X-Team

· ·

· ·

*A*s a sports fan, I enjoy watching all kinds of team sports, whether football, basketball, baseball, or an Olympic team competition. I've noticed that regardless of the sport, great teams have two things in common. First, they have very talented individuals on them. Second, they function well as a team; I find hardly anything more thrilling in sports than seeing a squad of talented athletes working together cohesively. (Of course, it goes without saying that the *most* exciting part of sports is the "I'm going to Disneyworld" commercials!)

Although this book focuses on eXtensible Stylesheet Language Transformations, or XSLT, you'll quickly discover that XSLT is an important component of a closely related set of technologies that I affectionately call the X-Team. This "Dream X-Team" consists of: XML, XSL, XSLT, and XPath. (For the techies out there, that's shorthand for eXtensible Markup Language, eXtensible Stylesheet Language, XSL Transformations, and XML Path Language.) Each of these technologies is powerful, but each gets its true strength through interrelationships. So, although I concentrate much of the attention in this book on XSLT, never think of it as something independent of its teammates.

As you start your XSLT journey, I begin by introducing you to the X-Team members, each of which has a separate but intertwined responsibility.

XML: Storing Your Data

The original member of the X-Team is eXtensible Markup Language (XML), the granddaddy of them all. All other X-Team members are designed to work with or act upon XML. A relatively recent innovation, XML was conceived primarily by Jon Bosak as a way to make working with information delivered over the Web easier. Then in 1998, XML was standardized by the World Wide Web Consortium (W3C), the international standards body for the Web.

Since its beginnings, the Web has used HyperText Markup Language (HTML) to display content. HTML documents are stored on Web servers and then sent on demand to a Web browser, such as Microsoft Internet Explorer or Netscape Navigator. The browser then displays the HTML as a Web page. Figure 1-1 illustrates this process.

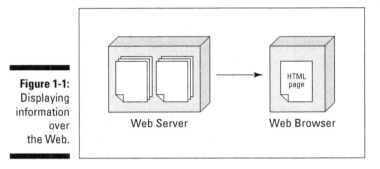

Figure 1-1:
Displaying
information
over
the Web.

HTML comes up short

HTML has become so wildly popular largely because it's very easy to learn and work with; heck, even my 7-year-old can create a Web page using Microsoft FrontPage, and my 9-year-old can write HTML by hand. The markup language was originally designed purely as a way to format and lay out information. However, because people have wanted to use the Web for nearly every task under the sun, HTML has been forced to do far more than was ever intended.

Consider a familiar scenario: A company wants to put information stored in a database onto its Web site. A sampling of its data might look something like Table 1-1.

Table 1-1		Sample Customer Database		
ID	**Name**	**City**	**State**	**Zip**
100	Ray Kinsella	Anderson	IN	46011
101	Rick Blaine	Manchester	NH	02522

To present this information on the Web, these database records must be converted into HTML text and formatted properly as a table so that they can be viewed in a Web browser.

```
<table border="1">
  <tr>
    <th>ID</th>
    <th>Name</th>
    <th>City</th>
    <th>St</th>
    <th>Zip</th>
  </tr>
  <tr>
    <td>100</td>
    <td>Ray Kinsella</td>
    <td>Anderson</td>
    <td>IN</td>
    <td>46011</td>
  </tr>
  <tr>
    <td>101</td>
    <td>Rick Blaine</td>
    <td>Manchester</td>
    <td>NH</td>
    <td>02522</td>
  </tr>
</table>
```

Look closely at the above code to see how HTML falls short. I turn meaningful clusters of information into a format that looks good in a browser but isn't useful for much else. In a database, related fields such as ID, Name, and Address make up a customer record, but after they have been converted to HTML, they're just row and column formatting instructions and their contents — thus, the concept of a *customer* is gone.

Such a solution would be acceptable if you only want to display information in a Web browser, but many people are discovering needs that go far beyond that. For example, searching for information within an HTML document is very limited. How would I be able to retrieve from my HTML file the names of all of my customers from Indiana who spend over $1,000 annually? That kind of query is far beyond the scope of HTML. And, even if I were to develop some convoluted way to get this information through JavaScript, I'd have to throw all that away if I ever wanted to move my information to another non-HTML environment, such as a Java application, Windows program, or even a cellular phone.

Think of HTML as a sort of information blender: Add a dash of data and a pinch of formatting instructions into the pitcher, turn the power on high, and out comes a pureed mixture of the two. Like creating a milkshake by mixing ice cream, chocolate syrup, vanilla, and milk in a blender, imagine the impossibility of trying to extract the vanilla from the milkshake after it's been blended. This no-win backward mobility is the futile attempt to mine useful information from HTML documents.

In other words: Yes, the shake tastes great, but don't try to use the raw materials again for a different purpose.

XML to the rescue

Developed as a response to the information-blender effect of HTML, XML is simply a practical way to work with structured information on the Web. The motivation of its inventors was to assemble structured data into something that was similar to HTML — so that data could be easily readable by people like you and me — but different enough from HTML so that it's freely expandable to effectively describe the data that it contains.

Whether you realize it or not, almost all the information used on the Web has a natural structure or organization to it and thus can be expressed using XML. Some everyday examples include:

✓ **The contents of a letter**

```
<letter>
  <date>March 31, 2002</date>
  <salutation>Dear Sir:</salutation>
  <text>Thanks for your recent article on Swiss Cheese
        chips.
  However, I don't think you gave enough credit to the
        farmer
  who invented the Swiss Cheese chip - Charley
        Cowley.</text>
  <closing>Warm Regards,</closing>
  <signature>Mrs. Charlie Cowley</signature>
</letter>
```

✓ **Dialogue from a movie**

```
        <dialogue>
  <rick>I'm saying it because it's true. Inside of us, we
        both know you belong with Victor. You're part of
        his work, the thing that keeps him going. If that
        plane leaves the ground and you're not with him,
        you'll regret it. Maybe not today. Maybe not
        tomorrow, but soon and for the rest of your
        life.</rick>
  <ilsa>But what about us?</ilsa>
  <rick>We'll always have Paris. We didn't have, we, we
        lost it until you came to Casablanca. We got it
        back last night.</rick>
```

```
<ilsa>When I said I would never leave you.</ilsa>
<rick> And you never will. But I've got a job to do,
       too. Where I'm going, you can't follow. What I've
       got to do, you can't be any part of. Ilsa, I'm no
       good at being noble, but it doesn't take much to
       see that the problems of three little people
       don't amount to a hill of beans in this crazy
       world. Someday you'll understand that. Now,
       now... Here's looking at you kid.</rick>
</dialogue>
```

✔ **Those customer records of Ray and Rick**

```
<customers>
  <customer>
    <id>100</id>
    <name>Ray Kinsella</name>
    <city>Anderson</city>
    <state>IN</state>
    <zip>46011</zip>
  </customer>
  <customer>
    <id>101</id>
    <name>Rick Blaine</name>
    <city>Manchester</city>
    <state>NH</state>
    <zip>02522</zip>
  </customer>
</customers>
```

✔ **A Web page**

```
<html>
  <head>
    <title>My Home Page</title>
  </head>
  <body>
    <h1>Heading</h1>
  </body>
</html>
```

From these examples, you can see that XML describes information in a very logical and straightforward manner. Put descriptive tags before and after the text values and you've just about got an XML document. XML isn't rocket science!

HTML is standardized with a fixed set of formatting tags or *elements* to define different parts of a document. An <h1> element identifies a Level 1 Header, and <b> denotes bolded text. In contrast, the only thing standardized about XML is its syntax rules, not its actual tags; this is what makes XML so flexible. For example, a bank can define a set of XML tags to describe its financial data:

```
<account id="10001010">
  <type>Checking</type>
  <rating level="-5"/>
  <customer preferred="no way, hosea">
    <firstname>John</firstname>
    <lastname>Charles</lastname>
    <address>123 Main Street</address>
    <city>Fremont</city>
    <state>CA</state>
    <zip>94425</zip>
  </customer>
</account>
```

Or, a pizza store chain can come up with its own set of XML elements that describes their pizzas.

```
<pizza>
  <size value="Mega"/>
  <crust type="Thick and Chewy"/>
  <toppings>Olives, Sausage, Pepperoni, Lima Beans</toppings>
  <cookingtime>30</cookingtime>
</pizza>
```

A set of defined XML tags used for a particular purpose is an *XML vocabulary*.

However, as great as it is at organizing information, XML by its very nature is a raw material. XML is of little use by itself and needs help from its X-Team teammates to actually make its information usable in the real world.

XSL: Presenting XML Data

Time to pass the baton to the second member of the X-Team: Extensible Stylesheet Language (XSL). XSL is charged with styling or laying out XML documents into a form that makes sense to its intended audience. As shown in Figure 1-2, you use XSL to define a set of formatting rules that are referred to when an XML document is processed.

For example, if I want to format the letter from the preceding "XML to the rescue" section, I use XSL to create a few rules, such as

✔ **When a** `<date>` **element is found, italicize the date's text.**

✔ **When a** `<salutation>` **element is found, indent salutation's text.**

✔ **When a** `<closing>` **element is found, add an extra line after it.**

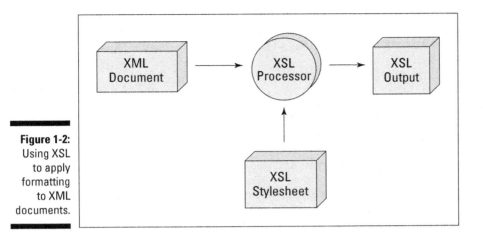

XSL rules like these are contained in an *XSL Stylesheet*, which is just a plain text file filled with formatting instructions that look like the following example.

```
<fo:page-sequence master-name="easy">
     <fo:flow flow-name="xsl-region-body">
          <fo:block font-family="Serif">Serif
     font</fo:block>
     </fo:flow>
</fo:page-sequence>
```

Note that this XSL is written in something that resembles XML. That is more than mere coincidence because, ironically, XSL is actually written in XML and is itself an XML vocabulary.

If your head is spinning around, hang on. XSL is used to format XML, which in turn is used as the language for defining XSL. The circular logic can be confusing, but fortunately, you don't need to worry about the particulars of how that all works — just know that it does. Actually, the fact that XSL uses XML to describe its instructions makes it far easier to learn than trying to grasp yet another language syntax.

When XSL was conceived by the W3C, the original intention of XSL was simply to provide a way to format XML data. However, after people began to use XML in the real world, it was discovered that something more was needed besides assigning font colors and margin indentions to the content. True, developers needed to be able to style XML in a way that was easily readable, but they also discovered a need to change an XML document from one XML structure to another, as well as to have the ability to easily convert

XML into HTML and other output options. Taking up this charge, the W3C expanded the scope of XSL to support transforming, and in doing so, gave birth to XSL Transformations (XSLT).

XSLT: Transforming Your XML Data

The third member of the X-Team is XSL Transformations (XSLT). XSLT is analogous to that high-priced rookie on a professional sports team that unseats the veteran player: XSL was supposed to be the killer technology to enable XML to achieve widespread adoption, but XSLT's ability to convert XML data into any wanted output has proven so compelling that it essentially swallowed up XSL. In fact, when people today talk about XSL, they're almost always referring to XSLT.

XSL is actually composed of two independent parts: XSLT for transforming XML from one structure to another; and XSL Formatting Objects and Formatting Properties for formatting XML documents.

The key reason for all this enthusiasm in support of XSLT is that XML documents often need to serve multiple audiences. The XML needs to be formatted so that it can be viewed in a Web browser, and the same XML may need to be tweaked to conform to a new trading partner's own XML structure. See Figure 1-3 for an illustration of this relationship.

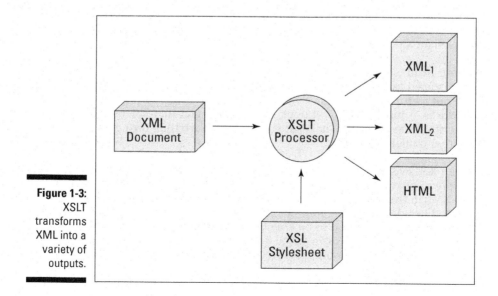

Figure 1-3:
XSLT
transforms
XML into a
variety of
outputs.

To illustrate, suppose that I want to change the XML definition of a customer from the original format of

```
<customer>
<id>101</id>
<name>Rick Blaine</name>
<city>Manchester</city>
<state>NH</state>
<zip>02522</zip>
</customer>
```

into this:

```
<customer id="101">
<fullname>Rick Blaine</fullname>
<address city="Manchester" state="NH"
zipcode="02522"/>
</customer>
```

Before XSLT came along, I'd have to dust off my programming software, bury myself in a cave for a day, and write a program to do this migration process. However, with XSLT, I can transform the data from one XML format to another nearly instantly, with no true programming required.

XSLT is not a programming language as such. In fact, when written out, it doesn't even look anything like C++, Java, or Visual Basic. Like its XSL parent, XSLT rules and templates are defined by using XML.

Most programming languages transform data structures through blood, sweat, and tears. In contrast, XSLT does this work in what can best be described as *transforming by example* — you provide an example of what kind of information you'd like to see, and XSLT does the rest. For example, the following XSLT snippet changes the name element to fullname in the output document.

```
<xsl:template match="name">
  <fullname>
  <xsl:apply-templates/>
  </fullname>
</xsl:template>
```

(I get into the specifics of how XSLT template rules work in Chapter 4.)

However, as powerful as XSLT is, it needs help to do its transformational magic from our last X-Team member: XPath. XPath specializes in picking out the specific nuggets of information from one XML document in order for XSLT to fit it neatly into another one.

XPath: Seeking Out Your Data

XPath is the spy or seeker of the X-Team who is charged with going into an XML document and picking out the requested information for XSLT. Without the ability to precisely locate information in an XML document, the ability to transform or do anything special with XML is minimal.

Any XSLT transformation must be set up to answer two questions:

✔ **Input:** What information from the original XML document do you want?

✔ **Output:** How would you like that information structured in the output document?

XSLT relies on XPath to answer the first question, as shown in Figure 1-4.

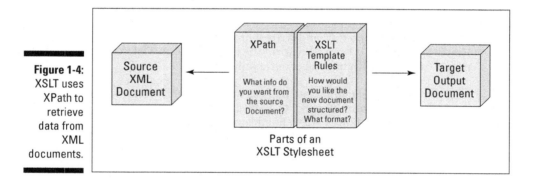

Figure 1-4: XSLT uses XPath to retrieve data from XML documents.

XSLT looks at an XML document element by element, so XPath expressions are used to tell what your XSLT stylesheet should look for as it goes through the XML document. Looking closer at the preceding XSLT example, the XPath expression `name` tells XSLT what information to look for, which in this case is to look for all `name` elements.

```
<xsl:template match="name">
  <fullname>
  <xsl:apply-templates/>
  </fullname>
</xsl:template>
```

This XPath expression is intuitive and easy to understand, but for more hearty needs, the syntax can be quite arcane and challenging. (I discuss XPath in detail in Chapter 5.)

Interestingly, much of the effort required to develop XSLT stylesheets is related to the input side of the equation, so throughout this book, I spend a sizeable amount of time on how to use XPath.

The X-Team through HTML Eyes

You may be approaching the X-Team after having already worked with HTML. If so, when you look at XML and XSLT, it's natural to view these new technologies through HTML eyes. Having a knowledge of HTML definitely gives you a head start in learning XML syntax; noting the similarities and differences between them is important.

Although I compare HTML and XML in this section, remember that XSL and XSLT stylesheets are both written using XML, so the same rules apply to them as to XML.

XML looks a lot like HTML . . .

If you can read HTML, you quickly see that XML looks an awful lot like HTML in terms of its syntax. For example, a document title in HTML is defined as

```
<title>My Document Title</title>
```

Like HTML, the element is the primary building block of XML. Therefore, a book title in XML might be defined to look something like this:

```
<book>War and Peace</book>
```

Additionally, XML follows HTML in using name-value pairs inside elements to provide additional descriptive information about an element.

```
<invoice id="110">
  <company>Polar Salsa Corporation</company>
</invoice>
```

In this XML snippet, the id attribute provides additional information related to the invoice element.

But XML isn't the same as HTML . . .

HTML and XML have a definite likeness, but you should watch out for some significant variations in syntax rules. The three most important are as follows.

XML is well-formed

HTML has always been lenient in some of its syntax requirements, not always forcing you to have closing tags on some of the elements, such as the paragraph (<p>) element. For example, both of the following lines are valid HTML:

```
<p>Hello. My name is Inigo Montoya. You killed my father.
          Prepare to die.
```

and

```
<p>Hello. My name is Inigo Montoya. You killed my father.
          Prepare to die.</p>
```

In contrast, XML is much more rigid: All XML documents must be *well-formed*, meaning that every begin tag needs to have a matching end tag:

```
<president>Andrew Jackson</president>
```

XML allows shortcuts

Although XML requires any element to have a start and end tag pair, it does allow you to combine the two tags if the element is *empty,* meaning that no text is provided between the start and end tags. For example, the following two lines are equivalent.

```
<device id="3838-2020"></device>
```

and

```
<device id="3838-2020"/>
```

XML is case sensitive

HTML is case insensitive, so long as you spell out the tag syntax correctly, the document is processed appropriately. Each of the following are valid HTML statements.

```
<body bgcolor="#FFFFFF"></body>
<BODY BGCOLOR="#FFFFFF"></BODY>
<Body Bgcolor="#FFFFFF"></Body>
```

On the other hand, XML is case sensitive, so the following statements aren't considered equal.

```
<quote>Get used to disappointment.</quote>
<QUOTE>Get used to disappointment.</QUOTE>
```

To avoid confusion, you should consistently use either all lower- or uppercase characters for the XML, XSL, and XSLT documents that you create. However, I recommend consistently using lowercase characters because this is the convention that nearly everyone follows.

Chapter 2

Writing Your First XSLT Stylesheet

* *

In This Chapter

▶ Preparing your XSLT working environment

▶ Creating a simple XML document

▶ Writing an XSLT stylesheet

▶ Running an XSLT processor

▶ Creating a result tree

* *

Grasping XSLT is kind of like putting together a jigsaw puzzle. Even my 7-year-old knows that the best way to approach a puzzle is to first connect all the pieces of the outer border and then work your way inside, eventually filling in all the missing spaces.

In a sense, this book follows that same pattern. Chapter 1 defines the "conceptual" edges of the XSLT puzzle by talking about the cast of characters, the X-team. This chapter fills in the remaining edge pieces as it deals with the "mechanics" of XSLT — the materials you need and the process you follow for doing transformations. After you finish this chapter, the puzzle edge will all be connected; the rest of the book then focuses on filling in all that's left of this jigsaw puzzle.

Preparing Your XSLT Working Environment

Every craftsman needs tools to perform his or her job adequately, and as a new XSL transformer, you are no exception. You need two primary software programs to add to your tool belt — a text editor and an XSLT processor.

Some software tools actually combine the capabilities of the text editor and XSLT processor within a single application. X-Factor, a tool I describe in the next section, is such an example.

Text editor

XML and XSLT documents are ordinary text files, so finding software that allows you to create and edit them is a breeze. You simply need a text editor. If you are Windows user, you can use Notepad. Or if you already have a favorite editor, then feel free to use it.

However, to help make the task of learning XSLT easier, I recommend you start by using X-Factor as your editor. X-Factor is an easy-to-use software program specifically designed to be a learning tool for XSLT. The application enables you to open up your XML source and XSLT stylesheet at the same time, perform transformations with the click of a button, and view the results of the transformation inside the application window (see Figure 2-1).

X-Factor is available as a free download from the *XSLT For Dummies* Web site at `www.dummies.com/extras/xsltfd` or from Nombas, Inc. at `www.nombas.com`. To set up X-Factor, download the setup file from either of the preceding locations and run setup.exe on your computer. The X-Factor setup program guides you through the installation process.

XSLT processor

The second piece of software that you need for transformations is an XSLT processor. This essential component takes the source XML document, looks at the rules you have set up in your stylesheet, performs the transformation, and outputs the results to a new file.

An XSLT processor is quite different than a text editor, such as Notepad. It usually has no real user interface or window to work with. Instead, most are command-line tools — things you'd work with only inside a command prompt window (you know, the DOS-like window that takes you back to the 1980s). In Chapter 20, I list ten XSLT processors you can download from the Web. Although you can feel free to use any of those to transform stylesheets, if you use X-Factor, the Instant SAXON processor is included with it, so you don't need to install or configure it.

An XSLT processor parallels the engine of an automobile. When you drive a car, you're aware that the engine is there, but it's usually hidden from view under the hood. You interact with the engine, but minimally. You don't say much more than "speed up" or "slow down." In the same way, if you work with an XSLT processor directly, you give an XSLT processor the names of your XML document and XSLT stylesheet to process and tell it where you want to put the results, and it does the rest. However, if you use X-Factor, it manages the processor for you so you never have to call the processor directly.

```
X-Factor                                                    _ □ ×
File Edit Help

         XML                xsi  XSLT Stylesheet
      XML Source       <xsl:stylesheet xmlns:xsl="http://www.w3.org/1999/XSL/Transform" versi

         XSL           <!-- Template rule to convert child elements to attributes -->
                       <xsl:template match="score">
     XSLT Stylesheet       <score id="{@id}" film="{film}" composer="{composer}" releasedate="{
                           <xsl:apply-templates/>
                       </xsl:template>

       Results         <!-- Remove child elements from appearing as usual in the result docum
                       <xsl:template match="grade"></xsl:template>
                       <xsl:template match="film"></xsl:template>
                       <xsl:template match="year"></xsl:template>
                       <xsl:template match="composer"></xsl:template>

                       <!-- Maintain the scores element -->
                       <xsl:template match="scores">
                          <scores>
                          <xsl:apply-templates/>
                          </scores>
                       </xsl:template>

     Transform ▷
                       </xsl:stylesheet>
```

Figure 2-1:
You can use
X-Factor to
edit XSLT
stylesheets.

Many XSLT commercial-grade software tools are available that provide more functionality than X-Factor. Visit the Web sites discussed in Chapter 19 to find out more about these enhanced tools.

Creating a Simple XML Document

An XSLT stylesheet never acts alone. It's always applied to an XML document. So your first step in beginning XSL transformations is to create a simple XML document you can use as a sample.

Start out by creating a working folder on your computer into which you can put in documents and stylesheets you create or download from the *XSLT For Dummies* Web site. I recommend creating a new folder called *xslt* on your root C: drive (c:\xslt), although feel free to place it anywhere convenient.

To create an XML document, open X-Factor and choose New XML Source File from the File menu. Enter the following code in the XML editor window:

```
<?xml version="1.0" encoding="UTF-16"?>

<scores>

  <score id="1">
    <film>A Little Princess</film>
```

```
      <composer>Patrick Doyle</composer>
      <year>1995</year>
      <grade>100</grade>
   </score>

   <score id="2">
      <film>Chocolat</film>
      <composer>Rachel Portman</composer>
      <year>2001</year>
      <grade>90</grade>
   </score>

   <score id="3">
      <film>Vertigo</film>
      <composer>Bernard Herrmann</composer>
      <year>1956</year>
      <grade>95</grade>
   </score>

   <score id="4">
      <film>Field of Dreams</film>
      <composer>James Horner</composer>
      <year>1989</year>
      <grade>96</grade>
   </score>

   <score id="5">
      <film>Dead Again</film>
      <composer>Patrick Doyle</composer>
      <year>1991</year>
      <grade>97</grade>
   </score>

</scores>
```

XML files use an .xml extension, so save the file as score.xml.

You can save time typing in the XML by downloading the score.xml file from the *XSLT For Dummies* Web site.

In this sample XML document, the first line contains what is called a *processor directive* <?xml version="1.0"?>. This is simply a statement telling an XML processor: "Hello, I am an XML file. Please process me."

The rest of the document contains the actual XML data. XML information is hierarchical: The outermost elements contain the elements that are inside of them. Therefore, the scores element contains five score elements in what is known as a *parent-child relationship*. (I discuss element relationships more in Chapter 3.)

Each score element has an attribute that provides an id value and has four child elements: film, composer, year, and grade.

Knowing the End Result

XSLT transforms XML documents into something new. But before you can write an XSLT stylesheet, you need to have a pretty good idea about what you want that something to look like. So, for this first example, suppose you need to create a new version of the scores.xml document that has three changes from the original:

✔ The children of each `score` element are turned into attributes.

✔ The `grade` element is removed.

✔ The `year` element is renamed `releasedate`.

Take the first element as an example:

```
<score id="1">
  <film>A Little Princess</film>
  <composer>Patrick Doyle</composer>
  <year>1995</year>
  <grade>100</grade>
</score>
```

With these changes applied, the new element looks like this:

```
<score id="1" film="A Little Princess" composer="Patrick
        Doyle" releasedate="1995"/>
```

All the preliminaries are now set. You created your source XML file. You know what the target document needs to look like. You are now ready to become a XSL transformer. Yippee!

Writing an XSLT Stylesheet

As you find out in Chapter 1, XSLT code is written inside an XSLT stylesheet. To create a new stylesheet, return to X-Factor and choose New XSLT Stylesheet from the File menu. Begin by entering:

```
<xsl:stylesheet xmlns:xsl="http://www.w3.org/1999/XSL/
        Transform" version="1.0">
```

Everything within an XSLT stylesheet is contained inside of an `xsl:stylesheet` element. Don't worry about the meaning of the `xmlns` attribute for now. Just type it in. You find out more about it in Chapter 3.

An XSLT stylesheet contains template rules that define what information from the original document goes into the new one and how that information is structured there.

Take a quick look at the XSLT code in this example to get a high-level overview of what XSLT is like. But don't get too bogged down by the particulars just yet. Heck, you have the rest of the book for that.

Your first template rule converts the score element's children into attributes:

```
<xsl:template match="score">
  <score id="{@id}" film="{film}" composer="{composer}"
         releasedate="{year}"></score>
  <xsl:apply-templates/>
</xsl:template>
```

This template rule tells the processor to look for each score element in the document and, when the processor encounters one, to replace the score element's original content with this new structure. The {@id} plugs in the value of the score element's id attribute. The {film}, {composer}, and {year} expressions fill in the value of the child element that matches the text inside the brackets.

Additional template rules are defined to remove original child elements from appearing in the result document:

```
<xsl:template match="grade"/>
<xsl:template match="film"/>
<xsl:template match="year"/>
<xsl:template match="composer"/>
```

Each of these template rules says: "Hey, Mr. Processor. I'll sit this one out. Just treat me as if I were not here." Adding these lines is important, because the processor automatically assumes that element values want to "go with the flow" and be included in the output — unless you specifically tell it *not* to include them. So, if you don't add these rules, the processor includes their content in the output document both as elements (their original form) and as attributes (the new form defined in the preceding score template rule).

The final section of the stylesheet is added to maintain scores as the parent of the score elements:

```
<xsl:template match="scores">
  <scores>
  <xsl:apply-templates/>
  </scores>
</xsl:template>
</xsl:stylesheet>
```

In this template rule, the apply-templates element tells the processor to include the contents of the scores element in the output. However, apply-templates doesn't include the tags of the element — only what's inside the tags. Therefore, I reapply the tags to the output document by placing apply-templates in between the scores start and end tags.

An end `xsl:stylesheet` tag is added at the bottom of the stylesheet:

```
</xsl:stylesheet>
```

Listing 2-1 shows the complete XSLT stylesheet.

Listing 2-1:   A Complete XSLT Stylesheet

```
<xsl:stylesheet
        xmlns:xsl="http://www.w3.org/1999/XSL/Transform"
        version="1.0">

<!-- Template rule to convert child elements to attributes --
        >
<xsl:template match="score">
  <score id="{@id}" film="{film}" composer="{composer}"
        releasedate="{year}"/>
  <xsl:apply-templates/>
</xsl:template>

<!-- Remove child elements from appearing as usual in the
        result document -->
<xsl:template match="grade"/>
<xsl:template match="film"/>
<xsl:template match="year"/>
<xsl:template match="composer"/>

<!-- Maintain the scores element -->
<xsl:template match="scores">
  <scores>
  <xsl:apply-templates/>
  </scores>
</xsl:template>
</xsl:stylesheet>
```

Type this code and save it as `score.xsl` in the same location as your `score.xml` file. By convention, an XSLT stylesheet has an extension of .xsl. Alternatively, you can save time and download the `score.xsl` file from the *XSLT For Dummies* Web site.

Processing the Stylesheet

You are now officially ready to transform your first XML document. Given this momentous occasion, I feel compelled to offer a sense of ceremony:

"Ladies and gentlemen, start your processors. Let the transforming begin!"

Ok, now that the formalities are over . . .

If you're using X-Factor, you can apply the XSLT stylesheet to the XML source document you created by clicking the Transform button. X-Factor kicks off the Instant SAXON processor behind-the-scenes to process the transformation.

Viewing the Results

After the transformation finishes in X-Factor, you have a brand spankin' new XML document that appears in the Results view, as shown in Figure 2-2.

In its raw XML form, this new file looks like the following XML snippet:

```
<scores>
<score id="1" film="A Little Princess" composer="Patrick
        Doyle" releasedate="1995"/>
<score id="2" film="Chocolat" composer="Rachel Portman"
        releasedate="2001"/>
<score id="3" film="Vertigo" composer="Bernard Herrmann"
        releasedate="1956"/>
<score id="4" film="Field of Dreams" composer="James
        Horner" releasedate="1989"/>
<score id="5" film="Dead Again" composer="Patrick Doyle"
        releasedate="1991"/>
</scores>
```

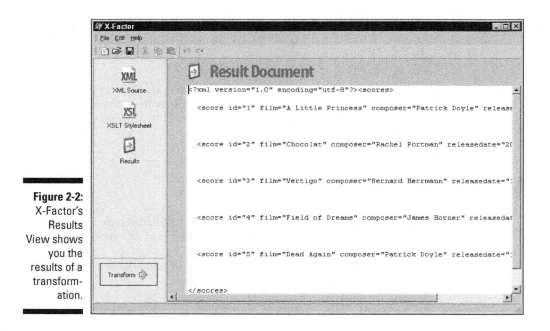

Figure 2-2:
X-Factor's
Results
View shows
you the
results of a
transform-
ation.

You see added spaces between the `score` elements in your file. Don't concern yourself with them; an XML or XSLT processor ignores these spaces. However, you can get rid of extra white space when you need to, which I discuss in more detail in Chapter 13.

In X-Factor, you can save the result document by choosing Save Result Document from the File menu. Because this is the second version of score.xml, call it score2.xml.

Interestingly, you can also view the score2.xml in Internet Explorer 5.5 or higher. Using its built-in XML processor, Internet Explorer displays the resulting XML in a tree-like manner.

Part II

Becoming an XSLT Transformer

The 5th Wave   By Rich Tennant

Hmm — Nice result tree.

In this part . . .

*I*t's time to roll up your sleeves and become an XSLT transformer. In this part, you find out all about three parts of the XSLT universe: the container (stylesheet), the basic building block (template rule), and the node selector (match pattern).

Chapter 3

Transforming with Style (Stylesheets, That Is)

. . . .

. . . .

XSLT plays in a sandbox called a stylesheet, and you stay within that sandbox for the rest of this book. You could skip across this sandbox with childlike fervor, but that would be messy and get sand everywhere. I suggest taking off your shoes and taking one step (or building one part of your castle) at a time. This way, you can divide and conquer the three major areas of XSLT: stylesheets, template rules, and XPath patterns. And that step-by-step approach is exactly the goal of the next three chapters.

In this chapter, you start off by finding out about stylesheets and focusing on the major issues related to stylesheets as a whole.

Structure of a Stylesheet

An XSLT stylesheet has a well-defined structure. Perhaps the easiest way to make sense of this structure is to compare it to something you are familiar with already, such as an ordinary document.

A document is made up of one or more paragraphs. A paragraph is a division of a document that contains one or more sentences that express a unified thought. However, not all sentences in a well-crafted paragraph are created equal. Traditionally, the first sentence holds a unique responsibility to lead the rest of the sentences by introducing a new subject or idea. The rest of the paragraph then expands upon this idea.

When you look at an XSLT stylesheet, you'll find a comparable structure. At the top level is a *stylesheet*, which acts as the overall container for XSLT code, much like a document serves as a container for all the sentences inside it. Whereas a paragraph is the primary component of a document, a *template rule* is the basic building block of a stylesheet. And, like the first sentence in a paragraph, the *match pattern* defines where the template rule is going. Figure 3-1 highlights these layers of a stylesheet.

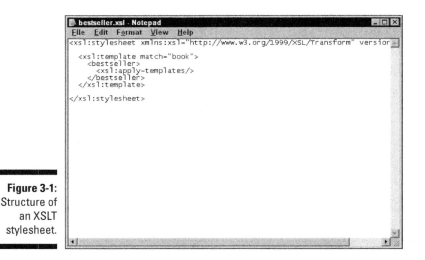

Figure 3-1:
Structure of
an XSLT
stylesheet.

Taking this analogy a step further, there are some elements in a document that aren't paragraphs per se. In a normal business letter, for example, the return address, date, greeting, and signature are all distinct, required elements but do not fit the definition of a paragraph. In the same way, an XSLT stylesheet has additional elements, such as `xsl:output`, that are valid to use but do not fit inside template rules.

Constructing Your XSLT Stylesheet

As you read in Chapter 1, an XSLT stylesheet is a well-formed XML document. By convention, it has an .xsl file extension.

xsl:stylesheet element

The `xsl:stylesheet` element serves as the topmost element (or document element) of an XSLT stylesheet. The shell of any XSLT stylesheet consists of:

```
<xsl:stylesheet
        xmlns:xsl="http://www.w3.org/1999/XSL/Transform"
        version="1.0">

<!-- XLST code goes here-->

</xsl:stylesheet>
```

As you can see in the preceding snippet, an `xsl:stylesheet` element must have two parts defined:

- ✔ **Namespace:** In the preceding code, the XSLT namespace is defined as `xmlns:xsl="http://www.w3.org/1999/XSL/Transform"` (Don't worry about what a namespace is just yet; you'll find out about namespaces later in this chapter.)
- ✔ **Version:** The `version` attribute defined providing the version of XSLT used, which is currently 1.0.

This information tells the XSLT processor how to process the stylesheet.

Alternatively, you can also use the `xsl:transform` element, which is synonymous to `xsl:stylesheet`:

```
<xsl:transform
        xmlns:xsl="http://www.w3.org/1999/XSL/Transform"
        version="1.0">

<!-- XLST code goes here-->

</xsl:transform>
```

Although both `xsl:stylesheet` and `xsl:transform` are valid, `xsl:stylesheet` is by far the most commonly used of the two elements. I use `xsl:stylesheet` throughout this book.

Top-level elements

An `xsl:stylesheet` element contains all the XSLT code that appears in the stylesheet. By and large, the basic building block of the stylesheet is the template rule, defined by using the xsl:template, but you can actually add 11 additional XSLT elements directly inside the xsl:stylesheet element. These elements are called *top-level elements* and are shown in Table 3-1.

Table 3-1	Top-level XSLT Elements
Element	*Definition*
xsl:template	Defines a template rule.
xsl:output	Specifies the output format for the result document.
xsl:variable	Defines a variable.
xsl:param	Defines a parameter, which is a special kind of variable.
xsl:import	Loads an external stylesheet.
xsl:include	Loads an external stylesheet as part of the current stylesheet.
xsl:preserve-space	Preserves whitespace in the result document.
xsl:strip-space	Removes whitespace in the result document.
xsl:key	Defines a key that can be used to link together XML elements.
xsl:decimal-format	Defines the decimal format to use when converting numbers to strings.
xsl:namespace-alias	Maps a namespace to another namespace.
xsl:attribute-set	Defines a named set of attributes for use in the result document.

The following code snippet shows an XSLT stylesheet with some of these top-level elements defined:

```
<xsl:stylesheet
          xmlns:xsl="http://www.w3.org/1999/XSL/Transform"
          version="1.0">
  <xsl:output method="html"/>
  <xsl:preserve-space elements="chapters"/>
  <xsl:template match="book">
    <p><xsl:apply-templates/></p>
  </xsl:template>
  <xsl:include href="moretemplates.xsl"/>
</xsl:stylesheet>
```

Generally, you can put the top-level elements in any sequence you wish. The XSLT processor processes these elements the same way regardless of order. For example, if I move the elements around, the code generates the same results as the original:

```
<xsl:stylesheet
        xmlns:xsl="http://www.w3.org/1999/XSL/Transform"
        version="1.0">
  <xsl:include href="moretemplates.xsl"/>
  <xsl:template match="book">
    <p><xsl:apply-templates/></p>
  </xsl:template>
  <xsl:preserve-space elements="chapters"/>
  <xsl:output method="html"/>
</xsl:stylesheet>
```

However, there are a couple of exceptions to this rule, which tend to occur only in advanced situations. Specifically, when you use the xsl:import element, it must be the first top-level element defined under xsl:stylesheet. Also, in some error checking routines, element placement can become critical.

Comments

A *comment* is text included in your stylesheet for behind-the-scenes use that the XSLT processor ignores during the transformation. In stylesheets, people typically use comments to label a template rule or other part of the code describing its functionality. Just like in HTML, a comment is any text surrounded by a <!-- prefix and --> suffix. For example, the heavily commented XSLT stylesheet shown here produces the same results as the preceding example:

```
<xsl:stylesheet
        xmlns:xsl="http://www.w3.org/1999/XSL/Transform"
        version="1.0">

  <!-- Developed by: R. Wagner -->
  <!-- Last modified: 04/22 -->

  <!-- This stylesheet will output an HTML document using
       several
       template rules, one defined in this file and the
       others from
       moretemplates.xsl -->

  <!-- Output document to HTML format -->
```

```
<xsl:output method="html"/>

<!-- Preserve space for chapters elements -->
<xsl:preserve-space elements="chapters"/>

<!--- For each book element, surround its content with
   HTML paragraph tags -->
<xsl:template match="book">
  <p><xsl:apply-templates/></p>
</xsl:template>

<!-- Include more template rules, which
     are stored in a separate file -->
<include href="moretemplates.xsl"/>

</xsl:stylesheet>
```

When I say the processor ignores any comment, I mean it. You can even insult the processor with `<!-- Hey processor, you're a loser! -->` and this still doesn't impact its performance. Now that's service.

Use comments freely. As you can see by the preceding examples, comments make XSLT code much more readable than without it. This is especially true if you are trying to read a stylesheet someone else wrote.

What's in a Name (space)?

You've probably noticed that something has come before each of the XSLT elements you have seen and worked with so far in this book. Yes, that `xsl:` prefix is part of what is known as a namespace. XML uses *namespaces* to distinguish one set of element names from another set.

The necessity for namespaces becomes clear when you think about the flexibility of the XML language. Because XML has no predefined set of element names, naming is totally up to each developer, whether he or she lives in San Jose, Lucerne, or Ouagadougou. So the possibility of two different developers using an identical element name is very high.

For example, suppose a satellite dish company develops an XML vocabulary using `dish` as an element, while a housewares company has its own `dish` element to describe the round thing off which you eat. Now, if these companies never exchange data with anyone outside their companies, they can use their XML vocabulary as is and don't need to use a namespace. But if they wish to exchange data with outside suppliers, the possibility of duplicate element names exists when this data is merged.

Namespaces were developed to avoid this name collision by linking a namespace identifier with a URI (Uniform Resource Identifier). A *URI* is the method in which resources on the Web are named, the most widespread form being URLs (Uniform Resource Locators), also known simply as Web addresses (for example, `http://www.dummies.com`). Because URIs are unique, you can be sure that the namespace associated with the URI is one of a kind.

When you define a namespace, you declare a URI once in a document and then refer to the namespace elsewhere in the document by using a *namespace prefix* (also known as namespace identifier or abbreviation), as shown in Figure 3-2.

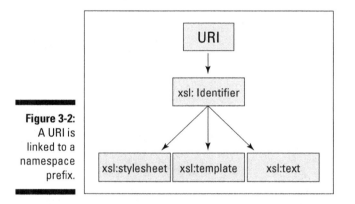

Figure 3-2:
A URI is linked to a namespace prefix.

Although you aren't required to use namespaces as part of an XML document, you must use them as part of an XSLT stylesheet. If you don't use namespaces in your stylesheet, for example, it would be impossible to tell if you wanted to use `<key>` to describe the XSLT key element or to refer to an item in a hardware store inventory.

XSLT stylesheets use the URI `http://www.w3.org/1999/XSL/Transform` and, by convention, assign this URI to an `xsl:` namespace identifier, as shown in Figure 3-3.

The mapping from the namespace identifier to the URI is what is important, not the literal namespace identifier `xsl:`. The `xsl:` identifier can actually be any label you choose. For example, the following is a perfectly valid XSLT stylesheet:

```
<richsmostexcellenttransform:stylesheet
          xmlns:richsmostexcellenttransform="http://www.w3.o
          rg/1999/XSL/Transform" version="1.0">
  <richsmostexcellenttransform:template match="book">
    <p><richsmostexcellenttransform:apply-templates/></p>
  </richsmostexcellenttransform:template>
</richsmostexcellenttransform:stylesheet>
```

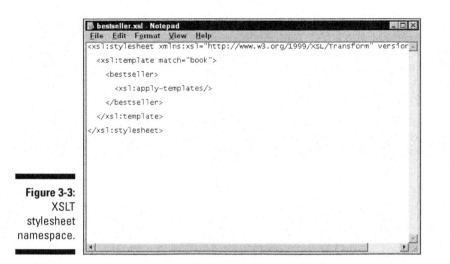

Figure 3-3:
XSLT
stylesheet
namespace.

Although you are free to use any prefix you like, I recommend sticking with xsl:. It is the prefix you'll see everywhere else. Using an alternative could easily lead to confusion.

Documents as Trees

XSLT processors don't read a document like you and I do. When I read a document, I start at the top of the page and read from left to right, line by line down the page to the end. I make sense of a document by reading its words, sentences, and paragraphs in sequence. (Okay, I admit it, I love those Dr. Seuss books the best, because I can get by just looking at pictures.)

In contrast, an XSLT processor does not read a document sequentially, but swallows it as a hierarchy of information. This hierarchy is best thought of as a *tree,* and in fact, XSLT uses tree lingo as a way to describe an XML document.

A solid grasp of document trees can help you realize that XSLT and XPath don't do their work by using smoke and mirrors, but actually follow a logical, understandable process. In fact, a good alternative title for this section is "Read This! This Section Is Important."

Treespeak

A common tree, be it a maple, oak, or elm, has a certain built-in structure or hierarchy to its various parts. At the bottom layer, a root system serves as the hidden foundation, supplying water and nutrients to the rest of the tree. Connected to the roots is the trunk, the most visible part of the support system. At the next level, you have branches of all shapes and sizes, which either connect to smaller branches or else directly to leaves. These smaller branches then lead to leaves or even tinier branches, and so on. Starting at the trunk, you can locate each branch and leaf somewhere in its complex hierarchy of parts.

An XML document follows this same pattern. Every XML document has its own counterpart to a trunk, an element commonly referred to as the *document element*. The document element encloses all the other elements inside its start and end tags. For example, doc in the snippet below is the document element because it contains all of the other elements in the document:

```
<doc>
  <para>Text1</para>
  <para>Text2</para>
</doc>
```

As you have seen already in this chapter, an xsl:stylesheet element contains template rules and all other parts of an XSLT stylesheet, so it acts as the document element of an XSLT stylesheet.

Just as a tree cannot have two trunks, neither can an XML document have two document elements. A well-formed XML document can have only a single document element that contains all of the other elements.

Top-level elements nested directly inside a document element are the equivalent of the first level of branches of a tree. Some of these elements (also called *nodes* in treespeak) contain additional elements, like smaller branches on a tree.

Even a tree's roots have an XML counterpart. Each document has something called a *root node* that contains all elements, including the document element. The root node, however, is invisible to your document, because no element or text represents the root node in the document.

Table 3-2 summarizes the comparison between a real tree and an XML one.

Table 3-2	Treespeak
Real World	*XML World*
Tree	Document
Roots	Root node

(continued)

Table 3-2 *(continued)*

Real World	XML World
Trunk	Document element
Branch	Node that contains more nodes or leaves
Leaf	A node that has no children (also called leaf)

Familyspeak

Just as a leaf cannot survive apart from a tree, a node cannot exist in isolation. Each node of a tree is related in some way to the other nodes that surround it in the document structure. The terminology used to describe these relationships comes straight from *The Waltons* or *The Simpsons*: ancestor, parent, sibling, and child. I like to call this terminology familyspeak.

Using familyspeak, you can say that a tree trunk is the *parent* of all the branches connected directly to it. Each of these attached branches is a *child* of the trunk and a *sibling* to the others. Any given branch typically has children as well, which may be either branches or leaves.

To illustrate the interrelationships of an XML document, consider a family tree expressed in XML:

```
<!-- familytree.xml -->
<family>
  <member firstname="Peter" surname="Selim" birth="1815">
    <spouse firstname="Maja" surname="Jonsdotter"/>
    <member firstname="Carl" surname="Selim" birth="1845">
      <spouse firstname="Joannah" surname="Lund"
          birth="1844"/>
      <member firstname="Hannah" surname="Selim"/>
      <member firstname="David" surname="Selim"/>
      <member firstname="Selma" surname="Selim"/>
      <member firstname="Ellen" surname="Selim"/>
      <member firstname="Charlie" surname="Selim"
          birth="1869">
        <spouse firstname="Hannah" surname="Carlsdotter"
            birth="1865"/>
        <member firstname="George" surname="Selim"
            birth="1898"></member>
          <spouse firstname="Dagmar" surname="Selim"
              birth="1898"/>
```

```
        <member firstname="Paul" surname="Selim"/>
        <member firstname="Pearl" surname="Rohden"
          birth="1897"/>
        <member firstname="Frances" surname="Lambert"
          birth="1903"/>
        <member firstname="Gladys" surname="Carlson"
          birth="1906"></member>
         <spouse firstname="Hilmer" surname="Carlson"
          birth="1906"/>
         <member firstname="Patricia" surname="Gustafson">
           <spouse firstname="Lauren" surname="Gustafson"/>
         </member>
         <member firstname="Wayne" surname="Carlson"/>
         <member firstname="Janet" surname="Olsen"/>
         <member firstname="Linda" surname="Zatkalik"/>
         <member firstname="Eunice" surname="Shafer">
        </member>
      </member>
    </member>
  </member>
</family>
```

This family tree has a parent element called family, which serves as the container for everything in that family. Peter Selim is the oldest recorded ancestor of this family, which is demonstrated by the <member firstname= "Peter" surname="Selim" birth="1815"> being the first member element of this family tree and serving as the ancestor for all the rest of the member elements.

Peter had a spouse named Maja and one son named Carl. Carl and his wife Joannah had five children, one of whom had children himself, and so on, down the family tree. So, for example, Eunice Shafer, the last child element on the tree had a parent named Gladys Carlson, and Eunice's siblings were Patricia, Wayne, Janet, and Linda. Peter Selim is a distant ancestor to Eunice.

Each of these family relationships — from Peter to Eunice — are interconnected. You find out later in this book that traversing this tree through these interrelationships is an important part of XSLT.

Nodes 'R' us

Now that you've got treespeak and familyspeak down, you can take a closer look at what a node is. In a general sense, a *node* is a point in a larger system. A leaf seems like an obvious node in a tree. However, in XML, each part of an XML document structure is a node, be it the trunk, branch, or leaf. Also, to make matters slightly more complicated, even attributes of a these parts are considered nodes. In fact, there are actually six different node types: element, attribute, namespace, processing instruction, comment, and text.

The XML snippet below contains several of these node types:

```
<?xml version="1.0" encoding="UTF-8"?>
<film name="Braveheart">
  <!-- Last modified 2/01 -->
  <storyline>William Wallace unites the 13th Century Scots in
             their battle to overthrow English
             rule.</storyline>

</film>
```

This snippet can be expressed as a tree structure, as shown in Figure 3-4.

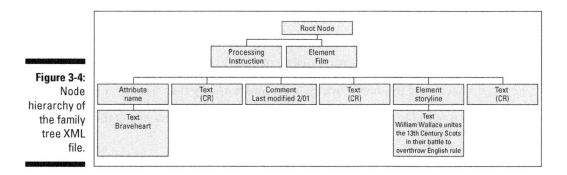

Figure 3-4:
Node hierarchy of the family tree XML file.

You'll notice one difference between the tree structure shown in Figure 3-4 and the XML code — the additional text nodes. These text nodes actually represent the "hidden text" in between the various elements. Although no actual text is between the `film` element and the comment or between the comment and the `storyline` element, invisible carriage return characters are present to start a new code line. These characters are considered part of the XML document by default, so they're not added to the document tree. (In Chapter 13 you find out how to tweak some of these whitespace settings.)

An XML document tree is often called a Document Object Model (or DOM). Although this may sound like technospeak, a DOM is only the exercise of looking at a document in a tree-like manner.

Because the XSLT processor reads the document as a tree, it has the entire tree available throughout the transformation process. This tree-like approach is much different than simpler XML parsers, such as the Simple API for XML (SAX), which reads an XML document sequentially and therefore deals with elements one at a time.

Working with trees

You need a solid understanding of document trees so that you know how XSLT works to get information from the XML source document and to output it in the result document. But, fortunately, you never actually have to worry about the mechanics of traversing the document tree (a practice sometimes called _tree walking_).

Many other programming languages make use of tree structures to describe hierarchical information. Yet working with trees can be a complex task if you have to write the code to actually walk through the tree, making sure every nook and cranny in it is found.

Certainly one of the tremendous benefits of XSLT is that it removes the burden of tree walking by doing all this hard stuff for you. You get to say, "I want all the nodes that match this pattern," and XSLT then goes off to handle the request. You don't need to concern yourself with the implementation details of this process.

Chapter 4

Templates Rule!

*T*emplate rules are the foundation of XSLT. Not only do they specify what information should be pulled from the source document, but template rules also define what the resulting document is going to look like. Think of them as the bricks of a chimney, the shingles of a roof, the pages of this book, nuggets in a 12-piece McNugget Value Meal. Well, you get the idea, right? Template rules are the basic building blocks of XSLT and nothing much happens in "transformation-land" without them. To use current slang, *templates rule!*

A Glorified Mail Merge

Template rules can be thought of as a glorified mail merge. Have you ever used the mail merge feature in a word processor? Even if you haven't, the concept is pretty simple. To do a mail merge that creates a personalized letter for each customer in a database, for example, you create a letter in a word processor that includes both normal text and data field placeholders. These fields in the word processed document are linked to an external customer database, so that when you print the document, the word processor prints a letter for each customer in the linked database. This mail merge process is very common; in fact, I am willing to bet you have mail sitting in your mailbox right now that was prepared in this manner.

The customer database serves as the source of the information. The word processor document serves as the template. And a printed letter results from the transformation in which the source and template are combined.

Similarly, an XML document acts as the source, while the XSLT stylesheet contains templates. The XSLT processor creates a result document based on the source XML document being applied to the stylesheet's template rules. Table 4-1 shows the parallels between the two processes.

Table 4-1	Comparing Mail Merge with XSLT Template Rules	
Item	*Mail Merge*	*XSLT*
Data Source	External database	XML document
Template	Word processor document with linked fields	XSLT stylesheet with template rules
Result	Printed letter with merged information	Result document, such as a web page

Some may argue that it is an oversimplification to compare XSLT transformations with a mail merge, but even if it is, the comparison isn't far off and is certainly a good starting point as you get your hands around template rules.

Basics of a Template Rule

A *template rule* transforms a set of XML nodes you specify from the source document into a new look. A "cookie cutter" template inside the template rule contains all the specifications for what this new look should be like. You create a temple rule using an xsl:template element with basic boilerplate code that looks like this:

```
<xsl:template match="">

</xsl:template>
```

As shown in Figure 4-1, each template rule consists of two key parts: the match pattern and the template.

```
score5.xsl - Notepad
File   Edit   Format   View   Help
<xsl:stylesheet xmlns:xsl="http://www.w3.org/1999/XSL/Transform" version
   <xsl:template match="score">
      <filmscore>
         <xsl:apply-templates/>
      </filmscore>
   </xsl:template>
</xsl:stylesheet>
```

Figure 4-1:
Parts of a
template
rule.

Pulling with match patterns

The *match pattern* is an XPath expression that pulls the nodes that you want
to transform from the source tree. Think of a match pattern as something like
the list your parents gave you to go to the supermarket for eggs, milk, and
cheese. When you entered the store, you would scurry up and down all of the
aisles searching for the specific groceries on the list. When you found an
item, you'd drop it into the basket and continue until everything was checked
off of the list. (And if you were like me, you probably threw in a candy bar for
good measure in the checkout aisle.)

In the same way, a match pattern defines a list of nodes that you want to be
included in the result document (also known as a *result tree*). It does so by
specifying the conditions you want a node to meet in order for it to be
included. The template rule uses the match pattern and scurries through the
source document looking for nodes that match these conditions. (However,
I've yet to see a template rule throw in a candy bar into the result document!)

To be used by the template rule, the match pattern is placed as the value of
the match attribute and takes the form of a specific XPath expression called
a location path.

XML source and result documents are treated as trees by XSLT because they
have a hierarchical tree-like structure to them. Therefore, for most purposes,
the terms *source document* and *source tree* are interchangeable, as are *result
document* and *result tree*. For more information on trees, see Chapter 3.

You can find out about XPath location paths in Chapter 5, but I can explain a bit now to help you get the gist of what they do for template rules. Consider the XML file in Listing 4-1.

Listing 4-1:   score.xml

```
<!-- score.xml -->
<scores>
  <score id="1">
    <film>A Little Princess</film>
    <composer>Patrick Doyle</composer>
    <year>1995</year>
    <grade>100</grade>
  </score>
  <score id="2">
    <film>Chocolat</film>
    <composer>Rachel Portman</composer>
    <year>2001</year>
    <grade>90</grade>
  </score>
  <score id="3">
    <film>Vertigo</film>
    <composer>Bernard Herrmann</composer>
    <year>1956</year>
    <grade>95</grade>
  </score>
  <score id="4">
    <film>Field of Dreams</film>
    <composer>James Horner</composer>
    <year>1989</year>
    <grade>96</grade>
  </score>
  <score id="5">
    <film>Dead Again</film>
    <composer>Patrick Doyle</composer>
    <year>1991</year>
    <grade>97</grade>
  </score>
</scores>
```

From this source document, suppose you want to get each of the `film` elements and do something with them. To do so, set your match element to be the name of the element:

```
<xsl:template match="film">
  <!-- Do something with the film elements -->
</xsl:template>
```

In plain English, this match pattern says:

> "Hey Mr. XSLT Processor, as you examine each of the nodes in the source tree, look for a child of the current node that is named *film*. If you find a match, please return the node to the template rule so that I can do something with it."

Each of the five film elements is processed by the template rule.

XPath location paths can get pretty . . . uh . . . shall I say "interesting." (Translation: They can look like gobbledygook!) Don't concern yourself too much with XPath location paths now. I save all that fun for Chapter 5.

Pushing with templates

Because of their similarity, the terms *template* and *template rule* are often confused and tend to be sloppily interchanged. But there is a fundamental difference in meaning: A *template rule* is the entire xsl:template element, and the *template* is everything inside the start and end tags of xsl:template. The purpose of the template is to define how the returning node set is pushed (or output) to the result tree.

A template contains two types of information:

- ✔ **Literal text:** Plain text that is simply copied to the result tree.
- ✔ **XSLT instructions:** XSLT instructions that generate text or nodes for the result tree. Common elements you use include xsl:apply-templates, xsl:copy, xsl:copy-of, and xsl:value-of.

In the following example, The film: is normal text, and the xsl:value-of instruction in an XSLT element that is evaluated at processing time to generate text:

```
<xsl:template match="score">
  The film: <xsl:value-of select="film"/>
</xsl:template>
```

How a template rule is processed

When a template rule is processed, the XSLT processor reads through an incoming XML document and assembles it as a tree. After this tree structure is defined, the processor starts walking through each node of the tree, looking for the most specific matching template rule for each node it encounters. When it finds a match, the processor uses the selected template as its guideline for how to add the node set to the result tree.

To illustrate, suppose you have the XML snippet shown in Listing 4-2.

Listing 4-2: tv.xml

```
<tv>
    <model>1010</model>
    <type>WideScreen</type>
    <aspectratio>16x9</aspectratio>
</tv>
```

And want to output it :

```
Model 1010 has an aspect ratio of 16x9.
```

The template rule that can do this transformation looks like:

```
<xsl:template match="tv">
   Model <xsl:value-of select="model"/> has an aspect ratio of
          <xsl:value-of select="aspectratio"/>.
</xsl:template>
```

When the XSLT processor performs this transformation, it first constructs a source tree like the one shown in Figure 4-2. Next, as it gets to each node, it checks to see if the node matches the lone template rule I've defined. The processor scores a bull's-eye when it gets to the root node, because the root node has a tv element node as its child.

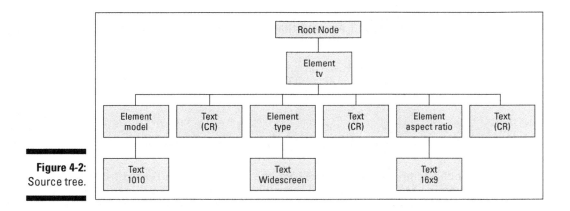

Figure 4-2:
Source tree.

The processor then gets the template rule's template and combines the literal text with the results of the two `xsl:value-of` elements (see Figure 4-3). These are combined into a single text node and added to the result tree's root node, as shown in Figure 4-4.

Figure 4-3:
Text nodes
of the
template.

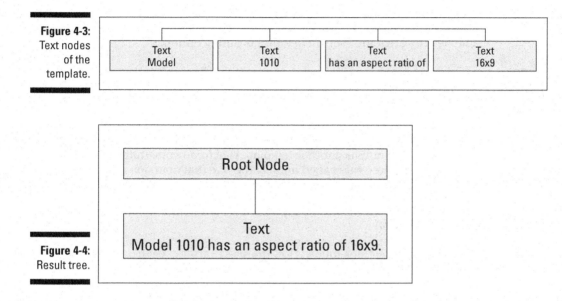

Figure 4-4:
Result tree.

When working with namespaces in your stylesheets, a good rule is that elements in a stylesheet in the xsl: namespace are part of the XSLT language, while non-xsl: elements within a template rule are literal elements put into the result tree.

Common Action Instructions

Within a template rule's template, a few key XSLT instructions do the yeoman's work of generating nodes for the result documents. These action instructions you use most often are `xsl:apply-templates`, `xsl:copy`, `xsl:copy-of`, and `xsl:value-of`.

In XSLTSpeak, top-level XSLT elements, such as `xsl:template` or `xsl:output` are called *elements,* whereas XSLT elements in the template rule that are used to create part of the result tree are called *instructions.*

xsl:apply-templates

The `xsl:apply-templates` element is perhaps the most commonly used instruction inside template rules. Its most basic syntax is:

```
<xsl:apply-templates select="expression"/>
```

The `select` attribute (shown in italic) is purely optional.

Think of `xsl:apply-templates` as something like a stereotypical factory supervisor. It doesn't really do anything by itself, but is charged with telling others, "Hey you, do this."

The purpose of `xsl:apply-templates` is to invoke the template rule most appropriate for the current node and its children. It doesn't really do anything by itself, but tells another template rule to do something. In some cases, the template rule called upon is the one that contains the `xsl:apply-templates` instruction. In other cases, it may be another template rule defined in your stylesheet. And, if nothing else is found, the XSLT processor applies one of XSLT's built-in template rules. (I discuss built-in template rules later in the chapter.)

Two obvious questions follow: How does `xsl:apply-templates` know which nodes to process? And after a node or node set is selected for processing, how does `xsl:apply-templates` decide which template rule to apply? I discuss the answers to these questions in the next two sections.

Scope of xsl:apply-templates

The `xsl:apply-templates` instruction processes nodes within its context or scope. When its `select` attribute is not defined, then its scope is the node set returned from the match pattern of the template rule it is inside of. For example, in the code snippet below, `xsl:apply-templates` processes the `tv` element and its children from the XML file shown in Listing 4-2:

```
<xsl:template match="tv">
  <xsl:apply-templates>
</xsl:template>
```

For each node in the node set, its template rule is applied along with all of its children's template rules.

Or, if `select` *is* defined, only the nodes that result from the expression are transformed, along with their children. For example, when the following template rule is processed on the tv.xml file in Listing 4-2, only the `aspectratio` element is applied by `xsl:apply-templates`, the `tv`, `model`, and `type` elements are ignored by this `xsl:apply-templates` instruction:

```
<xsl:template match="tv">
  <xsl:apply-templates select="aspectratio">
</xsl:template>
```

Looking for the best template rule

For each node that is processed by `xsl:apply-templates`, the XSLT processor looks for the best template rule to apply to it.

If the instruction's `select` attribute is defined, the processor will look for the most appropriate template rule for that node. But if `select` isn't defined, the template rule that contains `xsl:apply-templates` is chosen for the current node.

However, in both of these cases, don't forget about the children. The current node's children are also processed, so the XSLT processing engine goes through the same process of looking for the most appropriate template rule for each child. If a template rule is found matching that node, it will then be processed. But if not, then a built-in template rule is processed instead.

Here's a summary of the behavior of `xsl:apply-templates`:

✔ Looks for the most appropriate template rule to apply for each node in the node set. If no template rule has been defined, `xsl:apply-templates` will apply a built-in template rule.

✔ With no select attribute, processes all children.

In addition to elements, `xsl:apply-templates` also applies text nodes that are children of the current node.

Consider a few examples to get a better grasp of its intended actions. I use the following XML fragment in Listing 4-3 as the source document in each of these.

Listing 4-3:   miniscore.xml

```
<!-- miniscore.xml -->
<score id="1">
  <film>A Little Princess</film>
  <composer>Patrick Doyle</composer>
  <year>1995</year>
  <grade>100</grade>
</score>
```

Using `xsl:apply-templates` on the `score` element, the template rule is defined as:

```
<xsl:template match="score">
  <xsl:apply-templates/>
</xsl:template>
```

This template rule processes the score node and its children (using built-in templates, which I discuss later in the chapter) to send their content (in other words, text nodes) to the result tree. Because the score element has no text content, no text is added to the result tree. But, because the score element has four child elements that have text nodes, the child elements' content is transferred to the result document:

```
A Little Princess
Patrick Doyle
1995
100
```

Using xsl:apply-templates with a select attribute, the template rule supplied is defined as follows:

```
<xsl:template match="score">
  <xsl:apply-templates select="grade"/> is the critic's
         rating for the musical score of <xsl:apply-
         templates select="film"/>
</xsl:template>
```

In this template rule, I apply the template specifically on the grade and film elements to add their content to the result tree. In between these two, I add literal text to the output. The result is:

```
100 is the critic's rating for the musical score of A Little
         Princess
```

The other children of the score element (composer and year) were not added to the result tree, because the xsl:apply-templates's select attribute didn't match these elements.

If you use xsl:apply-templates on an element with no children, only that particular element is processed:

```
<xsl:template match="film">
  <movie><xsl:apply-templates/></movie>
</xsl:template>
```

The preceding template sends the following text to the result tree:

```
<movie>A Little Princess</movie>
```

xsl:copy

You can use the xsl:copy element to do just what you'd expect with a name like that — this element copies the current node. It has a basic syntax of:

```
<xsl:copy></xsl:copy>
```

However, keep in mind some specific behaviors to this xsl:copy instruction:

- ✔ Preserves the current node's start and end tags during processing.
- ✔ Doesn't copy children.
- ✔ Doesn't copy attributes.
- ✔ Includes content text only if you put an xsl:apply-templates inside the xsl:copy element. An empty xsl:copy (`<xsl:copy/>`) doesn't copy content.
- ✔ Has no select attribute, so it acts only on the result of the template rule's match pattern.

To illustrate, I use the miniscore.xml file (refer to Listing 4-3) as my source document. Using an empty xsl:copy element when the composer element is the match pattern, the code is defined as:

```
<xsl:template match="composer">
  <xsl:copy/>
</xsl:template>
```

The literal result of this template is `<composer></composer>`, but the XSLT processor shortens the empty tag to:

```
<composer/>
```

As you can see, the primary purpose of xsl:copy is to carry over the element tags. However, if you combine it with xsl:apply-templates, you copy both the tags and its content:

```
<xsl:template match="composer">
  <xsl:copy>
    <xsl:apply-templates/>
  </xsl:copy>
</xsl:template>
```

This template outputs:

```
<composer>Patrick Doyle</composer>
```

When you use xsl:copy and xsl:apply-templates on a current node that has children, the template rule copies the current node's tags and the content of the children. For example:

```
<xsl:template match="score">
  <xsl:copy>
    <xsl:apply-templates/>
  </xsl:copy>
</xsl:template>
```

Results in:

```
<score>
  A Little Princess
  Patrick Doyle
  1995
  100
</score>
```

xsl:copy-of

`xsl:copy-of` may be similar in name to `xsl:copy`, but its behavior is quite distinct. It has a basic syntax of:

```
<xsl:copy-of select="expression"/>
```

While `xsl:copy` provides a carbon copy of some parts of the returned node set, `xsl:copy-of` does more — it duplicates *everything* inside the current node. Specifically, `xsl:copy-of`:

- ✔ Copies all the nodes returned from its required `select` attribute.
- ✔ Preserves all element tags during processing.
- ✔ Copies children, attributes, and content.
- ✔ Keeps any comments or other processing instructions in the copy.

To copy the `score` element from the miniscore.xml (refer to Listing 4-3) to a new result document, I set up a new template rule. The template rule for copying the `score` element as is from the source tree to the result tree is defined as:

```
<xsl:template match="score">
  <xsl:copy-of select="."/>
</xsl:template>
```

The template rule's match pattern returns a `score` element, and the `.` expression inside the `select` attribute of the `xsl:copy-to` returns the current node (and all its children), producing the following output:

```
<score id="1">
  <film>A Little Princess</film>
  <composer>Patrick Doyle</composer>
  <year>1995</year>
  <grade>100</grade>
</score>
```

The `select` attribute of the `xsl:copy-of` element determines what is copied to the result tree. Suppose you define a more limited template rule:

```
<xsl:template match="score">
  <xsl:copy-of select="year"/>
</xsl:template>
```

This template rule results in a literal copy of only the `year` element (both tags and content):

```
<year>1995</year>
```

xsl:value-of

The `xsl:value-of` instruction is used when you want to convert part of the XML source to a string (plain text). It has a basic syntax of:

```
<xsl:value-of select="expression"/>
```

This instruction wants nothing to do with producing XML tags, so you never get elements or attributes when you use it. Specifically, the `xsl:value-of` element has the following behavior:

- ✔ Converts the result from its required `select` attribute to a string and adds it as a text node to the result tree. If the result is a single node, its contents are converted. If the result is a node set, the contents of the first node are used for processing.
- ✔ Removes element tags during processing.
- ✔ Doesn't convert attributes of the context node.
- ✔ Is combined with other text nodes that surround it before being added to the result tree.

Using the miniscore.xml file in Listing 4-3 as the source, if I use `xsl:value-of` on a single element (`film`), the template rule looks like:

```
<xsl:template match="score">
  <xsl:value-of select="film"/>
</xsl:template>
```

The film element is converted to text:

```
A Little Princess
```

`xsl:value-of` can also be used to convert an attribute to a string. For example, if I use a special @ character in the select attribute to denote an attribute:

```
<xsl:template match="score">
  <xsl:value-of select="@id"/>
</xsl:template>
```

It returns the following output:

```
1
```

Table 4-2 summarizes the behavior of `xsl:copy`, `xsl:copy-of`, and `xsl:value-of`.

Table 4-2	Parts Included in a Result Tree for Each Element				
Element	**Children**	**Attributes**	**Start/End tags**	**Content**	select attribute
`xsl:copy`	No	No	Yes	No (Yes, with `xsl:apply-templates`)	None
`xsl:copy-of`	Yes (all children)	Yes	Yes	Yes	Required
`xsl:value-of`	Yes	No	No	Yes	Required

A common mistake many XSLT stylesheet authors make is using a `match` attribute in place of the `select` attribute in an `xsl:copy-of`, `xsl:apply-templates`, or `xsl:value-of` instruction. You'll get a processing error if this occurs in your stylesheet.

Built-In Template Rules

As you begin to work with template rules, you need to know some behind-the-scenes activities I informally call "lazy man's template rules" because you don't have do anything in order to have them run. These actions are actually called *built-in template rules,* and the XSLT processor uses them to process any node that isn't matched with an explicitly defined template rule in your stylesheet. Different built-in template rules are applied to each node type.

The template rules you create in your stylesheet override built-in template rules.

Element nodes

For element nodes, I demonstrate the built-in template rule by using the ever-popular miniscore.xml file (refer to Listing 4-3) as the source document. Suppose you transform it by using an empty stylesheet:

```
<xsl:stylesheet
          xmlns:xsl="http://www.w3.org/1999/XSL/Transform"
          version="1.0">
</xsl:stylesheet>
```

The output is:

```
<?xml version="1.0" encoding="utf-8"?>
   A Little Princess
   Patrick Doyle
   1995
   100
```

Now, this output looks eerily familiar to the first example using `xsl:apply-templates`. That is no accident, because the built-in template that is run on element nodes and the root node looks like the following:

```
<xsl:template match="*|/">
   <xsl:apply-templates/>
</xsl:template>
```

The match pattern is a global catchall to process all nodes (child nodes of the current node and the root node), and `xsl:apply-templates` transforms each element and sheds the tags.

Text and attribute nodes

For text and attribute nodes, a built-in template rule copies their text through into the result tree:

```
<xsl:template match="text()|@*">
   <xsl:value-of select="."/>
</xsl:template>
```

In this rule, the match pattern returns all text nodes with `text()` and all attribute nodes with `@*`. The `xsl:value-of` instruction then transforms the current node to the result tree as text.

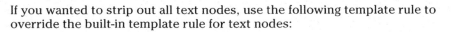

If you wanted to strip out all text nodes, use the following template rule to override the built-in template rule for text nodes:

```
<xsl:template match="text()"/>
```

Processing instructions, comments, and namespaces

A built-in template rule strips processing instructions and comments so that neither is carried over to the result tree:

```
<xsl:template match="processing-instruction()|comment()"/>
```

The match pattern returns every processing instruction and comment nodes; because the template is empty, nothing is added to the result tree.

Namespace nodes are also removed during processing. An XPath expression for matching a namespace node doesn't exist, so you can't express namespaces as a built-in template or override this built-in rule with your own.

You also have the option of *not* defining a template for a template rule. If you did so, the template rule looks like this:

```
<xsl:template match="film"></xsl:template>
```

or

```
<xsl:template match="film"/>
```

When this template rule is triggered, there is no template to output, so it outputs nothing.

When a template rule doesn't contain a template, the rule removes the match pattern from the output.

Matchmaker, Make Me a Match

So far in this chapter, I have been using examples that have had only a single template rule within the stylesheet. You can combine template rules in the same stylesheet, which is actually standard practice. However, suppose the processor evaluates a node in the source tree and finds that two or more of the template rules match. Which of the matches wins?

XSLT prioritizes template rules based on a fairly complex system of weighting, but Table 4-3 shows the more common cases (where Level 1 is highest priority, Level 4 is lowest):

Table 4-3	Priority of Common Template Rules	
Level	*Description of Rule*	*Example*
1 (most specific)	Element name with a filter	`<xsl:template match= "score[@id='1']">`
1	Element as part of a path	`<xsl:template match= "scores/score">`
2	Element name	`<xsl:template match= "score">`
3	Node test	`<xsl:template match= "node()">` or `<xsl: template match="*">`
4	Built-in template rule	`<xsl:template match="*|/">`

You can override the XSLT's built-in prioritization scheme by explicitly declaring your own priority for a template rule. You do this by using the `priority` attribute.

To illustrate, suppose I use the `score.xml` file (refer to Listing 4-1) as the source document and then want to apply the following XSLT stylesheet:

```
<xsl:stylesheet
          xmlns:xsl="http://www.w3.org/1999/XSL/Transform"
          version="1.0">

  <xsl:output method="xml" omit-xml-declaration="yes"/>

  <xsl:template match="score">
   Almost: <xsl:apply-templates select="film"/>
  </xsl:template>

  <xsl:template match="score[@id='1']">
   The Best: <xsl:apply-templates select="film"/>
  </xsl:template>

</xsl:stylesheet>
```

The first template rule returns a match when the current node has a `score` element node as a child. The second template rule returns a match when the current node has a `score` element node with an `id` attribute that equals 1.

So, when the source tree is evaluated, the XSLT processor finds two template rules that match when the current node is found to have a `score` element node with an `id` attribute equaling 1. However, the second template rule, being more specific to this particular node, is considered higher in priority; therefore, the node is matched to the second template rule, not the first. The result document looks like the following text output:

```
The Best: A Little Princess


Almost: Chocolat


Almost: Vertigo


Almost: Field of Dreams


Almost: Dead Again
```

Working with Attribute Value Templates

When your result document is XML or HTML format, you often have an occasion to plug in the result of an XPath expression as the value of an attribute. Designed specifically for this purpose, an *attribute value template* is located inside a template and surrounded by curly braces ({}).

For example, suppose I use the following XML snippet as the source:

```
<score>
  <film>A Little Princess</film>
  <composer>Patrick Doyle</composer>
  <year>1995</year>
  <grade>100</grade>
</score>
```

If I convert each of the `score`'s child elements to attributes of the `score` element, the end result looks like this:

```
<score year="1995" grade="100" composer="Patrick Doyle"
        film="A Little Princess"/>
```

To perform this transformation, I start by writing a new element as literal text in my template rule, putting empty quotes as the values:

```
<score year="" grade="" composer="" film=""/>
```

Using attribute value templates, I then enclose the name of each child node in curly braces. The curly braces tell the XSLT processor to evaluate what's inside each of them as an expression:

```
<xsl:template match="score">
  <score year="{year}" grade="{grade}"
         composer="{composer}" film="{film}"/>
  <xsl:apply-templates/>
</xsl:template>

<xsl:template match="film"/>
<xsl:template match="composer"/>
<xsl:template match="year"/>
<xsl:template match="grade"/>
```

As you can see, I also defined empty template rules for the child elements to remove them from the result tree. If I don't explicitly define these empty template rules, they are added as attributes (through the attribute value templates) and their text nodes (through xsl:apply-templates) are also added.

Working with Named Templates

A *named template* is an xsl:template element that has a name attribute but no defined match attribute. Normally, you declare a match attribute for a template rule so that when the processor encounters the rule, it processes the rule immediately based on this match pattern. In contrast, a named template doesn't contain a match attribute, so another template or instruction using xsl:call-template must explicitly call a named template.

To demonstrate, I use the miniscore.xml (refer to Listing 4-3) as the source. Suppose I want to append a text string to several of the template rules I apply to the source document. Rather than adding the same text string to each of the template rules, I can instead create a single named template that is called by each of the template rules and have the named template actually do the real work. Consider the following XSLT stylesheet:

```
<xsl:stylesheet
        xmlns:xsl="http://www.w3.org/1999/XSL/Transform"
        version="1.0">

  <xsl:template name="CreditLine">
    <xsl:value-of select="."/> - Brought to you by Tumplates,
         The Template People.
  </xsl:template>

  <xsl:template match="film">
    Film: <xsl:call-template name="CreditLine"/>
```

```
    </xsl:template>

    <xsl:template match="composer">
      Composer: <xsl:call-template name="CreditLine"/>
    </xsl:template>

    <xsl:template match="year"/>
    <xsl:template match="grade"/>

</xsl:stylesheet>
```

The first xsl:template element is the named template. When called, it adds text to the result document using xsl:value-of. However, without a match attribute defined, the XSLT processor has nothing to evaluate so the processor ignores the named template unless it's explicitly called somewhere else.

The next two template rules then use xsl:call-template to call the CreditLine named template, which executes based on the node set returned from the calling template's match pattern. The output then looks like:

```
    Film: A Little Princess - Brought to you by Tumplates, The
          Template People.

    Composer: Patrick Doyle - Brought to you by Tumplates, The
          Template People.
```

To find out how to use named templates in combination with parameters, see Chapter 8.

Chapter 5

XPath Espresso

- -

In This Chapter

▶ Understanding XPath's role in XSLT

▶ Creating XPath location steps

▶ Defining node relationships with axes

▶ Matching nodes with node tests

▶ Filtering node sets with predicates

▶ Creating absolute location steps

- -

My guess is that XPath is the espresso drinker of the X-Team. It's the high-energy workman that tirelessly treads through XML documents all hours of the day and night looking for those pesky nodes. Geez, with all that effort, it needs a good shot of espresso just to keep going!

Besides, XPath has another tie-in with coffee: Creating XPath expressions reminds me of ordering a drink at Starbucks. XPath is the one X-Teamer built from the ground up to decipher confusing instructions like: "I'd like a venti, triple shot, wet cappuccino with nonfat milk and a dash of cinnamon." This process of taking a specific request and going in and returning the right set of nodes (or cappuccinos) is what XPath is all about.

XPath, The X-Team's Commando

XPath is the language used by XSLT to describe how to locate nodes in a source XML document. Think of XPath as the spy or commando who is charged with going into foreign soil, picking out the requested information, and returning it to the XSLT homeland. Every template rule contains one of these XPath commando units that has a mission something like: "Go into the source tree and traverse each node. As you do so, look for a state parent that has city children. Bring each of the nodes that match back to me in this handy sack for further processing."

Unlike most languages, XPath has a vocabulary that is extremely targeted. Be it English, French, or Russian, any natural language spoken in the world has a rich, verbose vocabulary. Programming languages, like C or Java, are much more constrained, but you still can use these languages to create programs that have thousands or even millions of lines of code. In contrast, XPath's expressions are almost always placed on a single line.

XPath was originally part of the W3C's XSLT specification. But after the W3C working group discovered that other non-XSLT specifications, such as XPointer, can use XPath, the group pulled XPath out of the XSLT specification and standardized it on its own.

The primary use of XPath is to create location paths, which are instructions that specify what nodes to bring back to the template rule. More precisely, a *location path* is an XPath expression that is made up of a series of steps called *location steps.* A location path's return value is always a node set.

Dancing the Location Step

People using XSLT have their own dance called the Location Step. Ready? 1-2-3 . . . 1-2-3 . . . Well, even if you don't have happy feet, you can learn how to do this boogie. A *location step* is the basic unit that you use when creating XPath expressions and is central to everything done with XSLT. Each location step consists of an axis, a node test, and an optional predicate:

- ✔ The *axis* spells out the relationship of the nodes to be selected to the current node being processed.

- ✔ The *node test* identifies the particular nodes that the axis selected and that meet certain conditions.

- ✔ A *predicate* is an optional filter that sifts out some of the nodes returned by the axis and node test parts.

A location step takes the following form: `axis::nodetest[predicate]`. Figure 5-1 shows the XPath triumvirate.

Figure 5-1:
Parts of a location step.

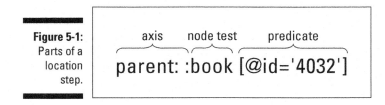

In earlier chapters, I have used the term *current node* (also commonly referred to as the *context node*) to describe the node that the XSLT processor is "on" during its traversal of the document tree. Although the term *current node* is accurate, it is also potentially confusing when you work with location steps, because the current node is not necessarily the selected node. The current node is a temporary "home base" that the XPath commandos start from to return a selection of nodes. On occasion, the location step returns the current node itself, but more often, it returns nodes that are only related in some way to the current node.

Steppin' through a funnel

You can think of a location step as a sifter (see Figure 5-2). For each source tree node encountered, the XSLT processor runs it through a location step. Starting at the topmost part of the sifter, the processor selects only those nodes that meet the axis specifications, throwing all others out before getting to the node test. In the middle section of the sifter, this node set is then further qualified against the criteria set by the node test. For all the remaining nodes of the set, they go through one final screen at the bottom of the sifter if a predicate is defined. What comes out at the bottom of the sifter is the end result of the location step.

For example, consider the following location step:

```
child::book[@id]
```

When a source tree is processed, for each node, the XSLT processor first uses the `child::` axis and returns all the current node's children as a node set. Next, the processor uses the `book` node test and returns just the child nodes that are `book` element nodes. Finally, from this smaller node set, it then uses the `@id` predicate to filter out all book elements that do not have an `id` attribute defined.

Steppin' up to a location path

As I mentioned earlier in this chapter, a location path consists of one or more location steps. If more than one location step is specified, then a `/` is used to separate each step. For example, `part/chapter` is a location path with two location steps (`part` and `chapter`). These two steps form a sequence that is examined from left to right, indicating that the second step is a child of the first. So, in this example, the `chapter` element is a child of the `part` element.

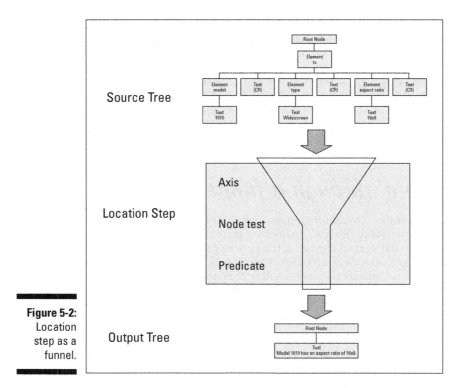

Defining Relationships with Axes

The axis part of a location step is all about defining relationships between the current node and the nodes that you wish to select. There are 13 possible axes, which are listed in Table 5-1. Some of these axes can be abbreviated; these abbreviations are shown in the Shortened Syntax column.

Table 5-1	Axes	
Axis	*Relationship to Current Node*	*Shortened Syntax*
child	Children of current node.	(no axis present denotes child axis)
self	Current node.	self::node() = .
parent	Parent of the current node. (always a single node)	parent:: node() = ..
attribute	All attributes of the current node.	@

Axis	Relationship to Current Node	Shortened Syntax
`descendant`	Children of current node, plus the children's children, and so on down the tree.	
`ancestor`	Parent of the current node, plus the parent's parent, and so on up to and including the root node.	
`following-sibling`	Siblings after the current node in the tree.	
`preceding-sibling`	Siblings before the current node in the tree.	
`following`	All nodes after the current node in the tree.	
`preceding`	All nodes before the current node in the tree.	
`namespace`	All namespace nodes of the current node.	
`descendant-or-self`	Current node and all its descendant nodes.	`descendant-or-self::node() = //`
`ancestor-or-self`	Current node and all its ancestor nodes.	

In addition to defining relationships, the axis also specifies the direction from the current node that the processor walks the tree to gather up nodes. Normally, tree walking goes top-to-bottom, left-to-right, much like you read a page in this book. However, certain axes — `ancestor`, `ancestor-or-self`, `preceding`, and `preceding-sibling` — travel in reverse order. (When working with `attribute` and `namespace` axes, the nodes are always unordered.)

For example, when processing a match pattern with a `descendant` axis, the XSLT processor starts with the first descendant defined in the source tree encountered and works its way downward until it reaches the last descendant for the current node. Or, when evaluating a `preceding` axis, the processor starts with the node just before the current node and works its way to the top of the document tree in reverse order. This directionality becomes important when you start thinking about the position of nodes within the node set that the axis returns. (I discuss node set positions later in this chapter.)

Child axis

Of the 13 available axes, the `child` axis is certainly the most common among them. It is used to select all the child nodes of the current node. The children are ordered based on the sequence in the document tree, as shown in Figure 5-3.

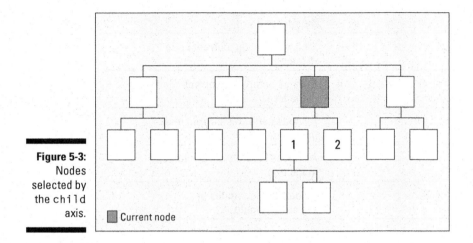

Figure 5-3:
Nodes
selected by
the `child`
axis.

■ Current node

For example, consider the following XML document shown in Listing 5-1, which is an XMLized version of this book's table of contents.

Listing 5-1:   **xsltfordummies-toc.xml**

```
<!-- xsltfordummies-toc.xml -->

<book title="XSLT For Dummies">

  <isbn>3651-6</isbn>

  <introduction/>

  <part number="I" name ="Getting Started With XSLT">

    <chapter number="1">
      <title>Introducing The X-Team</title>
      <summary>Introduce core XML/XSLT concepts</summary>
    </chapter>

    <chapter number="2">
      <title>Writing Your First XSLT Stylesheet</title>
```

```
         <summary>Getting feet wet with a simple, practical
               example of transforming</summary>
     </chapter>

</part>


<part number="II" name ="Becoming An XSLT Transformer">

   <chapter number="3">
     <title>Transforming With Style (Stylesheets, that
          is)</title>
     <summary>Cover topics related to top level "domain":
          the XSL Stylesheet</summary>
   </chapter>

   <chapter number="4">
     <title>Templates Rule!</title>
     <summary>Cover the second level domain:
          templates</summary>
   </chapter>


   <chapter number="5">
     <title>XPath Espresso</title>
     <summary>Focus on the third level domain: XPath
          Expressions</summary>
   </chapter>

   <chapter number="6">
     <title>We Want Results!</title>
     <summary>Provide practical examples to apply what was
          learned in Chapter 3-5</summary>
   </chapter>

</part>

<part number="III" name ="Prime Time XSLT">

   <chapter number="7">
     <title>Adding Programming Logic Isn't Just For
          Propheads</title>
     <summary>Add logic to template rules</summary>
   </chapter>

   <chapter number="8">
     <title>Variables in XSLT: A Breed Apart</title>
     <summary>Add variables/parameters to template
          rules</summary>
```

(continued)

Listing 5-1 *(continued)*

```
    </chapter>

    <chapter number="9">
      <title>Tweaking The Results To Get What You
          Want</title>
      <summary>Perform advanced data-related output
          options</summary>
    </chapter>

    <chapter number="10">
      <title>To HTML And Beyond!</title>
      <summary>Output to HTML and other formats</summary>
    </chapter>

    <chapter number="11">
      <title>Xpath Data Types and Functions</title>
      <summary>Cover practical examples of using built-in
          functions</summary>
    </chapter>

  </part>

  <part number="IV" name ="Extreme XSLT">

    <chapter number="12">
      <title>Combining XSLT Stylesheets</title>
      <summary>Using import and include</summary>
    </chapter>

    <chapter number="13">
      <title>"Gimme Some Space" And Other Output
          Issues</title>
      <summary>Perform advanced output options</summary>
    </chapter>

    <chapter number="14">
      <title>Keys and Cross-Referencing</title>
      <summary>Covers key and id usage</summary>
    </chapter>

    <chapter number="15">
      <title>Namespaces Revisited</title>
      <summary>More about namespaces</summary>
    </chapter>

    <chapter number="16">
      <title>Extending XSLT</title>
```

```
      <summary>Extensions for additional customization and
          power</summary>
   </chapter>

   <chapter number="17">
      <title>Debugging XSLT Transformations</title>
      <summary></summary>
   </chapter>

</part>

<part number="V" name ="Part of Tens">

   <chapter number="18">
      <title> Ten Most Confusing Things About XSLT </title>
   </chapter>

   <chapter number="19">
      <title>Ten All-Pro XSLT Resources On The Web</title>
   </chapter>

   <chapter number="20">
      <title>Ten XSLT Processors Available Online</title>
   </chapter>

</part>

<appendix number="A" name="Glossary"/>
</book>
```

Suppose you wanted to output a quick list of the book chapters. To do so, you could set up a template rule like this:

```
<xsl:template match="child::chapter">
  <xsl:apply-templates select="child::title"/>
</xsl:template>
```

Using the `child` axis as the starting point, the match pattern for the template looks for all `chapter` nodes that are children of the current node. For the returning node set, the template uses the `xsl:apply-templates` instruction, but does so by defining a `select` attribute to narrow the output to the child `title` elements of the returning node set. The output is:

```
Introducing The X-Team
Writing Your First XSLT Stylesheet
Transforming With Style (Stylesheets, That Is)
Templates Rule!
XPath Espresso
```

The location paths used inside the template of the template rule, such as in the `select` attributes of the `xsl:apply-templates` or `xsl:value-of` `instructions`, act off the returning node set, not the original document tree. Therefore, the current node of these `select` patterns is *not* the same as the current node of the template rule's match pattern.

You may find this fact surprising, but all the examples you have seen so far in this book have used the `child` axis. So why have you not seen `child::` before now? That is because `child` is the default axis for a location step, so that if you do not explicitly define an axis value, the `child` axis becomes the implicit axis. Therefore, if I drop `child::` from the template, I get an identical result:

```
<xsl:template match="chapter">
 <xsl:apply-templates select="title"/>
</xsl:template>
```

Attribute axis

The second most common axis type is `attribute`. The `attribute` axis selects all attributes of the current node. Like `child::`, `attribute::` has a shorter alternative, the @ symbol. Therefore, the following two are equivalent:

```
<xsl:value-of select="attribute::id"/>
```

and

```
<xsl:value-of select="@id"/>
```

XPath axes abbreviations

If you're like me and routinely frequent Starbucks, I suspect you too picked up the coffee lingo from the baristas. I have a favorite drink I order nearly every time I go to my local shop. I first start off by saying, "I'd like a grande café mocha with half of the chocolate syrup, nonfat milk, and extra whipped cream." But over time, I learned barista-speak. Now I say, "I want a grande light, nonfat, extra whipped mocha." Both are a mouthful, but the second one is quicker rolling off the tongue.

In the same way, XPath has some abbreviated ways to write axes values that make it quicker to write XPath expressions. These include:

`child::` axis doesn't need to be explicitly defined, so you can leave it off.

`attribute::` can be shortened to @.

`self::node()` is abbreviated to . (single period).

`parent::node()` is shortened to .. (double period).

`/descendant-or-self::node()/` is reduced to //.

Suppose, for example, you want to output a list of the book parts from the XML document shown in Listing 5-1. To do so, you set up a template rule like this:

```
<xsl:template match="part">
  Part <xsl:value-of select="@number"/>: <xsl:value-of
      select="@name"/>
</xsl:template>
```

Using the `child` axis as the starting point, the match pattern for the template looks for all `part` nodes that are children of the current node. The template uses `xsl:value-of` elements to output the `number` and `name` attributes of all returned `part` nodes as strings. The output is:

```
Part I: Getting Started With XSLT
Part II: Becoming An XSLT Transformer
Part III: Prime Time XSLT
Part IV: Extreme XSLT
Part V: Part of Tens
```

Parent axis

The `parent` axis specifies the parent of the current node (see Figure 5-4). Unlike most of the other axes, `parent` always refers to a single node, because a node never has two nodes as its immediate parent.

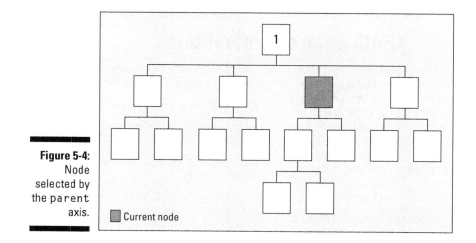

Figure 5-4:
Node
selected by
the parent
axis.

The `parent` axis is commonly abbreviated as `..` (double periods) when it is used in combination with the node test `node()`. (I don't want to get ahead of myself because I talk about node tests in the next part of the chapter, but understanding this point can help you as you find out about axes.) `node()` is a node test that matches any node whatever kind it is. So, `parent::node()` means, "Don't worry about its node type; just give me the parent of the current node." (Similarly, `child::node()` selects all the children of the current node no matter their node type.)

To illustrate the `parent` axis in action, suppose you want to transform `xsltfordummies-toc.xml` (shown in Listing 5-1) into a result document that looks like the following:

```
Chapter 1, "Introducing The X-Team", is in Part I
Chapter 2, "Writing Your First XSLT Stylesheet", is in Part I
Chapter 3, "Transforming With Style (Stylesheets, That Is)",
          is in Part II
Chapter 4, "Templates Rule!", is in Part II
Chapter 5, "XPath Espresso", is in Part II
Chapter 6, "We Want Results!", is in Part II
Chapter 7, "Adding Programming Logic Isn't Just For
          Propheads", is in Part III
Chapter 8, "Variables in XSLT: A Breed Apart", is in Part III
Chapter 9, "Tweaking The Results To Get What You Want", is in
          Part III
Chapter 10, "To HTML and Beyond!", is in Part III
Chapter 11, "XPath Data Types and Functions", is in Part III
Chapter 12, "Combining XSLT Stylesheets", is in Part IV
Chapter 13, "Gimme Some Space and Other Output Issues", is in
          Part IV
Chapter 14, "Keys And Cross-Referencing", is in Part IV
Chapter 15, "Namespaces Revisited", is in Part IV
Chapter 16, "Extending XSLT", is in Part IV
```

```
Chapter 17, "Debugging XSLT Transformations", is in Part IV
Chapter 18, "Ten Most Confusing Things About XSLT ", is in
        Part V
Chapter 19, "Ten All-Pro XSLT Resources On The Web", is in
        Part V
Chapter 20, "Ten XSLT Processors Available Online", is in
        Part V
```

To get this output, you can create a template rule that looks like this:

```
<xsl:template match="chapter">
  Chapter <xsl:value-of select="@number"/>, "<xsl:value-of
        select="title"/>", is in Part <xsl:value-of
        select="../@number"/>
</xsl:template>
```

This template rule returns the chapter elements using `match="chapter"`. Inside the template, literal text is mixed with the following three `xsl:value-of` elements to get the resulting text:

- `<xsl:value-of select="@number"/>` returns the `number` attribute for the `chapter` element.

- `<xsl:value-of select="title"/>` returns the `title` child of the `chapter` element. (Yes, you can write it `child::title`.)

- `<xsl:value-of select="../@number"/>` first points to the parent of the `chapter` element (which is always the `part` element) and then returns the parent's `number` attribute with `@number`. The `/` is used to express the hierarchical relationship between the `part` element and its child `number` attribute.

Self axis

You use the `self` axis to select the current node, as shown in Figure 5-5.

When used with the `node()` node test, `self::node()` is abbreviated as `.` (a single period), which in effect says, "Return the current node." For example, from Listing 5-1, to get the value of the `introduction` element and output it to a string, you can create a template rule like the following:

```
<xsl:template match="isbn">
  <xsl:value-of select="."/>
</xsl:template>
```

The match pattern returns the `isbn` element and the `select="."` uses the returned node itself in the `xsl:value-of` conversion. The end result is:

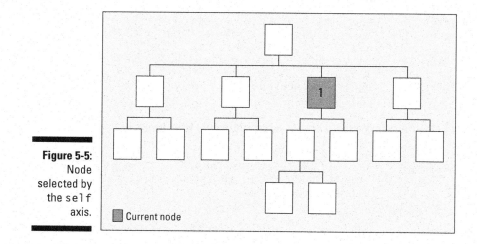

Figure 5-5:
Node
selected by
the self
axis.

Preceding-sibling and following-sibling axes

The preceding-sibling and following-sibling axes are used to select sibling nodes that come either before or after the current node (see Figures 5-6 and 5-7). Although the terms themselves are singular, preceding-sibling and following-sibling select *all* sibling nodes in the direction that is specified, not just the next or previous sibling.

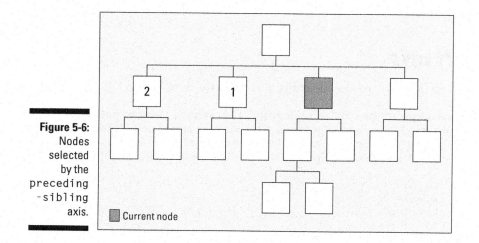

Figure 5-6:
Nodes
selected
by the
preceding
-sibling
axis.

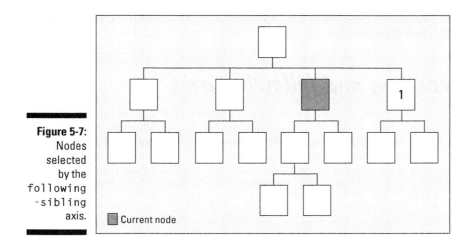

Figure 5-7:
Nodes
selected
by the
following
-sibling
axis.

Current node

For example, consider the following XML snippet:

```
<part number="II" name ="Becoming An XSLT Transformer">

   <chapter number="3">
     <title>Transforming With Style (Stylesheets, that
        is)</title>
   </chapter>

   <chapter number="4">
     <title>Templates Rule!</title>
   </chapter>

   <chapter number="5">
     <title>XPath Espresso</title>
   </chapter>

   <chapter number="6">
     <title>We Want Results!</title>
   </chapter>

</part>
```

Suppose your context node is the <chapter number="5"> element and you
want to get the value of the title element under <chapter number="6">.
To do so, you start out by using following-sibling::chapter to get the
next siblings and then a second location step that retrieves the title element
children:

```
<xsl:template match="chapter[@number='5']">
  <xsl:value-of select="following-sibling::chapter/title"/>
</xsl:template>
```

See the section, "Using Predicates to Get Specific," later in the chapter for a more detailed example of preceding-sibling and following-sibling.

Preceding and following axes

The preceding and following axes have a broader focus than do preceding-sibling and following-sibling. They return all the nodes, regardless of their hierarchy level, in the specified direction. preceding selects all the nodes before the current node on the tree, and following selects all the nodes after the current node. Figures 5-8 and 5-9 show these axes and their direction.

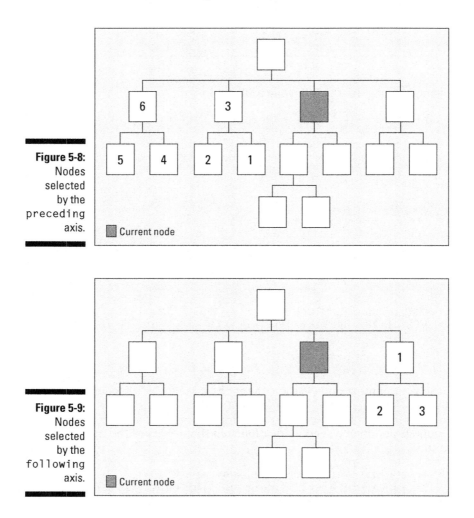

Figure 5-8:
Nodes
selected
by the
preceding
axis.

Figure 5-9:
Nodes
selected
by the
following
axis.

Descendant and descendant-or-self axes

The descendant axis selects all the nodes under the current node, whether they are children, grandchildren, great-grandchildren, and so on (see Figure 5-10). The descendant-or-self axis selects both the current node and all its descendants (see Figure 5-11). The descendant-or-self axis can be useful when you're uncertain of the number of levels between two nodes or if you simply want to bypass the intermediate levels.

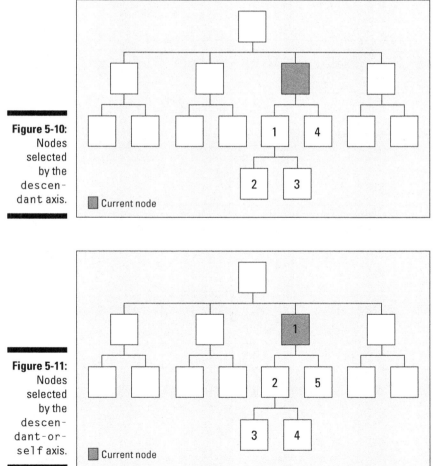

Figure 5-10: Nodes selected by the descendant axis.

Current node

Figure 5-11: Nodes selected by the descendant-or-self axis.

Current node

Another common XPath abbreviation is //, which is short for /descendant-or-self::node().

Ancestor and ancestor-or-self axes

The `ancestor` axis selects all the ancestors of the current node, and the `ancestor-or-self` axis selects both the current node plus all its ancestors. See Figures 5-12 and 5-13. Both axes are useful when you know a node is the current node or is above the current node in the document tree, but are not certain where.

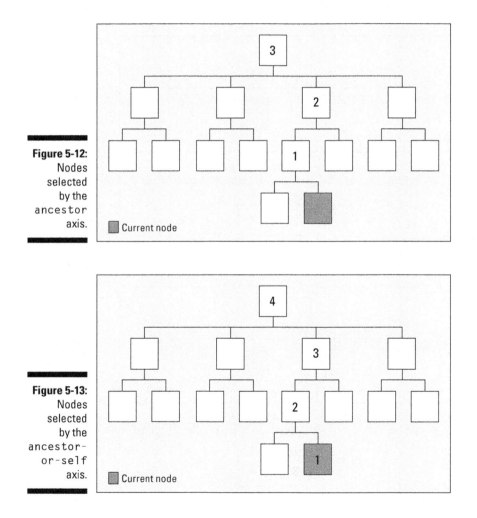

Figure 5-12: Nodes selected by the `ancestor` axis.

Figure 5-13: Nodes selected by the `ancestor-or-self` axis.

Namespace axis

The `namespace` axis selects all namespaces relevant for the current node.

Matching Nodes with Node Tests

The centerpiece of the location step is the *node test*. The axis is given a value if you don't define one, and the predicate is optional. The node test, however, must be part of every single location step you create. The node test looks at the node set given to it by the axis and says, "I want the nodes with this name or this type."

The most common node tests look for a match based on an element name. For example, the following XSLT snippet was used earlier in the chapter to return the chapter titles to the output tree:

```
<xsl:template match="title">
  <xsl:apply-templates/>
</xsl:template>
```

This node test, which should look fairly commonplace to you by now, says, "I want all the `title` elements from the node set given to me by the child axis."

In addition to using element names as the node test, you can also use several other node tests, as shown in Table 5-2.

Table 5-2	Node Tests
Node Test	*Description*
`elementname`	Matches `<elementname>` element nodes
`*`	Matches all nodes of the principal node type (for example, `child::*` returns all child element nodes and `attribute::*` returns all attribute nodes)
`node()`	Matches all nodes, regardless of their type
`text()`	Matches all text nodes
`comment()`	Matches all comment nodes
`namespace:elementname`	Matches `<elementname>` element nodes in the defined namespace
`namespace:*`	Matches all element nodes in the defined namespace
`processing-instruction()`	Matches processing instructions
`processing-instruction ('target')`	Matches processing instructions with the specified target `<?target ...?>`

Given that there are multiple types of nodes, you may be wondering how the processor knows that `title` from the preceding match pattern is referring to an element node rather than some other type. The reason is that every axis has a *principal node type* (or default node type). Most of the axes have a principal node type of an element, but there are a couple of exceptions: `attribute` axis has a principal node type of attribute and `namespace` axis has a principal node type of namespace. So, in the preceding example, because `child` — the implicit axis for `title` — has a principal node type of element, the processor knows that the match pattern is referring to an element node named `title`.

Using Predicates to Get Specific

The final part of the location step is the *predicate*, which can be optionally defined. If you use a predicate, it separates the wheat from the chaff in the resulting node set — keeping the wheat for the result tree and throwing away the chaff. After the processor evaluates the predicate, which is an XPath expression, the processor converts the result into a Boolean (true or false) value. Those nodes with a true value are included in the result tree, and those with a false value are not.

For example, using `xsltfordummies-toc.xml` (see Listing 5-1), suppose you wanted to output just the contents of Part V of the book in your result tree. Using a predicate, you define the template rule's match pattern as `part[@number='V']`, which tells the processor to return all the part elements that have a `number` attribute with the value of V. This template rule then returns only the specific part element you want. However, you also need to create an empty template rule to override the built-in template rule for the other `part` nodes:

```
<xsl:template match="part[@number='V']">
  Part V includes:
<xsl:apply-templates/>
</xsl:template>

<xsl:template match="isbn"/>
<xsl:template match="part"/>
```

The end result is:

```
Part V includes:
  Ten Most Confusing Things About XSLT
  Ten All-Pro XSLT Resources On The Web
  Ten Free XSLT Processors You Can Download
```

Both of these template rules have match patterns with the same axis::node test values, resulting in a conflict. However, because a predicate is defined for the first rule, it gets priority for any nodes that match both rules. (See Chapter 4 for more information on priorities.)

You can also use built-in XPath functions inside predicates. I talk about these in Chapter 11, but I use the `not()` built-in function here to give you a flavor for how you can use them. The `not()` function returns the opposite value of the XPath expression inside it. So, whereas the location step `book[@id]` is used to return all `book` elements that have an `id` attribute, `book[not(@id)]` returns all `book` elements that do *not* have an `id` attribute. Applying this principle to a full example, consider the following:

```
<xsl:template match="chapter">
  Chapter <xsl:apply-templates select="@number"/> : Summary
          provided
</xsl:template>

<xsl:template match="chapter[not(summary)]">
  Chapter <xsl:apply-templates select="@number"/> : No
          summary provided
</xsl:template>
```

This set of template rules formats the output differently based on whether or not the `chapter` element has a child `summary` element. Because Chapters 18 to 20 are the only ones that don't have a summary, the output looks like:

```
Chapter  1 : Summary provided
Chapter  2 : Summary provided
Chapter  3 : Summary provided
Chapter  4 : Summary provided
Chapter  5 : Summary provided
Chapter  6 : Summary provided
Chapter  7 : Summary provided
Chapter  8 : Summary provided
Chapter  9 : Summary provided
Chapter 10 : Summary provided
Chapter 11 : Summary provided
Chapter 12 : Summary provided
Chapter 13 : Summary provided
Chapter 14 : Summary provided
Chapter 15 : Summary provided
Chapter 16 : Summary provided
Chapter 17 : Summary provided
Chapter 18 : No summary provided
Chapter 19 : No summary provided
Chapter 20 : No summary provided
```

You can also use predicates to select a specific node based on its position in the node set. For example, if you want to select the first `chapter` child of the current node, you can use the `position()` built-in function:

```
chapter[position()=1]
```

As a shortcut, you can simply leave off the function name and just specify a position value:

```
chapter[1]
```

When the processor sees a numeric value by itself in the predicate, it implicitly adds the `position()=`.

Or to select the last chapter child, use another built-in function, `last()`:

```
chapter[last()]
```

As you work with positions in a node set, the order of the returning nodes becomes very important. So, when you use the reverse order axes (`ancestor`, `ancestor-or-self`, `preceding`, and `preceding-sibling`), remember that `[1]` selects the first node in reverse order. For example, consider the following XML snippet:

```
<part number="II" name ="Becoming An XSLT Transformer">

   <chapter number="3">
     <title>Transforming With Style (Stylesheets, that
         is)</title>
   </chapter>

   <chapter number="4">
     <title>Templates Rule!</title>
   </chapter>

   <chapter number="5">
     <title>XPath Espresso</title>
   </chapter>

   <chapter number="6">
     <title>We Want Results!</title>
   </chapter>

</part>
```

With `<chapter number="4">` element as the current node, `preceding-sibling` returns the `<chapter number="3">` and `following-sibling` returns a node set with `<chapter number="5">` and `<chapter number="6">` elements.

Using this snippet as the source, suppose you want to output the title of each chapter along with the titles of the previous and next chapter. The template rule is defined as follows:

```
<xsl:template match="chapter">
  Previous: <xsl:value-of select="preceding-
            sibling::chapter[1]/title"/>
  Current: <xsl:apply-templates select="title"/>
  Next: <xsl:value-of select="following-
            sibling::chapter[1]/title"/>
</xsl:template>
```

The template rule uses chapter as the location step to return all chapter elements for the template. Following the literal text Previous:, I use an xsl:value-of instruction to convert the result of select to a string. The preceding-sibling::chapter[1] step finds the first sibling that occurred before it on the source tree. The value of its child title element is then used by xsl:value-of. For the next chapter, I use following-sibling and apply the same logic as before. The end result is:

```
Previous:
Current: Transforming With Style (Stylesheets, that is)
Next: Templates Rule!

Previous: Transforming With Style (Stylesheets, that is)
Current: Templates Rule!
Next: XPath Espresso

Previous: Templates Rule!
Current: XPath Espresso
Next: We Want Results!

Previous: XPath Espresso
Current: We Want Results!
Next:
```

Take a Walk on the Absolute Side

If you work with directories and files on your computer, you're probably familiar with the concept of relative and absolute paths. For example, suppose I am in the c:\Windows\System32 directory and want to open up a file named espresso.txt in c:\Lattes. If I used a relative path, I would type the following to get to the file:

```
..\..\Lattes\espresso.txt
```

Or to use an absolute path, I would use:

```
C:\Lattes\espresso.txt
```

Like directory/file structures, location paths can either be relative or absolute. A *relative location path* is defined by the axis relation to the current node. Each of the preceding examples in this chapter is relative. In contrast, an *absolute location path* starts at the root node and then has specified steps to descend the tree to the desired axis. A / character, meaning "start at the root," is always placed at the start of an absolute location path. For example, to get the content of the introduction element from Listing 5-1, I can use the following absolute path:

```
<xsl:template match="/book/introduction">
<xsl:apply-templates/>
</xsl:template>
```

The match pattern starts with / to denote an absolute path and then looks for a book element node just under the root node with an introduction element node as its child. If found, the node set is applied using xsl:apply-templates.

An absolute path is also used when you want to specifically work with the root node. To demonstrate, suppose I want to surround all the contents of my xsltfordummies-toc.xml document (including the document element) with a new element called dummies. The following template rule does the trick:

```
<xsl:template match="/">
    <dummies genre="technology">
<xsl:copy-of select="."/>
    </dummies>
</xsl:template>
```

The match pattern of / selects the root node for the template and adds literal text before and after the result of the xsl:copy-of instruction.

Notice that some of the XPath syntax looks similar to traditional file system syntax – ., .., /, and //? That is more than a coincidence because the drafters of the XPath specification had directory/file syntax in mind when they defined the language.

Putting It All Together

The following bulleted lists give you a sampling of the various relative and absolute location paths I've talked about in this chapter.

Axis examples

- ✔ chapter or child::chapter selects the chapter element children of the current node.

- ✔ @name or attribute::name selects all the name attributes of the current node.

- ✔ .. or parent::node() selects the parent of the current node.

- ✔ . or self::node() selects the current node, regardless of its type.

- ✔ self::chapter selects the current node if it is a chapter element.

- ✔ descendant::chapter selects all the chapter descendants of the current node.

- ✔ descendant-or-self::page selects all the page element descendants of the current node and, if the current node is a page element, then include it as well.

- ✔ ancestor::page selects all the page element ancestors of the current node.

- ✔ ancestor-or-self::page selects all the page element ancestors of the current node and, if the current node is a page element, then include it as well.

- ✔ chapter/descendant::page selects the page descendants of the chapter element children of the current node.

Node test examples

- ✔ * or child::* selects all the element children of the current node.

- ✔ @* or attribute::* selects all the attributes of the current node.

- ✔ text() or child::text() selects all the text node children of the current node.

- ✔ node() or child::node() selects all the node children of the current node.

- ✔ */page selects all the page grandchildren of the current node.

Predicate examples

- ✔ chapter[1] or chapter[position()=1] selects the first chapter element child of the current node.

- ✔ chapter[last()] selects the last chapter element child of the current node.

- ✔ `following-sibling::chapter[1]` selects the next `chapter` element sibling of the current node.

- ✔ `preceding-sibling::chapter[1]` selects the previous `chapter` element sibling of the current node.

- ✔ `chapter[@level]` selects all the `chapter` element children of the current node that have a `level` attribute defined.

- ✔ `chapter[not(@level)]` selects all the `chapter` element children of the current node that don't have a `level` attribute defined.

- ✔ `chapter[@level='advanced']` selects all the `chapter` element children of the current node that have a `level` attribute with a value of `advanced`.

- ✔ `chapter[summary]` selects all the `chapter` element children of the current node that have one or more `summary` element children.

- ✔ `chapter[2][@level]` selects the second `chapter` element child of the current node if it has a `level` attribute defined.

- ✔ `chapter[@level][2]` selects the second `chapter` element child of the current node that has a `level` attribute defined.

Absolute path examples

- ✔ `/` selects the root node.

- ✔ `/descendant::chapter` selects all the chapter elements in the same document as the current node.

- ✔ `/descendant::summary[12]` selects the 12th `summary` element in the document.

Chapter 6

We Want Results!

S ports fans are a fickle sort. When their team is winning, the coach is a genius, the team leader is a superman, and the players are the toast of the town. But when the local team starts to lose, suddenly these one-time heroes become the focus of scorn and contempt, especially on those radio call-in shows. When it comes to their favorite team, fans want results.

In the same way, people like you and me come to XSLT for one thing: results. More than most other languages, XSLT is a highly focused, goal-oriented language. You don't use it to create games or expansive systems; you use it because you have XML and need to transform it into something else, perhaps another XML format, HTML, text, or whatever.

After you discover many of the basics of XSLT, it's time to get down to business. This chapter does just that by providing practical examples that show you how to perform the most common types of transformations using XSLT.

XSLT, Like Skinning a Cat

I'm sure you've heard the old expression, "There's more than one way to skin a cat." Although that adage may not make cat lovers like me happy (and may send my two cats hiding under the bed), it sure does apply to XSLT. As you grow more and more comfortable with the language, you find out that more than one way exists to generate the result you're seeking. What's more, for many tasks, there is no definitive right or wrong way to produce a transformed document.

Having said that, a seasoned XSLT developer knows that, in many instances, a specific technique may be more suitable or advantageous than another. Most of the time the decision comes down to a question of ease versus flexibility: Some methods are easier to do while others give you more power and flexibility.

Consider the following simple example. You can create a new element by using a literal text string within a template rule:

```
<cat>Siamese</cat>
```

But you can also get identical results by using the xsl:element instruction:

```
<xsl:element name="cat">Siamese</xsl:element>
```

Given that, why does XSLT have two or more methods that produce the same result? And which is the preferred way? For most purposes, the literal text approach is perfectly acceptable and is certainly the easiest to read and write. In contrast, the xsl:element instruction gives you more flexibility by allowing you to name an element, not just from a text string, but also to base it on the result of an XPath expression. Like everything else in life, knowing which technique is the most suitable simply comes with experience.

XML Source

To help you follow the XSLT stylesheet examples in this chapter, each example uses the coffee.xml source document shown in Listing 6-1 or, as appropriate, the smaller coffee-light.xml shown in Listing 6-2. Turn back to these code listings when you want to refer to the source.

Listing 6-1:   Coffee.xml

```
<?xml version="1.0"?>
<!-- coffee.xml -->
<coffees>
 <region name="Latin America">
  <coffee name="Guatemalan Express" origin="Guatemala">
    <taste>Curiously Mild And Bland</taste>
    <price>11.99</price>
    <availability>Year-round</availability>
```

```
      <bestwith>Breakfast</bestwith>
</coffee>
  <coffee name="Costa Rican Deacon" origin="Costa Rica">
    <taste>Solid Yet Understated</taste>
    <price>12.99</price>
    <availability>Year-round</availability>
    <bestwith>Dessert</bestwith>
  </coffee>
  </region>
  <region name="Africa">
  <coffee name="Ethiopian Sunset Supremo" origin="Ethiopia">
    <taste>Exotic And Untamed</taste>
    <price>14.99</price>
    <availability>Limited</availability>
    <bestwith>Chocolate</bestwith>
  </coffee>
  <coffee name="Kenyan Elephantismo" origin="Kenya">
    <taste>Thick And Chewy</taste>
    <price>9.99</price>
    <availability>Year-round</availability>
    <bestwith>Elephant Ears</bestwith>
  </coffee>
  </region>
</coffees>
```

Listing 6-2:   Coffee-light.xml

```
<?xml version="1.0"?>
<!-- coffee-light.xml -->
<coffee name="Guatemalan Express" origin="Guatemala">
  <taste>Curiously Mild And Bland</taste>
  <price>11.99</price>
  <availability>Year-round</availability>
  <bestwith>Breakfast</bestwith>
</coffee>
```

Pretty in pink?

The result documents in this chapter are formatted in a way that maximizes readability. Therefore, in many cases, when you run the stylesheet shown in the examples, the output looks slightly different, in terms of where line breaks or indenting occur. Don't worry about this for now; focus on the content first and later you can pretty up the results. When it comes to XML output, formatting is irrelevant more often than not, and is usually added only for readability. Having said that, I discuss how to format output in full detail in Chapter 13.

Copying an Element

XSLT is all about moving information from one place to another. Within all this hustle and bustle, the element is at the center of this activity. After all, most everything you move into the new document is an element or comes from an element in some way. When you want to perform a simple copy of an element's content or tags or even copy everything from one tree to another, use the techniques I discuss in the following sections.

Content only

In previous chapters, you find out that `xsl:apply-templates`, by calling the element's built-in templates, is used to push an element's content to the result tree, stripping away its tags in the process. I can use this technique to output just the content of the `price` element in the `coffee.xml` document by using the following stylesheet:

```
<!-- coffee-copy_elementcontent.xsl -->
<xsl:stylesheet
        xmlns:xsl="http://www.w3.org/1999/XSL/Transform"
        version="1.0">

<!-- Add just content -->
<xsl:template match="price"><xsl:text>
</xsl:text>
    <xsl:apply-templates/>
    </xsl:template>

<!-- Show just prices -->
<xsl:template match="coffees">
    <xsl:apply-templates select="region/coffee/price"/>
    </xsl:template>

</xsl:stylesheet>
```

The purpose of the first template rule is fairly simple; it outputs the `price` element's content. Using the `xsl:text` instruction, a line break is added before each line to separate the numbers that are generated in the transformation.

Although this template rule can produce the results I'm looking for, I have to keep in mind the context of the `price` element — it is a child of the `coffee` element, which is a child of `region`, which is a child of `coffees`. As a result, if I only use the `price` template rule in the stylesheet, I am going to get additional content in my result document that I'm not expecting. In case you're wondering why, remember the built-in template rules (which I discuss in Chapter 4) that are run on each transformation — an `xsl:apply-templates` is run by default on any element that doesn't have an explicitly defined template rule.

To prevent built-in templates from kicking in on the other elements, a second template rule is added that uses the coffees document element as the match pattern. However, I can't just create an empty template rule (`<xsl:element match="coffees"/>`) because it would override the built-in template rules not only for coffees but also its descendants as well. In essence, it would suffocate the price template rule I just defined. So, in this particular case, the easiest solution is to make sure that the xsl:apply-templates instruction is applied only to the price element by using region/coffee/price as the select attribute value.

The result that is generated is shown here:

```
11.99
12.99
14.99
9.99
```

Tags only

The xsl:copy instruction is one of two copy routines that XSLT has in its arsenal. I always consider it the decaffeinated version of the two, because it doesn't copy children or attributes and, by default, doesn't copy content either. Suppose you need to copy only the tags of a given element. If so, xsl:copy is a good candidate for the job. In the following code, my goal is to do the inverse of the preceding example: Output just the tags, not the content. To do so, I create a stylesheet that looks like the following:

```
<!-- coffee-copy_elementcontent.xsl -->
<xsl:stylesheet
        xmlns:xsl="http://www.w3.org/1999/XSL/Transform"
        version="1.0">

  <!-- Copy just tag -->
  <xsl:template match="price">
    <xsl:copy/>
  </xsl:template>

  <!-- Add parent, run on just price -->
  <xsl:template match="coffees">
    <prices>
      <xsl:apply-templates select="region/coffee/price"/>
    </prices>
  </xsl:template>

</xsl:stylesheet>
```

The price template rule contains an empty xsl:copy instruction to tell the XSLT processor to copy just the tags. Also, because I don't want any other parts of the coffee.xml document carried over, I use a similar template rule for `coffees` that I used in the previous example. However, because my result document is XML this time, I am going to add a `prices` document element into the result tree by adding literal text strings both before and after the `xsl:apply-templates` instruction. When an XSLT processor runs this stylesheet, the results generated are:

```
<?xml version="1.0" encoding="utf-8"?>
<prices>
  <price/>
  <price/>
  <price/>
  <price/>
</prices>
```

Copy all

If `xsl:copy` is the decaffeinated side of XSLT copying, `xsl:copy-of` must be like a venti-sized coffee at Starbucks: It packs a wallop! `xsl:copy-of` is surely the tool of choice when you want to copy the entire element and its various pieces. To copy both the tags and content of the `price` element, I can use the following XSLT code:

```
<!-- coffee-copy_elementfull.xsl -->
<xsl:stylesheet
          xmlns:xsl="http://www.w3.org/1999/XSL/Transform"
          version="1.0">

  <!-- Copy price element -->
  <xsl:template match="price">
    <xsl:copy-of select="."/>
  </xsl:template>

  <!-- Add parent, run on just price -->
  <xsl:template match="coffees">
    <prices>
      <xsl:apply-templates select="region/coffee/price"/>
    </prices>
  </xsl:template>

</xsl:stylesheet>
```

The XML output produced is shown here:

```
<?xml version="1.0" encoding="utf-8"?>
<prices>
  <price>11.99</price>
  <price>12.99</price>
  <price>14.99</price>
  <price>9.99</price>
</prices>
```

A second way to copy an element is through a method that can be called *reconstruction*. The gist of this method is that you use a combination of literal text and `xsl:value` instructions to reconstruct the pieces of the element. As shown in the following XSLT stylesheet, the `price` template rule uses the reconstruction technique to achieve identical results as the preceding `xsl:copy-of` example:

```
<!-- coffee-copy_elementrecreate.xsl -->
<xsl:stylesheet
          xmlns:xsl="http://www.w3.org/1999/XSL/Transform"
          version="1.0">

  <!-- Recreate element -->
  <xsl:template match="price">
    <price><xsl:value-of select="."/></price>
  </xsl:template>

  <!-- Add parent, run on just price -->
  <xsl:template match="coffees">
    <prices>
      <xsl:apply-templates select="region/coffee/price"/>
    </prices>
  </xsl:template>

</xsl:stylesheet>
```

Copying All Elements

To copy the entire set of elements in a document, you can use the same `xsl:copy-of` instruction that you use to copy a single element and its children. To copy the whole enchilada, use the `xsl:copy-of` instruction within the context of the root node (using / as the match pattern):

```
<!-- coffee-copy_tree.xsl -->
<xsl:stylesheet
          xmlns:xsl="http://www.w3.org/1999/XSL/Transform"
          version="1.0">

  <xsl:template match="/">
    <xsl:copy-of select="."/>
  </xsl:template>

</xsl:stylesheet>
```

When this template rule is run, the output looks identical to the original `coffee.xml` document tree. `xsl:copy-of` even brings along processing instructions and comments for the ride. Now that's service!

Adding a New Element

You can add a new element to the result tree by using one of two methods: literal text or the xsl:element instruction.

Using literal text

The simplest technique for creating a new element in your output is to simply create it in your stylesheet as literal text. Suppose, for example, that I want to add an online element as a child to the coffee element. This new element is used to indicate whether a particular type of coffee is available as an online purchase. In this example, all the coffees are defined the same, so I can define the element's content of Yes as literal text too.

I begin by showing you the long version for this process and then explain a more efficient technique after that. For starters, here is a stylesheet that can be used for this transformation:

```
<!-- coffee-addelement_literal.xsl -->
<xsl:stylesheet
          xmlns:xsl="http://www.w3.org/1999/XSL/Transform"
          version="1.0">

  <!-- Add new element -->
  <xsl:template match="coffee">
    <coffee>
      <taste><xsl:value-of select="taste"/></taste>
      <price><xsl:value-of select="price"/></price>
      <availability><xsl:value-of
            select="availability"/></availability>
      <bestwith><xsl:value-of select="taste"/></bestwith>
      <online>Yes</online>
    </coffee>
  </xsl:template>

  <!-- Recreate the top level node -->
  <xsl:template match="/">
    <coffees>
      <xsl:apply-templates/>
    </coffees>
  </xsl:template>

</xsl:stylesheet>
```

The coffee template rule uses the reconstruction method I showed you earlier — entering literal text to define the element tags and xsl:value-of to bring in the content of the matching child element from the source tree. The online element is simply added onto the end.

To retain coffees as the document element, I recreate it with the second template rule. Its purpose is to use xsl:apply-templates to apply to every element, surrounding those results with a coffees tag pair. (Remember, I need to add these tags back into the result document, because the built-in template rules automatically strip them out.) After the transformation is performed, the following result is produced:

```
<?xml version="1.0" encoding="utf-8"?>
<coffees>
  <coffee>
    <taste>Curiously Mild And Bland</taste>
    <price>11.99</price>
    <availability>Year-round</availability>
    <bestwith>Breakfast</bestwith>
    <online>Yes</online>
  </coffee>
  <coffee>
    <taste>Exotic and Untamed</taste>
    <price>12.99</price>
    <availability>Year-round</availability>
    <bestwith>Dessert</bestwith>
    <online>Yes</online>
  </coffee>
  <coffee>
    <taste>Exotic and Untamed</taste>
    <price>14.99</price>
    <availability>Limited</availability>
    <bestwith>Chocolate</bestwith>
    <online>Yes</online>
  </coffee>
  <coffee>
    <taste>Solid Yet Understated</taste>
    <price>9.99</price>
    <availability>Year-round</availability>
    <bestwith>Elephant Ears</bestwith>
    <online>Yes</online>
  </coffee>
</coffees>
```

The coffee template rule contains both literal text elements as well as XSLT instructions. A logical question you may be asking curiously is, "How does the XSLT processor know a literal element from an XSLT command?" The answer lies in the namespace: It treats all elements outside the xsl namespace as plain text and avoids trying to process them during transformations.

Although the previous example is perfectly valid and produces the intended results, it sure is a lot of work to reconstruct several elements that don't change at all from the source to the result document. A much more efficient way to do the same task is as follows:

```
<!-- coffee-addelement_literal2.xsl -->
<xsl:stylesheet
          xmlns:xsl="http://www.w3.org/1999/XSL/Transform"
          version="1.0">

  <!-- Add new element -->
  <xsl:template match="coffee">
    <coffee>
      <xsl:apply-templates/>
      <online>Yes</online>
    </coffee>
  </xsl:template>

  <!-- Copy everything else over -->
  <xsl:template match="@*|node()">
    <xsl:copy>
      <xsl:apply-templates select="@*|node()"/>
    </xsl:copy>
  </xsl:template>

</xsl:stylesheet>
```

This stylesheet produces the exact same result tree as the previous example. It does so by defining two template rules. The coffee template rule focuses on recreating the coffee element tags and adding the new online element. These literal text nodes are added to the result tree using xsl:applytemplates.

The second template rule is a nifty catchall template that is used to copy everything else over into the result document. It allows you to ignore the children elements that don't change as you create the coffee template rule.

Using xsl:element

In addition to adding elements using literal text, XSLT provides a specific instruction for adding elements: xsl:element. The xsl:element uses a name attribute to define the element's name while the content of the instruction defines the value. For example:

```
<xsl:element name="dog">Sheepdog</xsl:element>
```

This code produces the following element:

```
<dog>Sheepdog</dog>
```

I can use xsl:element to achieve the same result as with the previous example, simply by substituting the literal text for an xsl:element instruction:

```
<!-- coffee-addelement_instr.xsl -->
<xsl:stylesheet
          xmlns:xsl="http://www.w3.org/1999/XSL/Transform"
          version="1.0">

  <!-- Add new element using xsl:element -->
  <xsl:template match="coffee">
    <coffee>
      <xsl:apply-templates/>
      <xsl:element name="online">Yes</xsl:element>
    </coffee>
  </xsl:template>

  <!-- Copy everything else over -->
  <xsl:template match="@*|node()">
    <xsl:copy>
      <xsl:apply-templates select="@*|node()"/>
    </xsl:copy>
  </xsl:template>

</xsl:stylesheet>
```

Adding a Calculated Value

If you have used Excel or any database like Access, chances are you have
used calculated values before. A *calculated value* is a number that is produced through some sort of calculation. (Here's where all that math you
learned in school kicks in.) Placing a calculation within an XPath expression,
you can create a calculated value for your results document.

Suppose, for example, that I want to add a new child element for the coffee
element that provides a discounted price for the coffee. In this case, I'd like
to add a new discountprice element that is 20 percent off the price element value. The stylesheet is set up as follows:

```
<!-- coffee-addelement_calc.xsl -->
<xsl:stylesheet
          xmlns:xsl="http://www.w3.org/1999/XSL/Transform"
          version="1.0">

  <!-- Add new calculated element -->
  <xsl:template match="coffee">
    <coffee>
      <xsl:apply-templates/>
      <discountprice><xsl:value-of select="format-number(
          price*.8, '###.##' )"/></discountprice>
    </coffee>
```

```
  </xsl:template>

  <!-- Copy everything else over -->
  <xsl:template match="@*|node()">
    <xsl:copy>
      <xsl:apply-templates select="@*|node()"/>
    </xsl:copy>
  </xsl:template>

</xsl:stylesheet>
```

The first template rule I created uses `coffee` as the match pattern to
return the `coffee` element node set. Literal text is used to define the
`discountprice` tags. Because the value of the element needs to be generated during processing time, I need to use an XPath expression to generate
the value. An `xsl:value-of` instruction comes in handy at this point,
because you can use it to convert the result of an XPath expression into a
string.

To get the value I'm looking for, I can use a simple expression `price * .8`.
However, because this value needs to represent a currency amount, I need to
round the value to two decimal places. To do that, XPath conveniently has a
built-in function called `format-number` that allows you to define how you
want to format a number output. I talk more about `format-number` in
Chapter 11, but the important thing to know for this example is that the function has two parameters: The first is the number to format (`price*.8`) and
the second is the format picture (*###.##*, where *#* represents a numeric digit).

The results from the transformation are as follows:

```
<?xml version="1.0" encoding="utf-8"?>
<coffees>
 <region name="Latin America">
  <coffee>
    <taste>Curiously Mild And Bland</taste>
    <price>11.99</price>
    <availability>Year-round</availability>
    <bestwith>Breakfast</bestwith>
  <discountprice>9.59</discountprice>
  </coffee>
  <coffee>
    <taste>Exotic and Untamed</taste>
    <price>12.99</price>
    <availability>Year-round</availability>
    <bestwith>Dessert</bestwith>
  <discountprice>10.39</discountprice>
  </coffee>
 </region>
 <region name="Africa">
  <coffee>
```

```
      <taste>Exotic and Untamed</taste>
      <price>14.99</price>
      <availability>Limited</availability>
      <bestwith>Chocolate</bestwith>
      <discountprice>11.99</discountprice>
    </coffee>
    <coffee>
      <taste>Solid Yet Understated</taste>
      <price>9.99</price>
      <availability>Year-round</availability>
      <bestwith>Elephant Ears</bestwith>
      <discountprice>7.99</discountprice>
    </coffee>
  </region>
</coffees>
```

Renaming an Element

Renaming an element is another technique that involves the use of literal text and xsl:value-of combination. Suppose, for example, that I want to rename the taste element to description in the coffee-light.xml. Within the stylesheet, I can create a single template rule to perform this operation:

```
<!-- coffee-rename.xsl -->
<xsl:stylesheet
        xmlns:xsl="http://www.w3.org/1999/XSL/Transform"
        version="1.0">

  <!-- Rename taste to description -->
  <xsl:template match="taste">
    <description><xsl:value-of select="."/></description>
  </xsl:template>

</xsl:stylesheet>
```

The template rule uses a match pattern of taste to return all taste elements. The xsl:value-of instruction, with its select value of ., converts the content of each taste element to a string. The result is the following document:

```
<?xml version="1.0" encoding="utf-8"?>
<coffee name="Guatemalan Express" origin="Guatemala">
  <description>Curiously Mild And Bland</description>
  <price>11.99</price>
  <availability>Year-round</availability>
  <bestwith>Breakfast</bestwith>
</coffee>
```

Removing an Element

Because XSLT's built-in templates automatically add the content of elements, you frequently have occasions when you need to prevent an element from appearing in the result document. XSLT doesn't have a remove instruction, but you can ensure an element doesn't appear in the transformation by using one of two methods.

Explicitly removing an element

The first technique is to explicitly delete an element by defining an empty template rule and using the element as the rule's match pattern. An *empty template rule* is one that has a match pattern defined but no accompanying template. For example:

```
<xsl:template match="dog"/>
```

An empty template rule tells the processor to grab a node set and deliberately do nothing with it. As an illustration, I produce a result document that removes the taste and bestwith elements as part of the coffee element. After I set up my stylesheet, it looks like the following:

```
<!-- coffee-remove.xsl -->
<xsl:stylesheet
          xmlns:xsl="http://www.w3.org/1999/XSL/Transform"
          version="1.0">

  <!-- Remove taste element -->
  <xsl:template match="taste"/>
  <xsl:template match="bestwith"/>

  <!-- Copy everything else over -->
  <xsl:template match="@*|node()">
    <xsl:copy>
      <xsl:apply-templates select="@*|node()"/>
    </xsl:copy>
  </xsl:template>

</xsl:stylesheet>
```

By defining an empty template rule for the taste and bestwith elements, I remove these as part of the result. I can then use my "catch-all" template rule to simply copy everything else over. The XML code generated from the transformation looks like:

```
<?xml version="1.0" encoding="utf-8"?>
<coffees>
 <region name="Latin America">
```

```
      <coffee name="Guatemalan Express" origin="Guatemala">
        <price>11.99</price>
        <availability>Year-round</availability>
      </coffee>
      <coffee name="Costa Rican Deacon" origin="Costa Rica">
        <price>12.99</price>
        <availability>Year-round</availability>
      </coffee>
    </region>
    <region name="Africa">
      <coffee name="Ethiopian Sunset Supremo" origin="Ethiopia">
        <price>14.99</price>
        <availability>Limited</availability>
      </coffee>
      <coffee name="Kenyan Elephantismo" origin="Kenya">
        <price>9.99</price>
        <availability>Year-round</availability>
      </coffee>
    </region>
</coffees>
```

Because the `taste` and `bestwith` elements don't contain any other elements, running empty template rules on them only removed these two elements and nothing else. However, keep in mind, if you create an empty template rule for an element with children, the empty rule removes the specified element along with its children during the transformation. For example, running `<xsl:template match="coffees"/>` on the `coffee.xml` file generates an empty document, because `coffees` contains all other elements.

Implicitly removing an element

You can also implicitly remove an element by essentially ignoring it when template rules are applied. To demonstrate, imagine that you want to generate a new `selectcoffees` structure that removes the `region`, `taste`, and `bandwidth` elements. Here's the XSLT code that you use to do this operation:

```
<!-- coffee-remove2.xsl -->
<xsl:stylesheet
          xmlns:xsl="http://www.w3.org/1999/XSL/Transform"
          version="1.0">

  <xsl:template match="/">
    <selectcoffees>
      <xsl:apply-templates/>
    </selectcoffees>
  </xsl:template>

  <!-- Copy coffee and its price and availability children -->
  <xsl:template match="coffee">
```

```
    <coffee>
      <price><xsl:apply-templates select="price"/></price>
      <availability><xsl:apply-templates
          select="availability"/></availability>
    </coffee>
  </xsl:template>

</xsl:stylesheet>
```

A new document element named selectcoffees is created in the first template. The start and end tags of selectcoffees is plugged in before and after the xsl:apply-templates instruction, which is run on all descendants of the root node (the / match pattern).

The coffee template rule reconstructs the coffee element, but it does so by using literal text to redefine the price and availability tags and by using xsl:apply-templates to generate the child element's content. Notice that the context for these xsl:apply-templates instructions is very specific because the select attribute is defined for them, applying just the price and availability elements. As a result, taste and bestwith elements are summarily dropped from the result document. (Boy, XSLT is a tough business!)

I also want to get rid of the region element, but because it doesn't have any text nodes defined as content, I simply allowed the built-in template rule to do its thing; in doing so, the region element tags aren't added to the result document. The end result is a new selectcoffees structure:

```
<?xml version="1.0" encoding="utf-8"?>
<selectcoffees>
  <coffee>
    <price>11.99</price>
    <availability>Year-round</availability>
  </coffee>
  <coffee>
    <price>12.99</price>
    <availability>Year-round</availability>
  </coffee>
  <coffee>
    <price>14.99</price>
    <availability>Limited</availability>
  </coffee>
  <coffee>
    <price>9.99</price>
    <availability>Year-round</availability>
  </coffee>
</selectcoffees>
```

Removing an Attribute

So far in this chapter, I've been manipulating elements to generate the result documents, but you can similarly work with attributes as well. (If you recall, attributes are name/value pairs that describe the element it is associated with.)

Just as I showed you in the preceding section how to remove an element, an attribute can also be omitted from the result document in a variety of ways. One common technique is to reconstruct the element in a template rule, leaving behind any attributes you don't want to include. In the following stylesheet, I create a new derivative of coffee-light.xml that omits the origin attribute from the coffee element:

```
<xsl:stylesheet
          xmlns:xsl="http://www.w3.org/1999/XSL/Transform"
          version="1.0">

  <!-- Copy coffee but don't include the origin attribute -->
  <xsl:template match="coffee">
    <coffee name="{@name}">
      <xsl:apply-templates/>
    </coffee>
  </xsl:template>

  <!-- Copy everything else over -->
  <xsl:template match="@*|node()">
    <xsl:copy>
      <xsl:apply-templates select="@*|node()"/>
    </xsl:copy>
  </xsl:template>

</xsl:stylesheet>
```

The result is shown here:

```
<?xml version="1.0" encoding="utf-8"?>
<coffee name="Guatemalan Express">
  <taste>Mild and Bland</taste>
  <price>11.99</price>
  <availability>Year-round</availability>
  <bestwith>Breakfast</bestwith>
</coffee>
```

A second example that follows highlights another technique to remove attributes. Suppose I want to remove the attributes from the region element. I can do this with the following XSLT code:

```
<xsl:stylesheet
          xmlns:xsl="http://www.w3.org/1999/XSL/Transform"
          version="1.0">

  <!-- Copy region, but not its attributes -->
  <xsl:template match="region">
    <xsl:copy>
      <xsl:apply-templates select="*|node()"/>
    </xsl:copy>
  </xsl:template>

  <!-- Copy everything else over -->
  <xsl:template match="@*|node()">
    <xsl:copy>
      <xsl:apply-templates select="@*|node()"/>
    </xsl:copy>
  </xsl:template>

</xsl:stylesheet>
```

Looking closer at the stylesheet, the first template copies the region tags to the result document with xsl:copy. It also uses xsl:apply-templates to add its content to the output as well. However, the select attribute value of xsl:apply-templates selects elements and other nodes, but it specifically does *not* include attributes. The attribute-free result for region is shown here:

```
<?xml version="1.0" encoding="utf-8"?><coffees>
 <region>
  <coffee name="Guatemalan Express" origin="Guatemala">
    <taste>Mild and Bland</taste>
    <price>11.99</price>
    <availability>Year-round</availability>
    <bestwith>Breakfast</bestwith>
  </coffee>
  <coffee name="Costa Rican Deacon" origin="Costa Rica">
    <taste>Solid Yet Understated</taste>
    <price>12.99</price>
    <availability>Year-round</availability>
    <bestwith>Dessert</bestwith>
  </coffee>
 </region>
 <region>
  <coffee name="Ethiopian Sunset Supremo" origin="Ethiopia">
    <taste>Exotic and Untamed</taste>
    <price>14.99</price>
    <availability>Limited</availability>
    <bestwith>Chocolate</bestwith>
  </coffee>
  <coffee name="Kenyan Elephantismo" origin="Kenya">
```

```
    <taste>Thick And Chewy</taste>
    <price>9.99</price>
    <availability>Year-round</availability>
    <bestwith>ElephantEars</bestwith>
  </coffee>
  </region>
</coffees>
```

Reordering Elements

You can rearrange elements in the result document by recreating the element in the image of your choosing. For example, I can shuffle the children of the coffee element in the `coffee-light.xml` file by coding the following XSLT:

```
<!-- coffee-reorder.xsl -->
<xsl:stylesheet
          xmlns:xsl="http://www.w3.org/1999/XSL/Transform"
          version="1.0">

  <!-- Reorder elements -->
  <xsl:template match="coffee">
    <coffee>
      <availability><xsl:apply-templates
          select="availability"/></availability>
      <price><xsl:apply-templates select="price"/></price>
      <bestwith><xsl:apply-templates
          select="bestwith"/></bestwith>
      <taste><xsl:apply-templates select="taste"/></taste>
    </coffee>
  </xsl:template>

</xsl:stylesheet>
```

By using a combination of literal text and xsl:apply-templates instructions, I recreate each child within a new sequential order. The result is shown here:

```
<coffee>
  <availability>Year-round</availability>
  <price>11.99</price>
  <bestwith>Breakfast</bestwith>
  <taste>Curiously Mild And Bland</taste>
</coffee>
```

Not all reordering needs to be manually done. You can also automatically sort elements using the xsl:sort instruction. I discuss sorting in Chapter 9.

Merging Elements

You can combine elements in various fashions to form new elements. For instance, suppose I want to create a new tagline element for the coffee element in coffee-light.xml. I want to use this new element as a one-line advertisement to market the coffee. With the taste and bestwith elements, I already have bits of marketing information that can be used in the tagline. By combining these elements and adding additional text, I can produce a dynamically generated tagline for each coffee in a flash — and do so without any help whatsoever from an ad agency. The stylesheet to do this task is as follows:

```
<!-- coffee-merge.xsl -->
<xsl:stylesheet
        xmlns:xsl="http://www.w3.org/1999/XSL/Transform"
        version="1.0">

  <!-- Merge elements to create tagline element -->
  <xsl:template match="coffee">
    <coffee>
      <tagline>This Coffee Is <xsl:value-of select="taste"/>
          And Best Enjoyed With <xsl:value-of
          select="bestwith"/></tagline>
      <taste><xsl:value-of select="taste"/></taste>
      <price><xsl:value-of select="price"/></price>
      <availability><xsl:value-of
          select="availability"/></availability>
      <bestwith><xsl:value-of select="taste"/></bestwith>
    </coffee>
  </xsl:template>

</xsl:stylesheet>
```

As you can see, the tagline element is created using literal text and xsl:value-of instructions for both the taste and bestwith elements. The result is:

```
<?xml version="1.0" encoding="utf-8"?>
<coffee>
  <tagline>This Coffee Is Curiously Mild And Bland And Best
          Enjoyed With Breakfast</tagline>
  <taste>Curiously Mild And Bland</taste>
  <price>11.99</price>
  <availability>Year-round</availability>
  <bestwith>Curiously Mild And Bland</bestwith>
</coffee>
```

Adding Attributes

Like adding elements to your result document, you can add attributes in one of two ways. You can create attributes both through literal text as well as the xsl:attribute instruction.

Using literal text

Using the literal text method, I can add a currency attribute to the price element of the coffee-light.xml document by using the following stylesheet:

```
<!-- coffee-addattribute_literal.xsl -->
<xsl:stylesheet
          xmlns:xsl="http://www.w3.org/1999/XSL/Transform"
          version="1.0">

  <!-- Add currency attribute -->
  <xsl:template match="coffee">
    <coffee>
      <taste><xsl:value-of select="taste"/></taste>
      <price currency="$US"><xsl:value-of
          select="price"/></price>
      <availability><xsl:value-of
          select="availability"/></availability>
      <bestwith><xsl:value-of select="taste"/></bestwith>
    </coffee>
  </xsl:template>

</xsl:stylesheet>
```

The XML produced from the transformation is as follows:

```
<?xml version="1.0" encoding="utf-8"?>
<coffee>
  <taste>Curiously Mild And Bland</taste>
  <price currency="$US">11.99</price>
  <availability>Year-round</availability>
  <bestwith>Curiously Mild And Bland</bestwith>
</coffee>
```

Using xsl:attribute

The xsl:attribute can also be used to create an attribute. In the following example, I am creating a new salesevent element as a child of the coffee element, which has quarter, usregion, and supplier attributes:

```
<!-- coffee-addattribute_inst.xsl -->
<xsl:stylesheet
        xmlns:xsl="http://www.w3.org/1999/XSL/Transform"
        version="1.0">

  <!-- Add attribute using xsl:attribute instruction -->
  <xsl:template match="coffee">
    <coffee>
      <taste><xsl:value-of select="taste"/></taste>
      <price currency="$US"><xsl:value-of
          select="price"/></price>
      <availability><xsl:value-of
          select="availability"/></availability>
      <bestwith><xsl:value-of select="taste"/></bestwith>
      <xsl:element name="salesevent">
        <xsl:attribute name="quarter">Q3</xsl:attribute>
        <xsl:attribute name="usregion">New
            England</xsl:attribute>
        <xsl:attribute name="supplier">Horacio
            Zeeman</xsl:attribute>
      </xsl:element>
    </coffee>
  </xsl:template>
</xsl:stylesheet>
```

The result is shown here:

```
<?xml version="1.0" encoding="utf-8"?>
<coffee>
  <taste>Curiously Mild And Bland</taste>
  <price currency="$US">11.99</price>
  <availability>Year-round</availability>
  <bestwith>Curiously Mild And Bland</bestwith>
  <salesevent quarter="Q3" usregion="New England"
          supplier="Horacio Zeeman"/>
</coffee>
```

Moving an Attribute

An attribute describes something about the element in which it is contained and is treated as a child attribute node by the XSLT processor. On occasion, you may find it necessary to move an attribute from one element to another. To demonstrate, suppose I want to get rid of the region element in the coffee.xml document and replace it with a new region attribute in the coffees element. To do this, the value of the region element's name attribute needs to become the value of the region attribute by using the following stylesheet:

```
<!-- coffee-move_attr.xsl -->
<xsl:stylesheet
           xmlns:xsl="http://www.w3.org/1999/XSL/Transform"
           version="1.0">

  <!-- Move region name to be an attribute of coffees -->
  <xsl:template match="coffees">
    <coffees region="{region/@name}">
      <xsl:apply-templates/>
    </coffees>
  </xsl:template>

  <!-- Copy coffee elements as is -->
  <xsl:template match="coffee">
    <xsl:copy-of select="."/>
  </xsl:template>

</xsl:stylesheet>
```

The coffees template rule recreates the coffees element, and uses the
attribute value template {region/@name} to provide the value for the new
region attribute. The coffee elements are simply copied over using the
second template rule. These instructions produce output as shown here:

```
<?xml version="1.0" encoding="utf-8"?>
<coffees region="Latin America">
  <coffee name="Guatemalan Express" origin="Guatemala">
    <taste>Curiously Mild And Bland</taste>
    <price>11.99</price>
    <availability>Year-round</availability>
    <bestwith>Breakfast</bestwith>
  </coffee>
  <coffee name="Costa Rican Deacon" origin="Costa Rica">
    <taste>Solid Yet Understated</taste>
    <price>12.99</price>
    <availability>Year-round</availability>
    <bestwith>Dessert</bestwith>
  </coffee>
  <coffee name="Ethiopian Sunset Supremo" origin="Ethiopia">
    <taste>Exotic and Untamed</taste>
    <price>14.99</price>
    <availability>Limited</availability>
    <bestwith>Chocolate</bestwith>
  </coffee>
  <coffee name="Kenyan Elephantismo" origin="Kenya">
    <taste>Thick And Chewy</taste>
    <price>9.99</price>
    <availability>Year-round</availability>
    <bestwith>Elephant Ears</bestwith>
  </coffee>
</coffees>
```

Converting Elements into Attributes

The difference between what constitutes an attribute and what constitutes a child element is often arbitrary, because both describe its parent in some way. In the coffee.xml file, for example, I defined a coffee's name as an attribute of the coffee element, while its price is a child element. However, it could have just as easily been the reverse: name as a child element and price as an attribute. For my purposes here, I'm not concerned about which technique is best, but the important thing for XSLT is that moving from element to attribute and from attribute to element can be a typical scenario when transforming documents.

In the previous example, I move attributes from one element to another, but suppose I also want to tweak the structure of the coffee element too. In particular, I want to convert the price element into an attribute of coffee and add a new descriptions element that converts the taste and bestwith elements into attributes that describe coffee. I use the XSLT code shown here to do this task:

```
<!-- coffee-convert_to_attr.xsl -->
<xsl:stylesheet
          xmlns:xsl="http://www.w3.org/1999/XSL/Transform"
          version="1.0">

  <!-- Move region name to be an attribute of coffees -->
  <xsl:template match="coffees">
    <coffees region="{region/@name}">
      <xsl:apply-templates/>
    </coffees>
  </xsl:template>

  <xsl:template match="coffee">
    <coffee name="{@name}" origin="{@origin}"
          price="{price}">
      <availability><xsl:value-of
          select="availability"/></availability>
      <descriptions taste="{taste}" bestwith="{bestwith}"/>
    </coffee>
  </xsl:template>

</xsl:stylesheet>
```

Although the first template rule moves the region name to be the coffees region attribute, the second template is what I'd like to focus on. It reconstructs the coffee element attribute by using literal text and attribute value templates. The first two — name="{@name}" origin="{@origin}" — simply re-create the attributes that the coffee element already had. An attribute value template that returns the value of the price element creates the new price attribute. The descriptions element follows suit with the taste and bestwith attributes. The results look like this:

```
<?xml version="1.0" encoding="utf-8"?>
<coffees region="Latin America">
  <coffee name="Guatemalan Express" origin="Guatemala"
          price="11.99">
    <availability>Year-round</availability>
    <descriptions taste="Curiously Mild And Bland"
          bestwith="Breakfast"/>
  </coffee>
  <coffee name="Costa Rican Deacon" origin="Costa Rica"
          price="12.99">
    <availability>Year-round</availability>
    <descriptions taste="Solid Yet Understated"
          bestwith="Dessert"/>
  </coffee>
  <coffee name="Ethiopian Sunset Supremo" origin="Ethiopia"
          price="14.99">
    <availability>Limited</availability>
    <descriptions taste="Exotic and Untamed"
          bestwith="Chocolate"/>
  </coffee>
  <coffee name="Kenyan Elephantismo" origin="Kenya"
          price="9.99">
    <availability>Year-round</availability>
    <descriptions taste="Thick And Chewy" bestwith="Elephant
          Ears"/>
  </coffee>
</coffees>
```

In this example, the built-in template for the price element is not called, because I didn't use an xsl:apply-templates instruction in the coffee template rule. However, in cases in which the price element is applied, I need to define an empty template rule to prevent the price element's content from appearing both as an attribute and as an element.

Converting Attributes into Elements

You can also perform the opposite action and convert attributes into elements. As a demonstration of this technique as well as others I've shown in this chapter, I am going to create a new XML structure based on coffee.xml, but with several changes:

- ✔ Convert the region element's name attribute into a name child element.

- ✔ Add a new source element under coffee that gets its value based on the region element's name and the coffee element's origin attribute.

- ✔ Move the content of the price element to be the value of a new retail attribute and add a new wholesale attribute to price that is 60 percent of the retail value.

The following stylesheet sets up these conversions:

```
<!-- coffee-convert_to_elem.xsl.xsl -->
<xsl:stylesheet
          xmlns:xsl="http://www.w3.org/1999/XSL/Transform"
          version="1.0">

  <!-- Move region name to be a child element of region -->
  <xsl:template match="region">
    <region>
      <name><xsl:value-of select="@name"/></name>
      <xsl:apply-templates/>
    </region>
  </xsl:template>

  <!-- Convert coffee element -->
  <xsl:template match="coffee">
    <coffee>
      <price retail="{price}" wholesale="{format-number(
          price*.6, '###.##' )}"></price>
      <source><xsl:value-of select="../@name"/>|<xsl:value-of
          select="@origin"/></source>
      <availability><xsl:value-of
          select="availability"/></availability>
      <xsl:apply-templates/>
    </coffee>
  </xsl:template>

  <!-- Remove elements -->
  <xsl:template match="taste"/>
  <xsl:template match="price"/>
  <xsl:template match="availability"/>
  <xsl:template match="bestwith"/>

</xsl:stylesheet>
```

When this stylesheet is run against the `coffee.xml` file, the results from the transformation are as follows:

```
<?xml version="1.0" encoding="utf-8"?>
 <region>
   <name>Latin America</name>
   <coffee>
     <price retail="11.99" wholesale="7.19"/>
     <source>Latin America|Guatemala</source>
     <availability>Year-round</availability>
   </coffee>
   <coffee>
     <price retail="12.99" wholesale="7.79"/>
     <source>Latin America|Costa Rica</source>
```

```
      <availability>Year-round</availability>
  </coffee>
</region>

<region>
 <name>Africa</name>
 <coffee>
    <price retail="14.99" wholesale="8.99"/>
    <source>Africa|Ethiopia</source>
    <availability>Limited</availability>
 </coffee>
 <coffee>
    <price retail="9.99" wholesale="5.99"/>
     <source>Africa|Kenya</source>
     <availability>Year-round</availability>
 </coffee>
</region>
```

Part III
Prime Time XSLT

The 5th Wave   By Rich Tennant

"Can't I just give you riches or something?"

In this part . . .

*I*t's time for the big time. This section takes you beyond the basics and stretches your programming prowess by adding conditional logic and variables to your template rules. You can tweak result documents to your heart's content to get just the output you're looking for. Finally, you take the path less traveled by looking at XPath functions and data types.

Chapter 7

Adding Programming Logic Isn't Just for Propheads

In This Chapter

▶ Finding out about conditional and looping structures

▶ Testing for conditions with xsl:if

▶ Deciding among a set of conditions with xsl:choose

▶ Looping through a set of nodes with xsl:for-each

*A*re you a *prophead?* (Prophead is short for *propeller head* or *geek.*) If you aren't sure, I'm going to give you a simple test that can tell you exactly whether you qualify. Here goes:

```
if-else
for
while
switch-case
```

When you read those lines, what was your reaction? Did you have a quizzical look on your face? Did you groan? A nod of the head? Or perhaps you screamed out in excitement and felt your pulse racing?

Well, if you cried out in exultation and felt your heart skipping a beat, my guess is that you've got programming in your blood and are as "excited as a prophead" about getting into a discussion on adding programming logic to your XSLT stylesheets.

Kidding aside, no matter your reaction, I think you'll find this chapter to be extremely useful to expand the scope of what you can do with XSLT.

Conditional and Looping Statements

Conditional and looping commands, such as *if* and *for,* are essential to nearly every programming language on the planet. *Conditional structures* allow you to execute parts of a program when certain conditions are met. *Looping statements* enable you to cycle through a series of values or objects and perform actions with them. The practical effect is that both kinds give you greater control and flexibility to do what you are trying to do in your code.

Ever wonder how different XSLT is from traditional programming languages? Consider this: When you learn C++, Java, or Visual Basic, conditional and loop statements are some of the first things you learn about. In XSLT, however, conditionals and loops aren't as important, primarily because of the way XSLT makes use of template rules. A template rule certainly has something akin to conditional and looping structure built into it: For all the nodes that match its pattern, do something or else skip the template altogether.

Having said that, although you can do a heck of a lot in XSLT without ever touching these control structures, there are certain tasks you just cannot perform without them.

If and Only If

The most basic of all control structures is the if statement. It performs one or more actions if certain conditions are met. XSLT uses `xsl:if` instruction for this purpose:

```
<xsl:if test="expression">
  do something
</xsl:if>
```

In effect, this instruction says: if the `test` expression is true, then process the lines inside the start and end `xsl:if` tags.

For example, the following `xsl:if` instruction sends the literal text `Extra large size is required` to the result tree if the current node has a `size` attribute that equals `XL`:

```
<xsl:if test="@size='XL'">
  Extra large size is required.
</xsl:if>
```

`xsl:if` can be used only inside an `xsl:template` rule. Otherwise, you get an error.

Let me give you a fuller example to demonstrate `xsl:if`, starting with the `students.xml` file shown in Listing 7-1 as my source document.

Listing 7-1: students.xml

```xml
<?xml version="1.0"?>
<!-- students.xml -->
<school name="Elliot Academy">
  <student id="601" name="Jordan">
    <class name="Language Arts" days="5">Sentence
           diagramming</class>
    <class name="Reading" favorite="true" days="5">Lord Of
           The Rings</class>
    <class name="Writing" days="3">Colonial Times</class>
    <class name="Geography" days="2">African Sahel</class>
    <class name="Math" days="5"
           section="6.42">Decimals</class>
    <class name="Science" days="3"
           level="advanced">Volcanos</class>
    <class name="History" days="3">American
           Presidents</class>
    <class name="Art" days="1">Drawing</class>
  </student>
  <student id="401" name="Jared">
    <class name="Language Arts" days="5"
           section="4.56">Punctuation</class>
    <class name="Reading" days="5">Voyage Of The
           Dawntreader</class>
    <class name="Writing" days="3">Haiku Poetry</class>
    <class name="Geography" favorite="true" days="2">African
           Sahel</class>
    <class name="Math" days="5"
           section="4.45">Fractions</class>
    <class name="Science" days="3"
           level="basic">Insects</class>
    <class name="History" days="3">American
           Presidents</class>
    <class name="Art" days="1">Paper Mache</class>
  </student>
  <student id="301" name="Justus">
    <class name="Language Arts" days="5"
           section="3.80">Capitalization</class>
    <class name="Reading" days="5">Sherlock Holmes Solves
           Them All</class>
    <class name="Writing" days="3">Penmanship</class>
    <class name="Geography" days="2">African Sahel</class>
    <class name="Math" favorite="true" days="5"
           section="3.30">Division</class>
    <class name="Science" days="3"
           level="basic">Vertebrates</class>
    <class name="History" days="3">American
           Presidents</class>
    <class name="Art" days="1">Clay Sculptures</class>
  </student>
</school>
```

Suppose I want to create a text-based report for each of the three students. If the desired output were the same for each of them, then I could use a normal template rule along with `xsl:apply-templates` or `xsl:value-of`. However, in this case, I'd actually like to provide literal text that is customized for each student and make variations in my output based on each student. Given these requirements, `xsl:if` becomes a great tool at my disposal, because I can use it to test for a specific student, and if that expression has a true value, then I can tell the processor to write the customized output to the result tree. For example, for a student named Jordan, the following `xsl:if` instruction is used:

```
<xsl:template match="student">
  <xsl:if test="@name='Jordan'">
  *******************************************
    Jordan is a 6th grader with an id
    of <xsl:value-of select="@id"/>

    Emphasizing:
     Reading: <xsl:value-of
        select="class[@name='Reading']"/>
     Writing: <xsl:value-of
        select="class[@name='Writing']"/>
  *******************************************
  </xsl:if>
</xsl:template>
```

As the template rule is processed and run on each `student` element, the XSLT processor faces a fork in the road for each node when it gets to the `xsl:if` statement. Either the conditions of `test` are met or they are not. If so, then the text inside is added to the result document. If not, then it is ignored. Here's what the complete stylesheet, which contains a test for each student, looks like:

```
<!-- students.xsl -->
<xsl:stylesheet version="1.0"
        xmlns:xsl="http://www.w3.org/1999/XSL/Transform">

  <xsl:output method="text"/>

  <xsl:template match="student">

    <xsl:if test="@name='Jordan'">
    *******************************************
      Jordan is a 6th grader with an id
      of <xsl:value-of select="@id"/>

      Emphasizing:
       Reading: <xsl:value-of
          select="class[@name='Reading']"/>
       Writing: <xsl:value-of
          select="class[@name='Writing']"/>
    *******************************************
```

```
      </xsl:if>

      <xsl:if test="@name='Jared'">
      ***********************************************
        Jared is a 4th grader with an id
        of <xsl:value-of select="@id"/>

        Emphasizing:
         Language: <xsl:value-of select="class[@name='Language
            Arts']"/>
         Writing: <xsl:value-of
            select="class[@name='Writing']"/>
      ***********************************************
      </xsl:if>

      <xsl:if test="@name='Justus'">
      ***********************************************
        Justus is a 3rd grader with an id
        of <xsl:value-of select="@id"/>

        Emphasizing:
         Reading: <xsl:value-of
            select="class[@name='Reading']"/>
         Geography: <xsl:value-of
            select="class[@name='Geography']"/>
      ***********************************************
      </xsl:if>

   </xsl:template>

</xsl:stylesheet>
```

The text document generated looks like this:

```
      ***********************************************
        Jordan is a 6th grader with an id
        of 601

        Emphasizing:
         Reading: Lord Of The Rings
         Writing: Colonial Times
      ***********************************************


      ***********************************************
        Jared is a 4th grader with an id
        of 401

        Emphasizing:
         Language: Punctuation
         Writing: Haiku Poetry
      ***********************************************
```

```
*************************************************
   Justus is a 3rd grader with an id
   of 301

   Emphasizing:
     Reading: Sherlock Holmes Solves Them All
     Geography: African Sahel
*************************************************
```

Unlike most other programming languages, XSLT does *not* have an else state-ment to go along with if. Use a series of xsl:if statements or else the xsl:choose instruction instead.

Testing Expressions with Logical Operators

Arguably the most important part of any xsl:if instruction is its test attribute. Its expression must be true in order for the xsl:if content to be processed. In addition to looking for a specific element or attribute value as I did in the preceding example, you can do a variety of tests inside the expression.

To test if an attribute exists, you use:

```
<xsl:if test="@favorite">
```

Alternatively, you can use the XPath's built-in function not() to test for the opposite value:

```
<xsl:if test="not(@favorite)">
```

XPath also allows you to use or and and operators to enable you to test more than one condition. If you want just one of two or more expressions to evalu-ate to true, then use or. But if you want all expressions to evaluate to true, then use and. For example, the following test expression is looking for an element with a name attribute that has a value of Language Arts, Reading, *or* Writing:

```
<xsl:if test="(@name='Language Arts') or (@name='Reading') or
              (@name='Writing')">
```

To show the use of the and operator, the test expression that follows is look-ing for an element that has a days attribute of 5 *and* has a parent with a name attribute that equals Justus:

```
<xsl:if test="(@days='5') and (../@name='Justus')">
```

To evaluate numeric expressions, you can use the traditional forms of comparison that you learned back in 3rd grade math: <, <=, >, >=, and =. However, in XML, you can't use the < character in your XSLT stylesheet, because XML reserves this character for marking the start of an element tag. If you need to use the less than sign, use <. For example, rather than using 6 < 9, you use what's in the following expression:

```
<xsl:if test="6 &lt; 9">
```

Additionally, in place of using <= to mean "less than or equal to," you use 6 <= 9.

The complete list of comparison operators is shown in Table 7-1.

Table 7-1	XPath Comparison Operators
Operator	*Means*
>	Greater than
>=	Greater than or equal to
<	Less than
<=	Less than or equal to
=	Equals
!=	Not equal

I have been using the equals sign in previous examples, but I can use its opposite — the != operator — to test for results that aren't equal. So, if I want to search on elements with days attributes that aren't equal to 5, then I use:

```
<xsl:if test="@days != 5">
```

The following stylesheet uses each of these xsl:if instructions:

```
<?xml version="1.0"?>
<xsl:stylesheet version="1.0"
          xmlns:xsl="http://www.w3.org/1999/XSL/Transform">
  <xsl:output method="text"/>

  <xsl:template match="class">

    <!-- if favorite attribute exists -->
    <xsl:if test="@favorite">
```

```
      <xsl:value-of select="@name"/> is the favorite class of
          <xsl:value-of select="../@name"/><xsl:text>
  </xsl:text>
  </xsl:if>

  <!-- if favorite attribute does not exist -->
  <xsl:if test="not(@favorite)">
    <xsl:value-of select="@name"/> is not the favorite
        class of <xsl:value-of
        select="../@name"/><xsl:text>
  </xsl:text>
  </xsl:if>

  <!-- if name is language arts, reading, or writing -->
  <xsl:if test="(@name='Language Arts') or
        (@name='Reading') or (@name='Writing')">
      <xsl:text>English class topic: </xsl:text><xsl:value-
          of select="."/><xsl:text>
  </xsl:text>
  </xsl:if>

  <!-- if favorite attribute exists -->
  <xsl:if test="(@days='5') and (../@name='Justus')">
      <xsl:text>One of Justus' 5-day/week classes:
          </xsl:text><xsl:value-of
          select="@name"/><xsl:text>
  </xsl:text>
  </xsl:if>

  <!-- if days less than 3 -->
  <xsl:if test="@days &lt; 3">
      <xsl:text>Minor subject: </xsl:text><xsl:value-of
          select="@name"/><xsl:text>
  </xsl:text>
  </xsl:if>

  <!-- if days greater than or equal to 3 -->
  <xsl:if test="@days >= 3">
      <xsl:text>Major subject: </xsl:text><xsl:value-of
          select="@name"/><xsl:text>
  </xsl:text>
  </xsl:if>

  <!-- if days does not equal 5 -->
  <xsl:if test="@days != 5">
      <xsl:text>Not a full-time subject:
          </xsl:text><xsl:value-of
          select="@name"/><xsl:text>
  </xsl:text>
  </xsl:if>

  </xsl:template>

</xsl:stylesheet>
```

When applied to the XML source shown in Listing 7-1, the following output is then generated:

```
Language Arts is not the favorite class of Jordan
English class topic: Sentence diagramming
Major subject: Language Arts

Reading is the favorite class of Jordan
English class topic: Lord Of The Rings
Major subject: Reading

Writing is not the favorite class of Jordan
English class topic: Colonial Times
Major subject: Writing
Not a full-time subject: Writing

Geography is not the favorite class of Jordan
Minor subject: Geography
Not a full-time subject: Geography

Math is not the favorite class of Jordan
Major subject: Math

Science is not the favorite class of Jordan
Major subject: Science
Not a full-time subject: Science

History is not the favorite class of Jordan
Major subject: History
Not a full-time subject: History

Art is not the favorite class of Jordan
Minor subject: Art
Not a full-time subject: Art

Language Arts is not the favorite class of Jared
English class topic: Punctuation
Major subject: Language Arts

Reading is not the favorite class of Jared
English class topic: Voyage Of The Dawntreader
Major subject: Reading

Writing is not the favorite class of Jared
English class topic: Haiku Poetry
Major subject: Writing
Not a full-time subject: Writing

Geography is the favorite class of Jared
Minor subject: Geography
Not a full-time subject: Geography

Math is not the favorite class of Jared
Major subject: Math
```

```
Science is not the favorite class of Jared
Major subject: Science
Not a full-time subject: Science

History is not the favorite class of Jared
Major subject: History
Not a full-time subject: History

Art is not the favorite class of Jared
Minor subject: Art
Not a full-time subject: Art

Language Arts is not the favorite class of Justus
English class topic: Capitalization
One of Justus' 5-day/week classes: Language Arts
Major subject: Language Arts

Reading is not the favorite class of Justus
English class topic: Sherlock Holmes Solves Them All
One of Justus' 5-day/week classes: Reading
Major subject: Reading

Writing is not the favorite class of Justus
English class topic: Penmanship
Major subject: Writing
Not a full-time subject: Writing

Geography is not the favorite class of Justus
Minor subject: Geography
Not a full-time subject: Geography

Math is the favorite class of Justus
One of Justus' 5-day/week classes: Math
Major subject: Math

Science is not the favorite class of Justus
Major subject: Science
Not a full-time subject: Science

History is not the favorite class of Justus
Major subject: History
Not a full-time subject: History

Art is not the favorite class of Justus
Minor subject: Art
Not a full-time subject: Art
```

Why Choosy People Choose xsl:choose

The second type of control statement in XSLT is the `xsl:choose` instruction. While `xsl:if` is the equivalent of a true/false test, `xsl:choose` is akin to a multiple choice test. Using it, you can choose among two or more options or optionally default to an alternative if no other condition is met.

`xsl:choose` is the equivalent of the `case` or `switch` statement found in many other programming languages.

`xsl:choose` has a `xsl:when` subelement that is used to test for each condition and an optional `xsl:otherwise` to specify a default response. The `xsl:choose` syntax looks like:

```
<xsl:choose>
  <xsl:when test="expression">
    do something
  </xsl:when>
  <xsl:when test="expression2">
    do something
  </xsl:when>
  <xsl:when test="expression3">
    do something
  </xsl:when>
  <xsl:otherwise>
    do something
  </xsl:when>
</xsl:choose>
```

When the XSLT processor encounters an `xsl:choose` element, the processor evaluates each `xsl:when` instruction in sequential order looking for a `true` result of the `test` expression. When the first `true` result is found, then that `xsl:when`'s content is processed, and the processor bypasses the remaining `xsl:when` and `xsl:otherwise` elements of the `xsl:choose` instruction. If no `xsl:when` evaluates to true, then the `xsl:otherwise` element is used.

For example, suppose the following code snippet is run against an element that has a `name` attribute with a value of `Larry` (such as `<emp name="Larry">`):

```
<xsl:choose>
  <xsl:when test="@name='Moe'">
    My name is Moe
  </xsl:when>
  <xsl:when test="@name='Curly'">
    My name is Curly
  </xsl:when>
```

```
      <xsl:when test="@name='Larry'">
        My name is Larry
      </xsl:when>
      <xsl:otherwise>
        I am not a stooge!
      </xsl:when>
    </xsl:choose>
```

The XSLT processor evaluates the first xsl:when statement, but continues after it returns a false value. The same thing happens with the second xsl:when. But when the processor gets to the third xsl:when instruction, it returns a true value, so the literal string My name is Larry is output to the result tree. The xsl:otherwise is ignored in this case, because a true test expression was already found.

As with xsl:if, you can use xsl:choose only within a template rule.

To demonstrate xsl:choose, I transform the XML document in Listing 7-1 into a new XML fallclasses structure. The changes are as follows:

- ✔ For class name="Reading" elements, new schedule="9am" and priority="A" attributes are added.

- ✔ For class name="Writing" elements, new schedule="10am" and priority="B" attributes are added.

- ✔ For class name="Math" elements, new schedule="11am" and priority="C" attributes are added.

- ✔ For every other class element, new schedule="postlunch" and priority="D" attributes are added.

The stylesheet to perform this transformation is as follows:

```
<?xml version="1.0"?>
<xsl:stylesheet version="1.0"
          xmlns:xsl="http://www.w3.org/1999/XSL/Transform">

  <xsl:output method="xml"/>

  <!-- Replace school element with fallclasses -->
  <xsl:template match="/">
  <xsl:text>
</xsl:text><fallclasses teacher="ksw">
      <xsl:apply-templates/>
    </fallclasses>
  </xsl:template>

  <!-- Transform class elements -->
  <xsl:template match="class">
    <xsl:choose>
      <xsl:when test="@name='Reading'">
        <class student="{../@name}" subject="{@name}"
            assignment="{.}" schedule="9am" priority="A"/>
```

```
        </xsl:when>
        <xsl:when test="@name='Writing'">
          <class student="{../@name}" subject="{@name}"
              assignment="{.}" schedule="10am" priority="B"/>
        </xsl:when>
        <xsl:when test="@name='Math'">
          <class student="{../@name}" subject="{@name}"
              assignment="{.}" schedule="11am" priority="C"/>
        </xsl:when>
        <xsl:otherwise>
          <class student="{../@name}" subject="{@name}"
              assignment="{.}" schedule="postlunch"
              priority="D"/>
        </xsl:otherwise>
      </xsl:choose>
    </xsl:template>

</xsl:stylesheet>
```

In the first template rule, the school document element is replaced by adding a fallclasses element. In the second rule, the xsl:choose instruction is run against each class element. For all Reading class elements, the first xsl:when statement is run, while Writing class elements act on the second and Math elements on the third. For the remaining elements, the xsl:otherwise is triggered.

After the transformation, I have a shiny new XML document:

```
<?xml version="1.0" encoding="utf-8"?>
<fallclasses teacher="ksw">

    <class student="Jordan" subject="Language Arts"
            assignment="Sentence diagramming"
            schedule="postlunch" priority="D"/>
    <class student="Jordan" subject="Reading"
            assignment="Lord Of The Rings" schedule="9am"
            priority="A"/>
    <class student="Jordan" subject="Writing"
            assignment="Colonial Times" schedule="10am"
            priority="B"/>
    <class student="Jordan" subject="Geography"
            assignment="African Sahal" schedule="postlunch"
            priority="D"/>
    <class student="Jordan" subject="Math"
            assignment="Decimals" schedule="11am"
            priority="C"/>
    <class student="Jordan" subject="Science"
            assignment="Volcanos" schedule="postlunch"
            priority="D"/>
    <class student="Jordan" subject="History"
            assignment="American Presidents"
            schedule="postlunch" priority="D"/>
    <class student="Jordan" subject="Art" assignment="Drawing"
            schedule="postlunch" priority="D"/>
```

```
        <class student="Jared" subject="Language Arts"
            assignment="Punctuation" schedule="postlunch"
            priority="D"/>
        <class student="Jared" subject="Reading"
            assignment="Voyage Of The Dawntreader"
            schedule="9am" priority="A"/>
        <class student="Jared" subject="Writing"
            assignment="Haiku Poetry" schedule="10am"
            priority="B"/>
        <class student="Jared" subject="Geography"
            assignment="African Sahal" schedule="postlunch"
            priority="D"/>
        <class student="Jared" subject="Math"
            assignment="Fractions" schedule="11am"
            priority="C"/>
        <class student="Jared" subject="Science"
            assignment="Insects" schedule="postlunch"
            priority="D"/>
        <class student="Jared" subject="History"
            assignment="American Presidents"
            schedule="postlunch" priority="D"/>
        <class student="Jared" subject="Art" assignment="Paper
            Mache" schedule="postlunch" priority="D"/>


        <class student="Justus" subject="Language Arts"
            assignment="Capitalization" schedule="postlunch"
            priority="D"/>
        <class student="Justus" subject="Reading"
            assignment="Sherlock Holmes Solves Them All"
            schedule="9am" priority="A"/>
        <class student="Justus" subject="Writing"
            assignment="Penmanship" schedule="10am"
            priority="B"/>
        <class student="Justus" subject="Geography"
            assignment="African Sahel" schedule="postlunch"
            priority="D"/>
        <class student="Justus" subject="Math"
            assignment="Division" schedule="11am"
            priority="C"/>
        <class student="Justus" subject="Science"
            assignment="Vertebrates" schedule="postlunch"
            priority="D"/>
        <class student="Justus" subject="History"
            assignment="American Presidents"
            schedule="postlunch" priority="D"/>
        <class student="Justus" subject="Art" assignment="Clay
            Sculptures" schedule="postlunch" priority="D"/>

</fallclasses>
```

Going Loopy with xsl:for-each

The `xsl:for-each` element allows you to perform a set of instructions on each node returned from its `select` attribute. Its syntax is:

```
<xsl:for-each select="expression">
  do something
</xsl:for-each>
```

Essentially, the `xsl:for-each` element means that for each of the nodes returned by the `select` expression, perform the instructions in between the start and end tags.

I'm not trying to be a spoilsport, but like `xsl:if` and `xsl:choose`, you can use `xsl:for-each` only inside an `xsl:template` rule.

`xsl:for-each` is a loose equivalent to the `for` statement found in other programming languages.

At this point, you may be asking yourself, "Doesn't a template rule do the same thing as `xsl:for-each`?" After all, a template rule processes the template instructions for each node returned from its match pattern. It is certainly true that template rules perform similar operations and are usually the best way to perform routines in XSLT. In fact, before automatically using `xsl:for-each`, see if you can do the same task with an ordinary template rule.

A common mistake many newcomers to XSLT make if they've programmed in other languages is to overuse `xsl:for-each` rather than simply using template rules. After all, `xsl:for-each` looks much more familiar to a programmer than does `xsl:template`. However, XSLT asks you to think differently.

I've found the `xsl:for-each instruction` works best when you need to loop through a set of nodes at the same time you are applying a template to another node.

To illustrate `xsl:for-each` in action, suppose I want to create a list of classes for each student in the Listing 7-1 document. I use the following stylesheet to accomplish this task:

```
<xsl:stylesheet version="1.0"
        xmlns:xsl="http://www.w3.org/1999/XSL/Transform">

<xsl:output method="text"/>

<!-- Create list of classes for each student -->
<xsl:template match="student">
```

```
    <xsl:value-of select="@name"/>'s Classes:
    <xsl:for-each select="class">
      <xsl:value-of select="@name"/>
      <xsl:if test="position()!=last()">
        <xsl:text>, </xsl:text>
      </xsl:if>
    </xsl:for-each>
    <xsl:text>
    </xsl:text>
  </xsl:template>

</xsl:stylesheet>
```

To compile a list for each student, a template rule is created to return the student element nodes. After using an xsl:value-of instruction to write the student's name, I use xsl:for-each to loop through each class element and print the class name to the output document.

In the result document, I'd like to separate each class name in the list with a comma, but if I just added <xsl:text>, <xsl:text> after the xsl:value-of instruction, I'd get a trailing comma at the end of my list. As a result, I add xsl:text inside an xsl:if instruction that tests using the built-in XPath functions position() and last() to determine whether the node is the last one in the given node set. (See Chapter 11 for a complete discussion on built-in functions.)

The result document is as follows:

```
Jordan's Classes:
   Language Arts, Reading, Writing, Geography, Math,
         Science, History, Art

Jared's Classes:
   Language Arts, Reading, Writing, Geography, Math,
         Science, History, Art

Justus's Classes:
   Language Arts, Reading, Writing, Geography, Math,
         Science, History, Art
```

For most practical purposes, you can think of xsl:for-each as looping through each node in the returned node set. However, to be completely accurate, xsl:for-each is technically not a loop, but a mapping. In other words, for each node encountered in the retuning node set, something is added to the output document.

Chapter 8

Variables in XSLT: A Breed Apart

. . . .

In This Chapter

▶ Declaring variables

▶ Setting variables in templates

▶ Using variables to save time

▶ Calculating values with variables

▶ Determining variable scope

. . . .

Do you like canned spinach? Unless you have a name that begins with a *P*, forearms the size of thighs, and a girlfriend named Olive Oyl, I suspect you'd much prefer a fresh spinach salad instead. Okay, maybe spinach is push-ing it, but I bet you'd at least go for the *fresh* part, right? Prepackaged goods are helpful when you need to prepare food in advance of their actual use, but people don't much like the notion of "canned" anything if they can help it.

In earlier chapters of this book, I walk you through a lot of XSLT. All the infor-mation plugged into result documents until this chapter has come from XML or from "canned" text. That works fine in the earlier chapters of this book, but just as one longs for fresh veggies after a weekend camping trip of SPAM and beef jerky, here I show you how to gather and utilize "fresh" data through the use of variables and parameters.

What Is a Variable?

A *variable* is a handy little gadget used in nearly every programming lan-guage. Not to be left out, XSLT has variables as well, but they're quite differ-ent from those you find in Visual Basic, JavaScript, C++, or Java. They are truly their own breed.

In XSLT, a variable is used to represent something — perhaps a chunk of text, a numeric value, boilerplate HyperText Markup Language (HTML), or even a collection of XML tree nodes. But, in a manner quite different from its cousins in other languages, an XSLT variable can't change its value after you declare it. Actually, if you want to draw any comparisons, an XSLT variable is perhaps closest to a *constant* in a traditional programming language.

XSLT is quite powerful by using template rules and XPath expressions to transform XML into pretty much any output that you can imagine. Variables help to augment these tools by enabling you to make what techies call *run-time* changes (or for the rest of us, changes that happen at the time the XSLT is processed).

Run-time changes enable your transformation to adapt to a condition that exists at the time of execution rather than having all the "canned" answers prepared beforehand. Admittedly, XSLT variables are limited in their ability to do many things on the fly because you can't modify them after they're defined.

Setting Variables

A variable is defined in XSLT in one of two ways: either as a *content variable* or a *select attribute variable*.

Content variables

The most straightforward way to set a variable is by using the `xsl:variable` element to assign a variable name to the content enclosed by its tags.

```
<xsl:variable name="mystate">Massachusetts</xsl:variable>
```

In the preceding example, the `mystate` variable represents the string value of `Massachusetts`. Variables come in handy when you don't want to type out long pieces of text over and over again in your stylesheet.

In order to use a content variable, you first need to let the XSLT processor know your intentions. You can't just enter the variable's name inside the stylesheet as is and expect it to be treated properly. XSLT processors are smart, but they don't know whether you want it to be handled as normal text or as a variable identifier. If you don't tell the processor that a variable is on its way, it opts for the easy road and treats it as ordinary text. Thus, to tell the processor that you want to use `mystate` as a variable, prefix it with a $ character.

```
$mystate
```

This fully prepared variable then needs to be plugged into your stylesheet in the appropriate context. Just exactly where you place it in your stylesheet depends on how you want the variable to be placed in the result document.

If you want to output the variable as text, use the `xsl:value-of` element,

```
<p>I love <xsl:value-of select="$mystate"/> in the Fall.</p>
```

which is spit out in HTML as

```
<p>I love Massachusetts in the Fall.</p>
```

(See Chapter 4 for more information on using the `xsl:value-of` instruction.)

Or, to insert the variable into your XML output as an attribute, use an attribute value template,

```
<location state="{$mystate}"/>
```

which results in

```
<location state="Massachusetts"/>
```

(See Chapter 5 for more information on attribute value templates.)

The value of a content variable is always the piece of text enclosed by the `xsl:variable` element. Even a number placed inside is converted to a string during transformation.

If you've been around computers much, you've probably heard the term WYSIWYG (What You See Is What You Get) — what you see on-screen looks the same as when it's printed. Content variables could similarly be described as WYSIWYG because what you see in the XSLT markup that you create is exactly what appears in the result document.

Select attribute variables

A second way to define a variable is to use the `xsl:variable` element with a `select` attribute added to it.

```
<xsl:variable name="mystate" select="'Massachusetts'"/>
```

This kind of variable is sometimes referred to as a select attribute variable. Whereas a content variable sees all values as text, a select attribute variable treats its value as the result of an expression. An *expression* is an XSLT statement that represents a value or is used to calculate a value. See Table 8-1 for some sample XSLT expressions and their results.

Table 8-1	Results of XSLT Expressions
Expression	*Result*
8-5	3
'Text'	Text
round(5.129)	5

Content variables are WYSIWYG, but select attribute variables often are not. As you can see in Table 8-1, the result of an expression typically looks different than the expression itself.

In the code sample at the beginning of this section, notice that I add single quotation marks around `Massachusetts` when placing it inside of a select attribute. If I don't add single quotation marks, XSLT tries to evaluate `Massachusetts` as an expression. Admittedly, I've certainly heard my share of expressions in Massachusetts — particularly from other drivers when I'm driving around downtown Boston — but that's not what I had in mind here. If I don't add the quotes, I get a goose egg from the XSLT processor when I try to plug in that variable into the stylesheet. But by including the quotes, I let the processor know that it should treat `Massachusetts` as a literal string.

Although you can use a select attribute variable anywhere that you would use a content variable for outputting text, its primary use is working with number values or node sets.

Remember these three final "gotchas" when you define variables:

✔ If you have a select attribute defined for an `xsl:variable`, you can't define any content (text between the start and end tags) or you get a processing error.

✔ Conversely, if the variable doesn't have any content defined and doesn't have a select attribute, its result is an empty string.

✔ A content variable needs to have a start and an end tag (`<xslt:variable name="x">y</xsl:variable>`), whereas a select attribute variable should use an empty tag (`<xslt:variable name="x" select="'y'"/>`) because it contains no content.

Uses of Variables

Variables play a less integral role in standard XSL transformations than their equivalents in C++ or Visual Basic do. But they remain useful devices — in particular, when you want to reuse values across your stylesheet and when you want to calculate values once and use the result in your output document.

Using a variable as a shortcut

Perhaps the most common purpose for XSLT variables is simply to use them as shortcuts to values that you intend to use multiple times across a document. For example, suppose that you have a standard footer that you want to place at the bottom of a result document that you produce. Save time and effort by defining a variable once, having it reference a chunk of HTML.

```
<xsl:variable name="footer">
<p><font size="8pt">Copyright (c)2001, Variably Speaking,
        Inc.</font></p>
<p><font size="8pt">Send us email at <a
        href="mailto:feedback@variably.com">feedback@varia
        bly.com</a></font>
</p>
</xsl:variable>
```

To use this `footer` variable, I reference it using the `xsl:value-of` element,

```
<xsl:value-of select="$footer"/>
```

which outputs the following HTML in the result document.

```
<p><font size="8pt">Copyright (c)2001, Variably Speaking,
        Inc.</font></p>
<p><font size="8pt">Send us email at <a
        href="mailto:feedback@variably.com">feedback@varia
        bly.com</a>
<font></p>
```

These shortcut variables are very easy to define and use in your XSLT stylesheets. They come in especially handy when you need to use hard-to-remember constants such as HTML color-code values or special characters.

Variables also come in handy when you need to reuse a value within the same stylesheet. For example, suppose that I want to transform the following XML snippet:

```
<film name="Henry V">
    <director>Kenneth Branagh</director>
    <writer>Kenneth Branagh, William Shakespeare</writer>
    <year>1989</year>
    <runtime>137</runtime>
    <sound>Stereo</sound>
    <genre>Drama</genre>
    <score>10.0</score>
    <mpaa>PG-13</mpaa>
</film>
```

and output it into this HTML:

```
<p>Highest movies by score:</p>
<b>
<font color="FF0000" size="2">Henry V by Kenneth
        Branagh</font>
</b>
<br/>
<i>
```

```
<font color="FF0000" size="-2">Received a score of:
        10.0</font>
</i>
<br/>
```

Looking at the resulting HTML, notice that the font color is used twice. And, although the two specified font sizes are different, they're relative to each other. Therefore, in my XSLT stylesheet, I can use variables to represent both the font color and size.

```
<xsl:variable name="myfontcolor">FF0000</xsl:variable>
<xsl:variable name="myfontsize" select="2"/>
```

To get the results for the first output section, I create a template rule for the director element, plugging in the myfontcolor and myfontsize variables.

```
<xsl:template match="director">
    <p>Highest movies by score:</p>
    <b><font color="{$myfontcolor}" size="{$myfontsize}">
    <xsl:value-of select="../@name"/>
    <xsl:text> by </xsl:text>
    <xsl:apply-templates/>
    </font></b><br/>
</xsl:template>
```

For the score template rule, the myfontcolor variable is simply placed as is. However, because I want the font size of this text to be four increments smaller than the myfontsize value, I subtract one from the variable. The XSLT processor evaluates {$myfontsize - 4} as an XPath expression and uses the result of the expression (-2) in the output document.

```
<xsl:template match="score">
    <i><font size="{$myfontsize-4}">
    Received a score of:
    <xsl:apply-templates/>
    </font></i><br/>
</xsl:template>
```

The complete XSL stylesheet is shown below.

```
<xsl:stylesheet
        xmlns:xsl="http://www.w3.org/1999/XSL/Transform"
        version="1.0">

<!-- Define variables -->
<xsl:variable name="myfontcolor">FF0000</xsl:variable>
<xsl:variable name="myfontsize" select="2"/>

<!-- Director template -->
```

```
<xsl:template match="director">
    <p>Highest movies by score:</p>
    <b><font size="{$myfontsize}" color="{$myfontcolor}">
    <xsl:value-of select="../@name"/>
    <xsl:text> by </xsl:text>
    <xsl:apply-templates/>
    </font></b><br/>
</xsl:template>

<!-- Score template -->
<xsl:template match="score">
    <i><font size="{$myfontsize - 4}">
    Received a score of:
    <xsl:apply-templates/>
    </font></i><br/>
</xsl:template>

<!-- Remove these elements from our results document -->
<xsl:template match="year"/>
<xsl:template match="writer"/>
<xsl:template match="sound"/>
<xsl:template match="genre"/>
<xsl:template match="mpaa"/>
<xsl:template match="runtime"/>

</xsl:stylesheet>
```

See the results on the transformation in Internet Explorer in Figure 8-1.

Figure 8-1:
Results of
the XSLT
transforma-
tion.

Using a variable as a calculator

Because select attribute variables return expressions rather than ordinary
text, they're handy when you want a little more firepower and flexibility, such
as the calculation of a value. Consider the following XML file in Listing 8-1.

Listing 8-1:   films.xml

```
<films>
  <film name="Henry V">
    <director>Kenneth Branagh</director>
    <writer>Kenneth Branagh, William Shakespeare</writer>
    <year>1989</year>
    <runtime>137</runtime>
    <sound>Stereo</sound>
    <genre>Drama</genre>
    <score>10.0</score>
    <mpaa>PG-13</mpaa>
  </film>
  <film name="Groundhog Day">
    <director>Harold Ramis</director>
    <writer>Danny Rubin</writer>
    <year>1993</year>
    <runtime>101</runtime>
    <sound>Dolby</sound>
    <genre>Romantic Comedy</genre>
    <score>9.0</score>
    <mpaa>PG</mpaa>
  </film>
  <film name="Man for All Seasons">

    <director>Fred Zinnemann</director>
    <writer>Robert Bolt</writer>
    <year>1966</year>
    <runtime>120</runtime>
    <sound>Mono</sound>
    <genre>Drama</genre>
    <score>8.0</score>
    <mpaa>PG</mpaa>
  </film>
  <film name="Field of Dreams">
    <director>Phil Alden Robinson</director>
    <writer>W.P.Kinsella, Phil Alden Robinson</writer>
    <year>1988</year>
    <runtime>107</runtime>
    <sound>Dolby</sound>
    <genre>Drama</genre>
    <score>9.8</score>
    <mpaa>PG</mpaa>
  </film>
  <film name="Babette&apos;s Feast">
    <director>Gabriel Axel</director>
    <writer>Gabriel Axel</writer>
    <year>1987</year>
    <runtime>102</runtime>
    <sound>Dolby</sound>
    <genre>Drama</genre>
    <score>9.5</score>
    <mpaa>PG</mpaa>
  </film>
</films>
```

Calculate the total number of PG-rated films in the list and then assign that value to a variable. You can tackle that problem by first defining a variable that uses an XPath expression to return the desired films.

```
<xsl:variable name="pgFilms" select="//film[mpaa='PG']"/>
```

The pgFilms variable uses the //film[mpaa='PG'] expression to tell the processor, "Gimme all the <film> elements in the document that have an <mpaa> child with the value of PG."

The pgFilms variable differs from others in that its value is not a string or number but rather a *result tree fragment*, or a collection of nodes that meet the stated requirements.

After you have a variable to represent the tree nodes, your next step is to declare a second variable that takes the value of the first to calculate the total number of PG films.

```
<xsl:variable name="totalNumOfPgFilms"
        select="count($pgFilms)"/>
```

In the preceding expression, the built-in XPath count() function adds up the total number of nodes contained in the result tree fragment stored in the pgFilms variable.

Keeping the output simple, you can use the variable like this:

```
<xsl:variable name="pgFilms" select="//film[mpaa='PG']"/>
<xsl:variable name="totalNumOfPgFilms"
        select="count($pgFilms)"/>
<xsl:template match="/">
   <p>The total number of PG films:
   <xsl:value-of select="$totalNumOfPgFilms"/>
   </p>
</xsl:template>
```

The end result in HTML is

```
The total number of PG films: 4
```

Think Globally, Act Locally

You've undoubtedly seen the slogan *Think globally, act locally* on bumper stickers. My personal favorite bumper sticker is *Visualize Whirled Peas*, but flying veggies are quite distracting when you try to work with variables, so I'll opt for the more environmentally sound expression.

Although the *Think globally, act locally* slogan is appropriate for conserving nature, it's also an ideal maxim for using variables because all variables have scope. A variable's *scope* is the area of the stylesheet in which the variable is available for use. Variables can be available to the entire document (globally) or simply to a specific region (locally).

Throughout previous chapters of this book, I define variables at the beginning of the XSLT stylesheets and then use them in templates defined at the same tree level. When you declare a variable at the top level of a document, however, you define a *global* variable, meaning that you can use this variable anywhere in the stylesheet and that it's always available.

You can also define variables inside of a given template rule. When you do so, this *local variable* is available to only that template rule or any elements that are inside of it. For example, the variable thinkGlobally can be used anywhere in this stylesheet:

```
<xsl:variable name="thinkGlobally">14pt</xsl:variable>

<xsl:template match="film">
   <font size="{$thinkGlobally}">
     <xsl:apply-templates select="writer"/>
   </font><xsl:text>
  </xsl:text>
   <xsl:variable name="actLocally">12pt</xsl:variable>
   <font size="{$actLocally}">
     <xsl:apply-templates select="director"/>
   </font>
</xsl:template>
```

to output the following HTML:

```
<font size="14">Kenneth Branagh, William Shakespeare</font>
<font size="12">Kenneth Branagh</font>
```

Although globals can be used anywhere, the actLocally variable can be used only inside the template rule in which it is defined. If you try to use it outside of the template rule it is in, the XSLT processor yells at you.

A second issue to consider when scoping variables is *precedence* when two variables have identical names. In other words, who wins the duel? In XSLT, the variable farthest down the hierarchy always wins; a local variable always overrides its global counterpart. So if you tweak the example and change the name of the local variable to also be thinkGlobally, the XSLT processor gives the writer element a value of 14pt and the director element a value of 12pt:

```
<xsl:template match="film">
   <font size="{$thinkGlobally}">
     <xsl:apply-templates select="writer"/>
   </font><xsl:text>
 </xsl:text>
   <xsl:variable name="thinkGlobally">12pt</xsl:variable>
   <font size="{$thinkGlobally}">
     <xsl:apply-templates select="director"/>
   </font>
</xsl:template>
```

with identical output as before:

```
<font size="14">Kenneth Branagh, William Shakespeare</font>
<font size="12">Kenneth Branagh</font>
```

Through these examples, you can see that *Think globally, act locally* holds true. Although you need to be aware of global variables that affect the stylesheet as a whole, in the end, the value of the variable being used depends wholly on the local conditions in the template rule in which it's being used.

Working with Parameters

XSLT packs another handy device called a *parameter*, which is a close cousin to a variable. Parameters follow the same general behavior of variables, but they have the added flexibility of being able to change their values at the time that the XSLT stylesheet is processed.

How parameters resemble variables

A parameter is defined in XSLT by using the `xsl:param` element and follows the same syntax rules of variables. Therefore, to define a content-based parameter, the `name` attribute of `xsl:param` specifies the parameter name and the text between the start and end tags provides its value.

```
<xsl:param name="style">Normal</xsl:param>
```

Or, to define a select attribute parameter, put the value inside the `select` attribute of `xsl:param`.

```
<xsl:param name="style" select="'Normal'"/>
```

Think of parameters as a superset of variables because they do everything that variables do — and more. For each of the preceding examples in this chapter, you can substitute `xsl:param` in place of `xsl:variable` and achieve the exact same results.

How parameters are different from variables

Parameters can be used in place of variables, but their main purpose is to provide a way to override default values at run-time, both from inside and outside of XSLT stylesheets.

Overriding parameters with the with-param element

To override the value of a parameter *within* a stylesheet, use the xsl:with-param element. This instruction is added to a template rule, mirroring the variable and parameter elements.

```
<xsl:with-param name="style">Enhanced</xsl:with-param>
```

Or you can add it like this:

```
<xsl:with-param name="style" select="'Enhanced'"/>
```

The typical use of xsl:with-param is to override a parameter that's been defined in a named template. To help you understand this, look at an example. Begin with the following XML fragment.

```
<film name="Field of Dreams">
  <director>Phil Alden Robinson</director>
  <writer>W.P.Kinsella, Phil Alden Robinson</writer>
  <year>1988</year>
  <runtime>107</runtime>
  <sound>Dolby</sound>
  <genre>Drama</genre>
  <score>9.8</score>
  <mpaa>PG</mpaa>
</film>
```

My objective is to generate an HTML document that transforms the values of the director, writer, and year elements and turns them into links (a elements), giving each link a unique URL.

```
<p><a href="legend.html#director">Phil Alden Robinson</a></p>
  <p><a href="legend.html#writer">W.P.Kinsella, Phil Alden
      Robinson</a></p>
  <p><a href="legend.html#year">1988</a></p>
```

Parameters are well suited for handling such a task because they allow you to change their value during the transformation.

Start by creating a named template called labels that contains a parameter value called legendUrl. The labels template defines the a element and the spot where the legendUrl parameter is plugged in.

```
<!-- Labels named template -->
<xsl:template name="labels">
  <xsl:param name="legendUrl">legend.html#main</xsl:param>
  <a href="{$legendUrl}"><xsl:apply-templates/></a>
</xsl:template>
```

After you define the `labels` template, add template rules for the `director`, `writer`, and `year` elements. For each of these, use an `xsl:call-template` instruction to call the `labels` template. Nestled comfortably inside of `xsl:call-template` is an `xsl:with-param` element that sends a new value to the `legendUrl` parameter. This value is then used as the `href` value in the resulting HTML.

```
<!-- Director -->
<xsl:template match="director">
  <xsl:call-template name="labels">
    <xsl:with-param
            name="legendUrl">legend.html#director</xsl:with-
            param>
  </xsl:call-template>
</xsl:template>

<!-- Writer -->
<xsl:template match="writer">
  <xsl:call-template name="labels">
    <xsl:with-param
            name="legendUrl">legend.html#writer</xsl:with-
            param>
  </xsl:call-template>
</xsl:template>

<!-- Year -->
<xsl:template match="year">
  <xsl:call-template name="labels">
    <xsl:with-param
            name="legendUrl">legend.html#year</xsl:with-param>
  </xsl:call-template>
</xsl:template>

<!-- Remove these elements from our results document -->
<xsl:template match="sound"/>
<xsl:template match="genre"/>
<xsl:template match="mpaa"/>
<xsl:template match="runtime"/>
<xsl:template match="score"/>
```

See Figure 8-2 for the formatted results of the transformation.

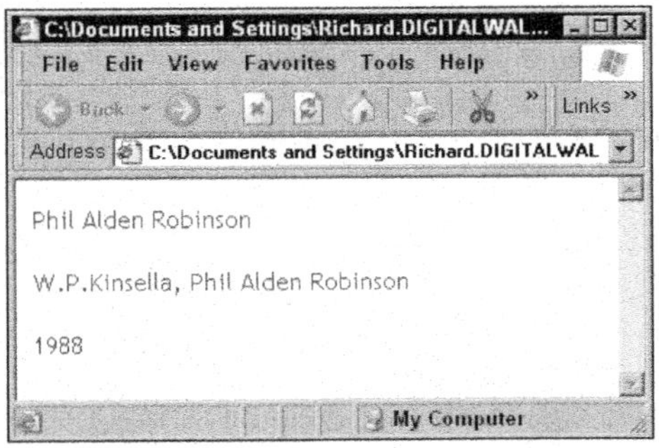

Figure 8-2:
Using
parameters
allows
values to
be updated
during
transforma-
tion.

Phil Alden Robinson

W.P.Kinsella, Phil Alden Robinson

1988

Overriding parameters from the XSLT processor

An invisible boundary for your XSLT work area throughout this book is the stylesheet itself; all the XSLT elements and instructions are contained inside the stylesheet document. However, parameters have the ability to be changed from The Great Beyond — outside the stylesheet — by passing in a new value from the XSLT processor. Exactly how you do this depends on the specific XSLT processor that you use.

For example, by using the SAXON processor, you can specify a parameter name-value pair as a command line parameter.

```
saxon xmlfile.xml xslfile.xsl param=value
```

If you want to pass in a value for a parameter called myfontsize, the command line is

```
saxon films.xml param2.xsl myfontsize=2
```

The XSLT processor passes the value of 2 to the myfontsize parameter, overriding any default values that were originally provided in the param2.xsl stylesheet.

Some XSLT processors may use a different method to pass parameter values to a stylesheet, but they all give you an identical result in the output document.

Much of the power of parameters lies in their ability to be changed from the outside. In so doing, parameters give you freedom to use values in your trans-formation that may not be known at the time when you're actually writing the XSLT stylesheet. Using parameters also enables you to run new transforma-tions without changing the underlying XSLT stylesheet one iota.

Chapter 9

Tweaking the Results to Get What You Want

I bet you've seen those commercials that promise you what you want when you need it: news at your fingertips, unmatched performance from your car, great taste, less filling. However, I don't need a firm voice and a well-groomed toupee or a slick song culled from a little-known album to convince you that you can get what you want from XSLT.

However, to do so might involve a little "tweaking" of your stylesheets. You will find the practice of tweaking to be both useful and necessary when working with XSLT result documents. In this chapter, I look at how you can refine and fine-tune your output documents by sorting and auto-numbering the results.

Sorting Elements in the Results Tree

Until now, all the nodes in the result trees have always been in the same order in which they appeared in the source document. But in many cases, you want to sort the results in a particular order. To this end, the xsl:sort instruction comes to the rescue, allowing you to greatly enhance your sorting capabilities when used with either xsl:apply-templates or xsl:for-each.

You can use the xsl:sort element only inside xsl:apply-templates and xsl:for-each instructions.

`xsl:sort` enables you to sort the nodes of a transformation based on the result of the XPath expression in its `select` attribute value. For example, the following instruction sorts the results based on the alphabetical value of the `name` child element returned for the current node:

```
<xsl:sort select="name"/>
```

In the preceding `xsl:sort` instruction, the `name` element is often called the *sort key.*

To illustrate how you can use `xsl:sort`, consider the following XML snippet:

```
<beverages>
  <beverage>Coffee</beverage>
  <beverage>Tea</beverage>
  <beverage>Milk</beverage>
  <beverage>Cola</beverage>
  <beverage>Diet Cola</beverage>
  <beverage>Root Beer</beverage>
  <beverage>Water</beverage>
  <beverage>Lemonade</beverage>
  <beverage>Iced Tea</beverage>
  <beverage>Wine</beverage>
</beverages>
```

Suppose you want to create a simple list of beverages from the preceding source document. To do so, create a template rule for the `beverage` element that prints its content as text:

```
<xsl:template match="beverage">
 * <xsl:value-of select="."/>
</xsl:template>
```

By using only this template, the list generated is in the same order as what is in the original source:

```
 * Coffee
 * Tea
 * Milk
 * Cola
 * Diet Cola
 * Root Beer
 * Water
 * Lemonade
 * Iced Tea
 * Wine
```

However, by adding `xsl:sort` to the stylesheet, you can spruce up the output to make this an alphabetized list of beverages. To do so, create a new template rule for the sorting:

```
<xsl:template match="beverages">
  <xsl:apply-templates>
    <xsl:sort select="."/>
  </xsl:apply-templates>
</xsl:template>
```

In this template rule, the parent element beverages is used as the match pattern. (I cannot use beverage as the pattern; it would conflict with the template rule I already defined.) Nestled within the xsl:apply-templates instruction is xsl:sort, which uses . as its select expression to sort by the value of the content for each beverage element. With this new template rule, the entire XSLT stylesheet looks like this:

```
<xsl:stylesheet
          xmlns:xsl="http://www.w3.org/1999/XSL/Transform"
          version="1.0">

<!-- Sort by beverage -->
<xsl:template match="beverages">
  <xsl:apply-templates>
    <xsl:sort select="."/>
  </xsl:apply-templates>
</xsl:template>

<!-- List beverage -->
<xsl:template match="beverage">
  * <xsl:value-of select="."/>
</xsl:template>

</xsl:stylesheet>
```

After the transformation, the sorted result is as follows:

```
* Coffee
* Cola
* Diet Cola
* Iced Tea
* Lemonade
* Milk
* Root Beer
* Tea
* Water
* Wine
```

Sorting by type

By default, the xsl:sort instruction decides how to sort based on the string result of the select attribute value. Because I'm working with alphabetical characters, this behavior is exactly what is expected in the preceding example. But this behavior becomes problematic when you want to sort with numeric values. Take, for example, the addition of a price attribute to the XML snippet:

```
<beverages>
  <beverage price="150">Coffee</beverage>
  <beverage price="90">Tea</beverage>
  <beverage price="80">Milk</beverage>
  <beverage price="80">Cola</beverage>
  <beverage price="80">Diet Cola</beverage>
  <beverage price="80">Root Beer</beverage>
  <beverage price="25">Water</beverage>
  <beverage price="125">Lemonade</beverage>
  <beverage price="90">Iced Tea</beverage>
  <beverage price="200">Wine</beverage>
</beverages>
```

By changing xsl:sort to arrange the output based on the value of the price attribute and adding the price to the resulting string, the updated stylesheet looks like:

```
<xsl:stylesheet
        xmlns:xsl="http://www.w3.org/1999/XSL/Transform"
        version="1.0">

<!-- Sort by beverage price -->
<xsl:template match="beverages">
  <xsl:apply-templates>
    <xsl:sort select="@price"/>
  </xsl:apply-templates>
</xsl:template>

<!-- List beverage -->
<xsl:template match="beverage">
  * <xsl:value-of select="."/> costs <xsl:value-of
        select="@price"/>
</xsl:template>

</xsl:stylesheet>
```

The list generated appears as follows:

```
    * Lemonade costs 125
    * Coffee costs 150
    * Wine costs 200
    * Water costs 25
    * Milk costs 80
    * Cola costs 80
    * Diet Cola costs 80
    * Root Beer costs 80
    * Tea costs 90
    * Iced Tea costs 90
```

Well, the list was sorted on price all right, but not the way I wanted it to. The reason is that sort is treating the price value as plain text. Alphabetical sorting rules evaluate each character in a string one at a time. Therefore, when a number is sorted using these rules, values which start with 1 come before 2, whether the number is 1, 10, or 1,000,000,000. Looking at the preceding example, although 125 is actually a higher number than 25, it is still placed earlier when the sort is alphabetical.

To get the results I want, I need to sort by actual numeric value. To do so, use the xsl:sort's data-type attribute to specify the type of sort. The two common data-type values are text and number:

✔ text denotes that the sort order is based on the alphabetical rules for the language specified by any declared lang value. (This is the default.)

✔ number specifies that the sort order is done by converting the result to a number and then sorting based on the numeric value.

By adding data-type to xsl:sort, I get:

```
<xsl:template match="beverages">
  <xsl:apply-templates>
    <xsl:sort select="@price" data-type="number"/>
  </xsl:apply-templates>
</xsl:template>
```

My updated list is now sorted based on price:

```
* Water costs 25
* Milk costs 80
* Cola costs 80
* Diet Cola costs 80
* Root Beer costs 80
* Tea costs 90
* Iced Tea costs 90
* Lemonade costs 125
* Coffee costs 150
* Wine costs 200
```

Changing sort order

The xsl:sort instruction has two additional attributes that enable you to further tweak the order in which the nodes are sorted:

✔ order specifies whether text is sorted in ascending or descending order.

✔ case-order specifies how text is sorted based on case. Use upper-first if you want all uppercase letters to sort before lowercase or lower-first for lowercase first.

TIP

The case-order attribute is ignored when you sort by number (use `data-type="number"`).

To demonstrate the `order` attribute, I've changed the sorting template rule to sort in descending order:

```
<xsl:template match="beverages">
  <xsl:apply-templates>
    <xsl:sort select="." data-type="text"
            order="descending"/>
  </xsl:apply-templates>
</xsl:template>

<xsl:template match="beverage">
  * <xsl:value-of select="."/>
</xsl:template>
```

The result is:

```
* Wine
* Water
* Tea
* Root Beer
* Milk
* Lemonade
* Iced Tea
* Diet Cola
* Cola
* Coffee
```

To illustrate the usage of the `case-order` attribute, I've modified the original XML code with some additional case-specific characters:

```
<beverages>
  <beverage>coffee</beverage>
  <beverage>COFFEE</beverage>
  <beverage>Tea</beverage>
  <beverage>milk</beverage>
  <beverage>Cola</beverage>
  <beverage>cola</beverage>
  <beverage>diet Cola</beverage>
  <beverage>Root Beer</beverage>
  <beverage>Water</beverage>
  <beverage>Lemonade</beverage>
  <beverage>Iced Tea</beverage>
  <beverage>WINE</beverage>
</beverages>
```

A `case-order` attribute is then added to `xsl:sort`:

```
<xsl:template match="beverages">
  <xsl:apply-templates>
    <xsl:sort select="." data-type="text" case-order="upper-
        first"/>
  </xsl:apply-templates>
</xsl:template>

<xsl:template match="beverage">
  * <xsl:value-of select="."/>
</xsl:template>
```

In the result that follows, notice that the sorting takes place with uppercase values going first:

```
* COFFEE
* coffee
* Cola
* cola
* diet Cola
* Iced Tea
* Lemonade
* milk
* Root Beer
* Tea
* Water
* WINE
```

Notice that case-order is applied *after* the main text sorting is finished. For example, take the second and third items in the list: coffee and Cola. Even though Cola has an uppercase *C,* it appears after coffee because the word *coffee* is sorted alphabetically before the word *cola.*

Think of case-order as a tie-breaker between similar values, not as the sole determinant of the xsl:sort instruction's sorting order.

Sorting with multiple keys

Two or more xsl:sort instructions can be applied to sort using multiple keys. When the XSLT processor encounters multiple xsl:sort instructions, it sorts first by the initial one encountered, then by the second, and so on.

Consider the following XML:

```
<customers>
  <customer id="100">
    <firstname>Joan</firstname>
    <lastname>Arc</lastname>
```

```
    </customer>
    <customer id="101">
      <firstname>Bill</firstname>
      <lastname>Shakespaire</lastname>
    </customer>
    <customer id="102">
      <firstname>Ned</firstname>
      <lastname>Ryerson</lastname>
    </customer>
    <customer id="103">
      <firstname>Gerald</firstname>
      <lastname>Smith</lastname>
    </customer>
    <customer id="104">
      <firstname>Rock</firstname>
      <lastname>Randels</lastname>
    </customer>
    <customer id="105">
      <firstname>Ted</firstname>
      <lastname>Narlybolyson</lastname>
    </customer>
    <customer id="106">
      <firstname>Tim</firstname>
      <lastname>Smith</lastname>
    </customer>
    <customer id="107">
      <firstname>Thomas</firstname>
      <lastname>Smith</lastname>
    </customer>
  </customers>
```

To create a list of customers sorted by the `lastname` and `firstname` elements, I set up the following stylesheet:

```
<xsl:stylesheet
        xmlns:xsl="http://www.w3.org/1999/XSL/Transform"
        version="1.0">

<!-- Sort by lastname and firstname -->
<xsl:template match="customers">
  <xsl:apply-templates>
    <xsl:sort select="lastname"/>
    <xsl:sort select="firstname"/>
  </xsl:apply-templates>
</xsl:template>

<!-- List customers -->
<xsl:template match="customer">
    <xsl:value-of select="lastname"/><xsl:text>,
        </xsl:text><xsl:value-of
        select="firstname"/><xsl:text>
```

```
   </xsl:text>
    </xsl:template>

  </xsl:stylesheet>
```

In the first template rule, two `xsl:sort` elements are added so that the list is sorted by `lastname` first and then by `firstname`. In the second template rule, I employ two `xsl:value-of` instructions to convert the content of `lastname` and `firstname` elements to strings. I use an `xsl:text` element to add a carriage return to the end of each line. The result is:

```
Arc, Joan
Narlybolyson, Ted
Randels, Rock
Ryerson, Ned
Shakespaire, Bill
Smith, Gerald
Smith, Thomas
Smith, Tim
```

Adding Automatic Numbering

People frequently need to automatically generate sequential numbers for tree nodes in order to create the results documents they want. My earlier examples are cases in point: I use ordinary asterisks before each list item to form a bulleted list. But suppose I want to get fancy and change the bulleted list to a numbered list. Consider the same XML snippet as the source:

```
<beverages>
  <beverage>Coffee</beverage>
  <beverage>Tea</beverage>
  <beverage>Milk</beverage>
  <beverage>Cola</beverage>
  <beverage>Diet Cola</beverage>
  <beverage>Root Beer</beverage>
  <beverage>Water</beverage>
  <beverage>Lemonade</beverage>
  <beverage>Iced Tea</beverage>
  <beverage>Wine</beverage>
</beverages>
```

The `xsl:number` element is used to generate a unique number for each item and write a formatted number to the result tree. For a basic list, I use just the instruction without any attributes:

```
<xsl:template match="beverage">
  <xsl:number/>. <xsl:apply-templates/>
</xsl:template>
```

The resulting output is:

```
 1. Coffee
 2. Tea
 3. Milk
 4. Cola
 5. Diet Cola
 6. Root Beer
 7. Water
 8. Lemonade
 9. Iced Tea
10. Wine
```

When you use xsl:number without any of its formatting attributes, the result is simply a number. Therefore, I added a . (period and space) as literal text between the xsl:number and xsl:value-of instructions to generate a formatted list. However, I show you in the next section how you can add those literal text formatting characters inside the xsl:number definition.

Adjusting the format

The default number format is a simple 1, 2, 3, and so on until the end of the nodes. However, xsl:number provides an optional format attribute to provide a kind of numbering template. The XSLT processor looks at the format attribute value and bases its auto-numbering output on it. There are three basic types of tokens:

- ✔ Numbers (1, 2, 3, and so on)
- ✔ Roman numerals (I, II, III, and so on or i, ii, iii, and so on)
- ✔ Letters (A, B, C, and so on or a, b, c, and so on)

You can intermix a token with literal text to create a template that you want reproduced for each xsl:number instruction processed. For example:

```
<xsl:number format="1. "/>
```

This format value has the 1 token along with literal text (a period and a space), so that when the instruction is converted to a string, a unique sequential number plus the literal text is added to the output.

Table 9-1 lists a variety of common format values and the sequences for each one.

Table 9-1	**Number Formats**		
format *Value*	*Sequence*		*Example Output*
format="1"	1, 2, 3 . . . 10, 11, 12 . . . 101, 102, 103 . . .		1Casablanca
format="01"	01, 02, 03 . . . 10, 11, 12 . . . 101, 102, 103 . . .		01Casablanca
format="001"	001, 002, 003 . . . 010, 011, 012 . . . 101, 102, 103 . . .		001Casablanca
format="1. "	1, 2, 3 . . . 10, 11, 12 . . . 101, 102, 103 . . .		1. Casablanca
format="(1) "	1, 2, 3 . . . 10, 11, 12 . . . 101, 102, 103 . . .		(1) Casablanca
format="I "	I, II, III, IV . . .		I Casablanca
format="i "	i, ii, iii, iv . . .		i Casablanca
format="i) "	i, ii, iii, iv . . .		i) Casablanca
format="A "	A, B, C . . . Z, AA, BB, CC . . .		A Casablanca
format="a "	a, b, c . . . z, aa, bb, cc . . .		a Casablanca

To illustrate, suppose you add a format attribute to the xsl:number element in the preceding example:

```
<xsl:template match="beverage">
  <xsl:number format="(01) "/>
  <xsl:apply-templates/>
</xsl:template>
```

The output is then changed to:

```
(01) Coffee
(02) Tea
(03) Milk
(04) Cola
(05) Diet Cola
(06) Root Beer
(07) Water
(08) Lemonade
(09) Iced Tea
(10) Wine
```

If you are numbering a result document that can count into the thousands or even millions, you can use `xsl:number`'s `grouping-size` and `grouping-separator` attributes to add grouping formatting:

- ✔ `grouping-size="number"` specifies the size of a group of digits. This value is normally 3.
- ✔ `grouping-separator="character"` defines the character used to separate the number groups. This value is normally a comma.

For example, if you used `grouping-size="3"` and `grouping-separator=","`, you get the following values: `1,000` and `1,000,000`.

Handling multiple levels

The `xsl:number` instruction provides a `level` attribute to enable you to handle numbering in a result document that needs numbering at multiple levels. For example, suppose I add a second level of `beverage` elements to the `beverages` structure:

```
<beverages>
  <beverage>Coffee
    <beverage>Drip Coffee</beverage>
    <beverage>Latte</beverage>
    <beverage>Espresso</beverage>
    <beverage>Cappuccino</beverage>
  </beverage>
  <beverage>Tea
    <beverage>Earl Grey</beverage>
    <beverage>Green Tea</beverage>
  </beverage>
  <beverage>Milk
    <beverage>Skim Milk</beverage>
    <beverage>2 Percent Milk</beverage>
    <beverage>Whole Milk</beverage>
  </beverage>
  <beverage>Cola
    <beverage>Coca Cola</beverage>
    <beverage>Pepsi</beverage>
    <beverage>RC</beverage>
  </beverage>
  <beverage>Diet Cola
    <beverage>Diet Coke</beverage>
    <beverage>Diet Pepsi</beverage>
  </beverage>
  <beverage>Root Beer</beverage>
  <beverage>Water
    <beverage>Sparking Mineral Water</beverage>
    <beverage>Spring Water</beverage>
```

```
    </beverage>
    <beverage>Lemonade</beverage>
    <beverage>Iced Tea</beverage>
    <beverage>Wine</beverage>
</beverages>
```

Using `xsl:number`'s `level` attribute, I can specify how I want to number the result document across these levels. The following template rule shows the `level` attribute being added:

```
<xsl:template match="beverage">
    <xsl:number format="1. " level="single"/>
    <xsl:apply-templates/>
</xsl:template>
```

The `level` attribute accepts three values:

✔ `level="single"` (the default) numbers each level on its own, ignoring other levels that may exist above it or below it. The resulting output is:

```
1. Coffee
    1. Drip Coffee
    2. Latte
    3. Espresso
    4. Cappuccino

2. Tea
    1. Earl Grey
    2. Green Tea

3. Milk
    1. Skim Milk
    2. 2 Percent Milk
    3. Whole Milk

4. Cola
    1. Coca Cola
    2. Pepsi
    3. RC

5. Diet Cola
    1. Diet Coke
    2. Diet Pepsi

6. Root Beer
7. Water
    1. Sparking Mineral Water
    2. Spring Water

8. Lemonade
9. Iced Tea
10. Wine
```

✔ `level="multiple"` treats the document as something like an outline, maintaining an interrelationship across hierarchical levels:

```
1. Coffee
   1.1. Drip Coffee
   1.2. Latte
   1.3. Espresso
   1.4. Cappuccino

2. Tea
   2.1. Earl Grey
   2.2. Green Tea

3. Milk
   3.1. Skim Milk
   3.2. 2 Percent Milk
   3.3. Whole Milk

4. Cola
   4.1. Coca Cola
   4.2. Pepsi
   4.3. RC

5. Diet Cola
   5.1. Diet Coke
   5.2. Diet Pepsi

6. Root Beer
7. Water
   7.1. Sparking Mineral Water
   7.2. Spring Water

8. Lemonade
9. Iced Tea
10. Wine
```

✔ `level="any"` ignores hierarchy altogether and simply numbers each matching node sequentially:

```
1. Coffee
   2. Drip Coffee
   3. Latte
   4. Espresso
   5. Cappuccino

6. Tea
   7. Earl Grey
   8. Green Tea

9. Milk
   10. Skim Milk
   11. 2 Percent Milk
   12. Whole Milk
```

```
13. Cola
   14. Coca Cola
   15. Pepsi
   16. RC

17. Diet Cola
   18. Diet Coke
   19. Diet Pepsi

20. Root Beer
21. Water
   22. Sparking Mineral Water
   23. Spring Water

24. Lemonade
25. Iced Tea
26. Wine
```

By default, the XSLT processor uses all the nodes it encounters that match the sort key in determining the list count. So, in the earlier template rule examples that returned beverage element nodes, the numbering scheme is based on this type of element. However, XSLT allows you to base the count on more than just the selected node by using its count attribute. The xsl:number's count attribute specifies the nodes that need to be counted at the levels defined by the level attribute.

I illustrate the usage of the count attribute by adding a size element to the beverages document:

```
<beverages>
  <beverage>Coffee
    <size>Small</size>
    <size>Medium</size>
    <size>Large</size>
    <size>Extra Large</size>
  </beverage>
  <beverage>Tea
    <size>Small</size>
    <size>Large</size>
  </beverage>
  <beverage>Milk
    <size>Small</size>
    <size>Large</size>
  </beverage>
  <beverage>Cola
    <size>Small</size>
    <size>Medium</size>
    <size>Large</size>
    <size>Extra Large</size>
  </beverage>
  <beverage>Diet Cola
```

```
        <size>Small</size>
        <size>Medium</size>
        <size>Large</size>
        <size>Extra Large</size>
    </beverage>
</beverages>
```

My objective is to number the result document like an outline (1., 1.1, 1.2, 2., 2.1, and so on), so I first add a `level="multiple"` attribute value. I want to base the first part of my `size` number on the position of the parent `beverage` element.

To do so, I am going to create two template rules: the first to number the `beverage` elements like I did before, and the second to number the `size` elements. In the `size` template rule, I add the `count` attribute to specify that the first number in a multilevel number is based on the number of the `beverage` element, while the second value is based on the `size` element:

```
<xsl:template match="beverage">
    <xsl:number format="1. " level="multiple"/>
    <xsl:apply-templates/>
</xsl:template>

<xsl:template match="size">
    <xsl:number format="1. " level="multiple"
            count="beverage|size"/>
    <xsl:apply-templates/>
</xsl:template>
```

The result of this transformation is as follows:

```
1. Coffee
    1.1. Small
    1.2. Medium
    1.3. Large
    1.4. Extra Large

2. Tea
    2.1. Small
    2.2. Large

3. Milk
    3.1. Small
    3.2. Large

4. Cola
    4.1. Small
    4.2. Medium
    4.3. Large
    4.4. Extra Large
```

```
5. Diet Cola
   5.1. Small
   5.2. Medium
   5.3. Large
   5.4. Extra Large
```

The following example shows how you can use count to span your sequencing across multiple levels and elements. By adding a types element to the beverages structure, the following XML snippet becomes the source:

```
<beverages>
 <types>Starbucks Crowd
  <beverage>Coffee
    <size>Small</size>
    <size>Medium</size>
    <size>Large</size>
    <size>Extra Large</size>
  </beverage>
  <beverage>Tea
    <size>Small</size>
    <size>Large</size>
  </beverage>
 </types>
 <types>Natural Types
  <beverage>Milk
    <size>Small</size>
    <size>Large</size>
  </beverage>
  <beverage>Water
    <size>Small</size>
    <size>Medium</size>
    <size>Large</size>
  </beverage>
 </types>
 <types>Popular Sodas
  <beverage>Cola
    <size>Small</size>
    <size>Medium</size>
    <size>Large</size>
    <size>Extra Large</size>
  </beverage>
  <beverage>Diet Cola
    <size>Small</size>
    <size>Medium</size>
    <size>Large</size>
    <size>Extra Large</size>
  </beverage>
  <beverage>Root Beer
    <size>Medium</size>
  </beverage>
 </types>
</beverages>
```

To use the number of the types element in the outline numbering scheme of the beverage and size elements, add the types element to the count attribute value:

```
<xsl:template match="beverage">
  <xsl:number format="1. " level="multiple"
          count="types|beverage"/>
  <xsl:apply-templates/>
</xsl:template>

<xsl:template match="size">
  <xsl:number format="1. " level="multiple"
          count="types|beverage|size"/>
  <xsl:apply-templates/>
</xsl:template>
```

The result is as follows:

```
Starbucks Crowd
  1.1. Coffee
     1.1.1. Small
     1.1.2. Medium
     1.1.3. Large
     1.1.4. Extra Large

  1.2. Tea
     1.2.1. Small
     1.2.2. Large


Natural Types
  2.1. Milk
     2.1.1. Small
     2.1.2. Large

  2.2. Water
     2.2.1. Small
     2.2.2. Medium
     2.2.3. Large


Popular Sodas
  3.1. Cola
     3.1.1. Small
     3.1.2. Medium
     3.1.3. Large
     3.1.4. Extra Large
```

```
3.2. Diet Cola
   3.2.1. Small
   3.2.2. Medium
   3.2.3. Large
   3.2.4. Extra Large

3.3. Root Beer
   3.3.1. Medium
```

In this example, the `types` elements aren't numbered, but their index value is factored into the overall number sequence of the `beverage` and `size` elements.

Chapter 10

To HTML and Beyond!

I'd like to nominate Buzz Lightyear as an honorary X-Team member. You know Buzz, don't you? He's the friendly spaceman of *Toy Story* fame. Buzz fits right in with the X-Team mates: He's a no-nonsense guy with a well-defined mission — to save the galaxy from the evil Zurg. Plus, he's the coolest and hippest of the *Toy Story* bunch (sorry, Woody). So too, the X-Team members are all cool, hip technologies with well-defined missions.

As you begin this chapter, it's time to expand this mission of XSLT to include outputting result documents as HTML. In this chapter, you find out all you need to know to transform XML into HTML, as well as find out ways to output into other formats. So, in the words of Buzz, "To HTML and beyond!"

XML and HTML

When you take a glance at HTML code, it sure does look an awful lot like an XML document, doesn't it? Ahhhhh, but a quick look like that can be deceiving, because HTML is not the same as XML. I overview the similarities and differences in Chapter 1, but I will dive deeper in this section.

HTML is a markup language with a collection of those familiar elements and attributes, but HTML is a lot more lax than its stricter XML cousin. Think of HTML as the laid-back surfer dude from California and XML as the New York accountant type.

Here are a few notable differences between HTML and XML:

✔ Many empty HTML elements such as `<p>`, `<br>`, and `<hr>` are used with no corresponding end tags.

✔ HTML doesn't recognize the XML shortcut syntax for an empty element, such as `<p/>`. The browser altogether ignores an empty element like this.

✔ In HTML, you don't need to enclose attribute values in quotes. You can if you want to, but HTML doesn't fuss if you don't.

✔ HTML is case-insensitive, whereas case matters for XML.

The core principle of XML is well-formedness (every start tag must have a matching end tag). And despite its markup language similarities to XML, HTML is not well-formed and should not be confused with XML. To tweak words once directed to Dan Quayle, I could say the following to HTML:

I knew XML. XML was a friend of mine. Senator, you're no XML.

To illustrate the difference between these two markup languages, consider the following HTML document. It is perfectly acceptable HTML, but breaks every rule in the book for XML:

```
<html>
<hEaD>
  <META NAME=Generator CONTENT='Star Web Page Commander'>
</HeAd>
<body BGCOLOR='#FFFFFF' link="#0000FF">
<p>Buzz: You are a sad, strange, little man. You have my
          pity. Farewell.
<hr>
</body>
```

A Web browser can display that HTML flawlessly, but you don't want to run this code through an XML processor. It would barf all over the place! To make the code XML friendly, you need to change it to:

```
<html>
<head>
  <meta name="Generator" content="Star Web Page Commander"/>
</head>
<body bgcolor="#FFFFFF" link="#0000FF">
<p>Buzz: You are a sad, strange, little man. You have my
          pity. Farewell.</p>
<hr/>
</body>
</html>
```

The problem is that, even in this simplest of examples, many browsers don't display the code exactly as you intended. For example, a browser doesn't recognize the `<hr/>` empty tag element as a horizontal rule element, because that is not part of HTML standard. Therefore, outputting tags as a pure XML document doesn't give you reliable formatting results.

Fortunately, you and I aren't the only ones who see these variations as problematic. To reconcile the differences between HTML and XML, there is a new W3C standard afoot called XHTML, which is an XMLized version of HTML. In other words, XHTML gives the California surfer a shirt and tie and aims to give it some semblance of discipline. Everyone has to grow up, sooner or later!

Over time, when the use of XHTML becomes widespread and browsers fully support it, switching between XML and HTML and displaying the results on the Web will be a breeze. But because older browsers will be around for some time to come, this XML Nirvana is still quite a ways off. Therefore, living with these nuances is something that you and I just have to get used to.

So how do these differences between HTML and XML impact you as an XSLT stylesheet author? The most important implication is on the input side: Before you can transform an HTML document with XSLT, you first need to make the HTML document well-formed. XSLT can't work with HTML documents that aren't well-formed.

HTML Tidy is a nifty utility that is freely available on the Web. You can use it to convert your HTML code into well-formed HTML. Go to `tidy.sourceforge.net` to download this utility. Also available is a Windows version of the tool called TidyGUI, which you can download at `perso.wanadoo.fr/ablavier/TidyGUI`.

Outputting to HTML

The disparities between HTML and XML may cause you to despair when you're inputting HTML documents. Happily, the output side is a completely different story. In fact, you don't even need to think about whether the resulting HTML code is well-formed when you create your XSLT stylesheets, because the XSLT processor handles all the messy conversions for you.

To demonstrate, I start with the `quotes.xml` file shown in Listing 10-1 as my source document.

Listing 10-1:   filmquotes.xml

```
<?xml version="1.0"?>
<filmquotes>
  <quote>
    <spokenby>Buzz Lightyear</spokenby>
    <source>Toy Story</source>
    <text>To infinity, and beyond!</text>
  </quote>
  <quote>
    <spokenby>Sam</spokenby>
    <source>Bennie and Joon</source>
```

(continued)

Listing 10-1 *(continued)*

```
    <text>It seems to me that, aside from being a little
          mentally ill, she's pretty normal.</text>
  </quote>
  <quote>
    <spokenby>Sabrina</spokenby>
    <source>Sabrina</source>
    <text>More isn't always better, Linus. Sometimes it's
          just more.</text>
  </quote>
  <quote>
    <spokenby>Rick Blaine</spokenby>
    <source>Casablanca</source>
    <text>Who are you really, and what were you before? What
          did you do, and what did you think, huh?</text>
  </quote>
  <quote>
    <spokenby>Phil Connors</spokenby>
    <source>Groundhog Day</source>
    <text>Well, it's Groundhog Day... again...</text>
  </quote>
  <quote>
    <spokenby>Wesley</spokenby>
    <source>Princess Bride</source>
    <text>To the pain...</text>
  </quote>
  <quote>
    <spokenby>Delmar</spokenby>
    <source>O Brother, Where Art Thou</source>
    <text>We thought you was a toad.</text>
  </quote>
  <quote>
    <spokenby>Inigo Montoya</spokenby>
    <source>Princess Bride</source>
    <text>Hello. My name is Inigo Montoya. You killed my
          father. Prepare to die.</text>
  </quote>
</filmquotes>
```

To transform this source file to an HTML document, my first step is to use the xsl:output element and define its method attribute to html:

```
<xsl:output method="html"/>
```

The xsl:output element is used to specify the structure of the result document. By default, XSLT outputs an XML file. But you can use the method attribute to also specify text or html. (Chapter 9 showed some examples of using xsl:output to create text files with method="text".) When you use html, the processor outputs standard HTML 4.0.

I now need to add the content to my HTML document. Because HTML knows only formatting elements, such as p or h1, I don't want to carry over any XML

element names into the result document. So, to start off, I change the
`filmquotes` document element into an HTML document "wrapper" with
`html` and `body` elements and apply the `filmquotes` element contents:

```
<!-- Wrap html and body elements around rest of document -
        ->
<xsl:template match="filmquotes">
  <html>
    <body>
      <xsl:apply-templates/>
    </body>
  </html>
</xsl:template>
```

For each `quote` element, I prepare a formatted template for its contents, listing the values of the three child elements:

```
<!-- Render each quote as HTML -->
<xsl:template match="quote">
  <h2><font color="#000099" face="Arial, Helvetica, sans-
        serif"><xsl:value-of select="source"/></font></h2>
  <font face="Georgia, Times New Roman, Times, serif">
  <p><xsl:value-of select="spokenby"/> said the following
        memorable line in <i><xsl:value-of
        select="source"/></i>:</p>
  <p>"<xsl:value-of select="text"/>"</p></font>
  <hr></hr>
</xsl:template>
```

The entire stylesheet is shown here:

```
<xsl:stylesheet version="1.0"
        xmlns:xsl="http://www.w3.org/1999/XSL/Transform">

<xsl:output method="html"/>

<!-- Wrap html and body elements around rest of document --
        >
<xsl:template match="filmquotes">
  <html>
    <body>
      <xsl:apply-templates/>
    </body>
  </html>
</xsl:template>

<!-- Render each quote as HTML -->
<xsl:template match="quote">
  <h2><font color="#000099" face="Arial, Helvetica, sans-
        serif"><xsl:value-of select="source"/></font></h2>
  <font face="Georgia, Times New Roman, Times, serif">
```

```
      <p><xsl:value-of select="spokenby"/> said the following
          memorable line in <i><xsl:value-of
          select="source"/></i>:</p>
      <p>"<xsl:value-of select="text"/>"</p></font>
      <hr/>
    </xsl:template>

</xsl:stylesheet>
```

Check out the HTML that the transformation generates:

```
<html>
    <body>

      <h2><font color="#000099" face="Arial, Helvetica, sans-
          serif">Toy Story</font></h2><font face="Georgia,
          Times New Roman, Times, serif">
      <p>Buzz Lightyear said the following memorable line
          in <i>Toy Story</i>:
      </p>
      <p>"To infinity, and beyond!"</p></font><hr>

      <h2><font color="#000099" face="Arial, Helvetica, sans-
          serif">Bennie and Joon</font></h2><font
          face="Georgia, Times New Roman, Times, serif">
      <p>Sam said the following memorable line in
          <i>Bennie and Joon</i>:
      </p>
      <p>"It seems to me that, aside from being a little
          mentally ill, she's pretty normal."</p></font><hr>

      <h2><font color="#000099" face="Arial, Helvetica, sans-
          serif">Sabrina</font></h2><font face="Georgia,
          Times New Roman, Times, serif">
      <p>Sabrina said the following memorable line in
          <i>Sabrina</i>:
      </p>
      <p>"More isn't always better, Linus. Sometimes it's
          just more."</p></font><hr>

      <h2><font color="#000099" face="Arial, Helvetica, sans-
          serif">Casablanca</font></h2><font face="Georgia,
          Times New Roman, Times, serif">
      <p>Rick Blaine said the following memorable line in
          <i>Casablanca</i>:
      </p>
      <p>"Who are you really, and what were you before?
          What did you do, and what did you think,
          huh?"</p></font><hr>
```

```
        <h2><font color="#000099" face="Arial, Helvetica, sans-
            serif">Groundhog Day</font></h2><font
            face="Georgia, Times New Roman, Times, serif">
<p>Phil Connors said the following memorable line in
            <i>Groundhog Day</i>:
        </p>
        <p>"Well, it's Groundhog Day...
            again..."</p></font><hr>

        <h2><font color="#000099" face="Arial, Helvetica, sans-
            serif">Princess Bride</font></h2><font
            face="Georgia, Times New Roman, Times, serif">
        <p>Wesley said the following memorable line in
            <i>Princess Bride</i>:
        </p>
        <p>"To the pain..."</p></font><hr>

        <h2><font color="#000099" face="Arial, Helvetica, sans-
            serif">O Brother, Where Art Thou</font></h2><font
            face="Georgia, Times New Roman, Times, serif">
        <p>Delmar said the following memorable line in <i>O
            Brother, Where Art Thou</i>:
        </p>
        <p>"We thought you was a toad."</p></font><hr>

        <h2><font color="#000099" face="Arial, Helvetica, sans-
            serif">Princess Bride</font></h2><font
            face="Georgia, Times New Roman, Times, serif">
        <p>Inigo Montoya said the following memorable line
            in <i>Princess Bride</i>:
        </p>
        <p>"Hello. My name is Inigo Montoya. You killed my
            father. Prepare to die."</p></font><hr>

    </body>
</html>
```

The XSLT processor not only formats the HTML nicely, but also converts the markup into the kind of HTML that gives browsers warm fuzzies. For example, my `<hr/>` element was automatically converted to `<hr>`. Figure 10-1 shows the resulting HTML document when you open it with Internet Explorer.

You aren't always required to specify `<xsl:output method="html"/>` to get HTML formatting in the result document. If `html` is your document element, the XSLT processor assumes that your file is supposed to be an HTML document and formats the document accordingly. However, it is good programming practice to use `xsl:output` anyway in order to ensure clarity and intent of your code.

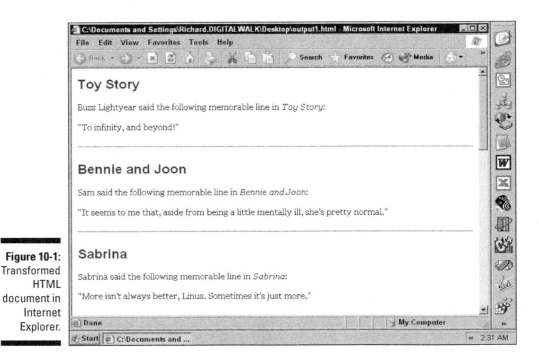

Figure 10-1:
Transformed
HTML
document in
Internet
Explorer.

Creating an HTML Table

Because of their well-formed structure, many XML documents naturally can be represented as a table. No, not the kind you eat off of in your kitchen, but the kind that has columns and rows. To show you how this process works, look again at the quotes.xml source document shown in Listing 10-1. I'd like to show these quotes inside an HTML table.

To start, I create a template rule that sets up the document container elements as I do in the example earlier in this chapter. That part is easy, because you always know that, for a given HTML document, there is always one html element and one body element. However, the number of rows in my table is based on the number of quote elements in my source document. Therefore, the common method of creating an HTML table lies in using an xsl:for-each instruction to create each of the table's rows. Consider the following stylesheet:

```
<?xml version="1.0"?>
<xsl:stylesheet version="1.0"
        xmlns:xsl="http://www.w3.org/1999/XSL/Transform">

  <xsl:output method="html"/>
```

```
<!-- Wrap html and body elements around rest of document --
     >
<xsl:template match="/">
  <html>
    <body bgcolor="#FFFFFF">
      <xsl:apply-templates/>
    </body>
  </html>
</xsl:template>

<!-- Create HTML table for quote elements -->
<xsl:template match="filmquotes">
  <table width="95%" border="1" cellspacing="2"
         cellpadding="2">
    <tr bgcolor="#FFCCCC">
      <th>Source</th>
      <th>Spoken By</th>
      <th width="60%">Quote</th>
    </tr>
    <xsl:for-each select="quote">
    <tr>
      <td><i><xsl:value-of select="source"/></i></td>
      <td><xsl:value-of select="spokenby"/></td>
      <td width="60%"><xsl:value-of select="text"/></td>
    </tr>
    </xsl:for-each>
    </table>
  </xsl:template>

</xsl:stylesheet>
```

In the `filmquotes` template rule, I use literal text to define the `table` element and the header row. I then add `xsl:for-each` to loop through each `quote` element in the source document. For each instance, a row is created, and the values of its `source`, `spokenby`, and `text` child elements are inserted as columns.

The result is shown here:

```
<html>
    <body bgcolor="#FFFFFF">
      <table width="95%" border="1" cellspacing="2"
             cellpadding="2">
        <tr bgcolor="#FFCCCC">
          <th>Source</th>
          <th>Spoken By</th>
          <th width="60%">Quote</th>
        </tr>
        <tr>
          <td><i>Toy Story</i></td>
          <td>Buzz Lightyear</td>
          <td width="60%">To infinity, and beyond!</td>
```

```
        </tr>
        <tr>
          <td><i>Bennie and Joon</i></td>
          <td>Sam</td>
          <td width="60%">It seems to me that, aside from
          being a little mentally ill, she's pretty
          normal.</td>
        </tr>
        <tr>
          <td><i>Sabrina</i></td>
          <td>Sabrina</td>
          <td width="60%">More isn't always better, Linus.
          Sometimes it's just more.</td>
        </tr>
        <tr>
          <td><i>Casablanca</i></td>
          <td>Rick Blaine</td>
          <td width="60%">Who are you really, and what were
          you before? What did you do, and what did you
          think, huh?</td>
        </tr>
        <tr>
          <td><i>Groundhog Day</i></td>
          <td>Phil Connors</td>
          <td width="60%">Well, it's Groundhog Day...
          again...</td>
        </tr>
        <tr>
          <td><i>Princess Bride</i></td>
          <td>Wesley</td>
          <td width="60%">To the pain...</td>
        </tr>
        <tr>
          <td><i>O Brother, Where Art Thou</i></td>
          <td>Delmar</td>
          <td width="60%">We thought you was a toad.</td>
        </tr>
        <tr>
          <td><i>Princess Bride</i></td>
          <td>Inigo Montoya</td>
          <td width="60%">Hello. My name is Inigo Montoya.
          You killed my father. Prepare to die.</td>
        </tr>
      </table>
    </body>
</html>
```

Figure 10-2 shows the table when you view it with a Web browser.

Source	Spoken By	Quote
Toy Story	Buzz Lightyear	To infinity, and beyond!
Bennie and Joon	Sam	It seems to me that, aside from being a little mentally ill, she's pretty normal.
Sabrina	Sabrina	More isn't always better, Linus. Sometimes it's just more.
Casablanca	Rick Blaine	Who are you really, and what were you before? What did you do, and what did you think, huh?
Groundhog Day	Phil Connors	Well, it's Groundhog Day... again...
Princess Bride	Wesley	To the pain...
O Brother, Where Art Thou	Delmar	We thought you was a toad.
Princess Bride	Inigo Montoya	Hello. My name is Inigo Montoya. You killed my father. Prepare to die.

Figure 10-2:
HTML table created from XML document.

Linking an XSLT Stylesheet with an XML Document

Under most circumstances, you link together an XML document with an XSLT stylesheet by specifying the .xml and .xsl files when you call the XSLT processor. However, XML offers a way to "direct connect" an XML file with an XSLT stylesheet by using the `xml-stylesheet` processing instruction. The instruction's basic syntax is:

```
<?xml-stylesheet href="lyon.xsl" type="text/xsl"?>
```

`xml-stylesheet` is an XML processing instruction, not an XSLT element.

When declared in an XML file, this instruction tells the processing engine to apply the specified stylesheet to the contents of the source XML. The instruction has two parameters:

- ✔ `href` specifies the URI of the XSLT stylesheet.
- ✔ `type` tells what kind of file the stylesheet is (or its MIME type). XSLT stylesheets have the type of `text/xsl`.

Therefore, if I want to apply the quotes.xsl stylesheet to the quotes.xml document when the XML file is processed, I add the xsl-stylesheet processing instruction to the top of the file (note that most of the quote elements are removed in this abbreviated Listing 10-2).

Listing 10-2:   quoteslink.xml

```
<?xml version="1.0"?>
<?xml-stylesheet href="quotes.xsl" type="text/xsl"?>
<filmquotes>
  <quote>
    <spokenby>Buzz Lightyear</spokenby>
    <source>Toy Story</source>
    <text>To infinity, and beyond!</text>
  </quote>
  <quote>
    <spokenby>Sam</spokenby>
    <source>Bennie and Joon</source>
    <text>It seems to me that, aside from being a little
          mentally ill, she's pretty normal.</text>
  </quote>
  <quote>
    <spokenby>Sabrina</spokenby>
    <source>Sabrina</source>
    <text>More isn't always better, Linus. Sometimes it's
          just more.</text>
  </quote>
</filmquotes>
```

You must place the xsl-stylesheet processing instruction at the top of the XML document, before the document element is declared.

Browser Support of XSLT

If you plan to convert your XML documents to HTML so that people can view your information with a Web browser, you have a decision to make: Where are you going to perform the transformation? You have three basic options:

✔ **Offline transformation:** If your transformation is a one-time or infrequent event, you can do a batch process of transforming your XML documents to HTML. The advantage to this option is that it enables you to do transformations before the result documents are ever accessed. You can then put the output HTML files in the appropriate location when done, and any Web browser can display the output. If your information changes constantly, the disadvantage is that the processing is not done in "real time," so the HTML documents may show stale information.

✔ **Server-side transformation:** If you need to have up-to-the-minute transformations when a user requests the Web page, you can perform the transformation when the user requests the XML file. The document can then be transformed on the server, and the resulting HTML is sent to the Web browser so that the user can view the document.

✔ **Client-side transformation:** A third option is to have the Web browser on the client do the transformations on the fly. In this case, a user receives an XML document from the server with a link to a stylesheet. The browser then performs the transformation, rendering the results in the Web browser as HTML. The advantage to this option is that it enables you to focus only the XML data and the XSLT stylesheet, and letting the browser concern itself with the transformation. However, the caveat is that the Web browser must support XSLT or else the transformation never happens.

If all Web browsers supported XSLT, then letting the transformation occur on the client would be a legitimate option. Take, for example, Internet Explorer 5.0 or higher. You can open up the preceding `quoteslink.xml` in Internet Explorer, and voilà! — the result document is a formatted Web page in full living color! So if you know all your users have an XSLT-capable browser, you can create an entire XML-based Web site and have Internet Explorer transform each page on the fly.

Yes, this idea rocks, but unfortunately you can't always count on all Web browsers to support XSLT. In fact, most don't. Microsoft Internet Explorer 5.0 and higher support XSLT 1.0, as does Netscape Navigator 6.1 and higher. But even these two browsers have some peculiarities and differences in how they display transformed XML documents. However, given XSLT's popularity, you will start to see more standardized and consistent support for XSLT within the major browsers.

The client-side transformation option can be an ideal solution within an office environment in which you can count on everyone using the same browser. Therefore, if an office is standardized on Internet Explorer 6.0 or higher, XML documents and XSLT stylesheets could be used in place of HTML files and get consistent results.

XSL transformations are usually best performed on the server rather than relying on the browser to do it for you. With a server-side solution, you do not need to concern yourself with browser compatibility issues, because you're sending vanilla HTML to it. Also, depending on the files involved, server-based transformation can be more efficient with respect to bandwidth, since you only need to send one HTML document to the browser rather than both XML and XSLT documents. (On the other hand, if your document has a lot of repetitive sections of HTML being created, the client-side loading could be significantly more efficient.) Additionally, if you want to reduce the load on the server, then pushing the transformation to the client browser may be a sound option, apart from the browser support nonsense.

For the latest on browser support, check out the XMLSoftware's Browser page at www.xmlsoftware.com/browsers.

To Infinity and Beyond (Into Other Formats)

XML is an excellent general-purpose language for storing structured data. Because XSLT has tremendous flexibility in how it can output XML data, you can create almost any kind of output imaginable. Consider a real-world case in point that I encountered recently. I needed to create JavaScript objects from XML elements, and then use those objects inside a Web page or other JavaScript application.

For this section, don't worry if you don't know JavaScript. The point of this example is to illustrate that XSLT can do much more than just output XML and HTML. You can do most anything, and JavaScript is but one example. Also, see Chapter 15 for an example on how to transform XML into a Microsoft Word document.

To demonstrate how I solved my JavaScript scenario, I'll use the employees.xml file shown in Listing 10-3.

Listing 10-3:   employees.xml

```xml
<?xml version="1.0"?>
<employees>
  <employee id="101">
    <lastname>Lamotte</lastname>
    <firstname>Mitch</firstname>
    <nickname>The Mitchster</nickname>
    <title>Director of Sales</title>
  </employee>
  <employee id="102">
    <lastname>Williams</lastname>
    <firstname>Tim</firstname>
    <nickname>Timmy Boy</nickname>
    <title>Director of Quality Assurance</title>
  </employee>
  <employee id="103">
    <lastname>Magruder</lastname>
    <firstname>Randy</firstname>
    <nickname>Randall</nickname>
    <title>Senior Engineer</title>
  </employee>
  <employee id="104">
    <lastname>Drohan</lastname>
    <firstname>Doug</firstname>
    <nickname>Tooltime</nickname>
    <title>Building Director</title>
  </employee>
  <employee id="105">
    <lastname>Burrer</lastname>
```

```
      <firstname>Phillip</firstname>
      <nickname>Flip</nickname>
      <title>Resident Physician</title>
   </employee>
</employees>
```

My goal is transform an `employee` element like this:

```
<employee id="101">
   <lastname>Lamotte</lastname>
   <firstname>Mitch</firstname>
   <nickname>The Mitchster</nickname>
   <title>Director of Sales</title>
</employee>
```

Into this JavaScript custom object:

```
// Mitch Lamotte object
emp_IDANZJS = new employee(
     "101",
     "Lamotte",
     "Mitch",
     "The Mitchster",
     "Director of Sales"
     )
```

After I transform the `employee` elements into JavaScript objects, I can access the employee information from inside my JavaScript code and work with it as native JavaScript, rather than parsing through XML data.

The result document I want to create is a text-based file with a .js extension. This type of file (called a JavaScript include file) is used to store JavaScript code and can be accessed from an HTML page using the `script` element.

I use the following stylesheet to perform the transformation:

```
<?xml version="1.0"?>
<xsl:stylesheet version="1.0"
         xmlns:xsl="http://www.w3.org/1999/XSL/Transform">

  <xsl:output method="text"/>

  <!-- Create constructor function and employees array -->
  <xsl:template match="/">

     // Employee constructor
     function employee( id, lastname, firstname, nickname,
           title )
     {
       this.id = id;
       this.lastname = lastname;
       this.firstname = firstname;
```

```
      this.nickname = nickname;
      this.title = title;
   }

var employees = new Array( <xsl:value-of select="count(
      //employee )"/> )
  <xsl:apply-templates/>
</xsl:template>

<!-- Create instances of JavaScript objects for each
      employee -->
<xsl:template match="employees">

  <xsl:for-each select="employee">
  // <xsl:value-of select="firstname"/><xsl:text>
      </xsl:text>
  <xsl:value-of select="lastname"/> object
  var emp_<xsl:value-of select="generate-id()"/> = new
      employee(
      "<xsl:value-of select="@id"/>",
      "<xsl:value-of select="lastname"/>",
      "<xsl:value-of select="firstname"/>",
      "<xsl:value-of select="nickname"/>",
      "<xsl:value-of select="title"/>"
      )
  employees[<xsl:value-of select="position()-1"/>] =
      emp_<xsl:value-of select="generate-id()"/>;
  </xsl:for-each>

</xsl:template>

</xsl:stylesheet>
```

In the first template rule in the preceding code, I declare JavaScript code that's needed to work with the new objects I'm creating. (If you're a JavaScripter, I will add that I'm defining the employee constructor and an array to store the employee objects that I'm creating.)

If my code contained reserved characters, such as <, which appear, for example, in a comparison expression, I would need to wrap that portion of my code in a <![CDATA[...]]> section or convert the reserved characters to their "escaped" version (for example, < for the < character).

In the employees template rule, I use an xsl:for-each instruction to write the JavaScript code needed to create an object instance for that employee. I use the generate-id() function to give each variable a unique name. After creating the object, I add it to an employees array where I could then reference it later.

Here's the resulting JavaScript code:

```
// Employee constructor
function employee( id, lastname, firstname, nickname,
        title )
{
  this.id = id;
  this.lastname = lastname;
  this.firstname = firstname;
  this.nickname = nickname;
  this.title = title;
}

var employees = new Array( 5 )

// Mitch Lamotte object
var emp_IDAGLJS = new employee(
        "101",
        "Lamotte",
        "Mitch",
        "The Mitchster",
        "Director of Sales"
        )
employees[0] = emp_IDAGLJS;

// Tim Williams object
var emp_IDAMLJS = new employee(
        "102",
        "Williams",
        "Tim",
        "Timmy Boy",
        "Director of Quality Assurance"
        )
employees[1] = emp_IDAMLJS;

// Randy Magruder object
var emp_IDASLJS = new employee(
        "103",
        "Magruder",
        "Randy",
        "Randall",
        "Senior Engineer"
        )
employees[2] = emp_IDASLJS;

// Doug Drohan object
var emp_IDAYLJS = new employee(
        "104",
        "Drohan",
        "Doug",
        "Tooltime",
        "Building Director"
        )
employees[3] = emp_IDAYLJS;
```

```
// Phillip Burrer object
var emp_IDA4LJS = new employee(
      "105",
      "Burrer",
      "Phillip",
      "Flip",
      "Resident Physician"
      )
employees[4] = emp_IDA4LJS;
```

Chapter 11

XPath Data Types and Functions

*T*he very first words I could read as a child were *free inside*. Those were the dear words that appeared on the front of cereal boxes and told kids like me what cool toy I could find when I ate the cereal. I remember caring far less about the cereal inside than the prize that was at the bottom of the box.

Everyone likes to get something for free, and with XSLT, you get a host of built-in functions for free inside XPath and XSLT. These functions give you a power boost that you can use when you create stylesheets.

Most of the built-in functions are categorized by the kind of data that they work with. The four primary data types in XSLT are: node sets, strings, numbers, and booleans. In this chapter, you find out all about the major built-in functions for these data types and about some general-purpose functions.

Throughout the chapter, I refer to the following menu.xml source document in Listing 11-1 to demonstrate the use of built-in functions.

Listing 11-1: menu.xml

```xml
<?xml version="1.0"?>
<menu>
  <entree name="Sunburnt Chicken">
    <diet>false</diet>
    <fatgrams>23</fatgrams>
    <features>Salad, Vegetables, Baked Potato, and
          Dessert</features>
    <description>Chicken prepared so hot by our master chef
          Georgio Faucher, you'll need a gallon of soda to
          wash it down. Bring sunscreen!</description>
```

Listing 11-1 *(continued)*

```
  </entree>
  <entree name="Filet Mig's None">
    <diet>true</diet>
    <fatgrams>0</fatgrams>
    <features>Soup, Vegetables, Baked Potato, and
           Dessert</features>
    <description>Our master chef Mig prepares a uniquely no-
           fat filet mignon. You won't believe how great it
           tastes!</description>
  </entree>
  <entree name="Chicken Parmashaun">
    <diet>false</diet>
    <fatgrams>20</fatgrams>
    <features>Soup, Pasta, Baked Potato, and
           Dessert</features>
    <description>Our award-winning Chicken Parmesan prepared
           especially for you by our master chef
           Shaun.</description>
  </entree>
  <entree name="Eggs Benelux">
    <diet>false</diet>
    <fatgrams>35</fatgrams>
    <features>Bacon, Sausage, and Toast</features>
    <description>No matter the time of day, enjoy our
           scrumptous breakfast cooked by our famous Belgian
           and Dutch master chefs.</description>
  </entree>
  <entree name="Jerk Chicken">
    <diet>true</diet>
    <fatgrams>5</fatgrams>
    <features>Soup, Vegetables, and Dessert</features>
    <description>A delicious hot Jamaican dish prepared by
           our most obnoxious master chef.</description>
  </entree>
  <entree name="Gusto Spaghetti">
    <diet>false</diet>
    <fatgrams>55</fatgrams>
    <features>Soup, Salad, and Dessert</features>
    <description>Our famous master chef Boyd Ardee prepares a
           succulent dish of spaghetti with zesty
           gusto!</description>
  </entree>
</menu>
```

Playing 'Heart and Soul' with Nodes

Nodes are the heart and soul of an XSLT transformation, because ultimately, the result document is some sort of arrangement of nodes, whether they are elements, attributes, text, or whatever. Naturally, then, being able to add capabilities beyond what you can do with XSLT elements alone is important. Several functions are available for working with nodes.

Getting the current element's position

The `position()` function returns the numeric position of the current element and has the following syntax:

```
number position()
```

In this syntax, *number* describes the return data type (or type of data returned) by the `position()` function. I show return data types in italics throughout this chapter.

The `position()` function always returns a value based on the current context, which can sometimes be misleading. For example, take the following template rule:

```
<xsl:template match="entree">
  <xsl:value-of select="@name"/>'s position: <xsl:value-of
          select="position()"/>
</xsl:template>
```

When applied to the `menu.xml` document (see Listing 11-1), you might guess that the result document looks something like this:

```
 Sunburnt Chicken's position: 1
Filet Mig's None's position: 2
Chicken Parmashaun's position: 3
Eggs Benelux's position: 4
Jerk Chicken's position: 5
Gusto Spaghetti's position: 6
```

Logical guess, perhaps, but a wrong one. Although the stylesheet focuses on `entree` elements, don't forget those hidden text nodes that appear between the element nodes. Look again at the source document, and this time I've removed the children of the `entree` elements for brevity:

```
<entree name="Sunburnt Chicken"></entree>
<entree name="Filet Mig's None"></entree>
<entree name="Chicken Parmashaun"></entree>
<entree name="Eggs Benelux"></entree>
<entree name="Jerk Chicken"></entree>
<entree name="Gusto Spaghetti"></entree>
```

When the processor goes through the XML document, it finds the nodes in the following positions:

```
[text node: 1]
Sunburnt Chicken's position: 2
[text node: 3]
Filet Mig's None's position: 4
[text node: 5]
Chicken Parmashaun's position: 6
[text node: 7]
Eggs Benelux's position: 8
[text node: 9]
Jerk Chicken's position: 10
[text node: 11]
Gusto Spaghetti's position: 12
```

The results that actually display in your result document are:

```
Sunburnt Chicken's position: 2
Filet Mig's None's position: 4
Chicken Parmashaun's position: 6
Eggs Benelux's position: 8
Jerk Chicken's position: 10
Gusto Spaghetti's position: 12
```

If you find text nodes getting in the way of your position() logic, you can use the xsl:strip-space element to remove them prior to your template rule. See Chapter 13 for more information on xsl:strip-space.

Getting the last element

You can use the last() function to return the final element of the current context. It has the following syntax:

```
number last()
```

The processor evaluates last() and all the other built-in functions when they are within an XPath expression, such as in the select attribute of the xsl:if or xsl:value-of instructions. You can't just type functions inside the template apart from an XSLT instruction; if you do so, the processor treats the function as literal text and doesn't evaluate it. As a general rule, remember that functions are defined only inside quotation marks. In fact, I think built-in functions could have their own *Rawhide*-like theme song: *"Quote 'em, quote 'em, quote 'em. Though the streams are swollen, Keep them doggies rollin', XSLT!"*

I can use the position() and last() functions together in the following example to list out the entrees in a sentence-like format. Specifically, I want to create a list of the entree elements in which a comma is inserted between entrees, except for the second-to-last entree — it has an and, added instead. For the final entree, a period is added to close the sentence. The template rule containing this logic is shown here:

```
<xsl:template match="menu">
  Tonight's entrees are the following:
  <xsl:for-each select="entree">
    <xsl:value-of select="@name"/>
    <xsl:choose>
      <xsl:when test="position()=last()">
      <xsl:text>.</xsl:text>
      </xsl:when>
      <xsl:when test="position()=last()-1">
        <xsl:text>, and </xsl:text>
      </xsl:when>
      <xsl:otherwise>
        <xsl:text>, </xsl:text>
      </xsl:otherwise>
    </xsl:choose>
  </xsl:for-each>
  <xsl:text>
  </xsl:text>
</xsl:template>
```

The xsl:choose element tests for the following three conditions:

✔ The first xsl:when uses position()=last() to return true if the current position equals the last position.

✔ The second xsl:when tests for the second-to-last node.

✔ xsl:otherwise is used for the remaining nodes.

The formatted results are:

```
Tonight's entrees are the following:
  Sunburnt Chicken, Filet Mig's None, Chicken Parmashaun,
       Eggs Benelux, Jerk Chicken, and Gusto Spaghetti.
```

Returning the current node

You can return the current node to your code by using the current() function:

```
nodeset current()
```

In the template rule that follows, the xsl:if instruction tests for an entree element that has a name attribute of Jerk Chicken. If so, then the xsl:copy-of instruction uses current() to copy the current node to the result tree:

```
<xsl:template match="entree">
  <xsl:if test="./@name='Jerk Chicken'">
    <xsl:copy-of select="current()"/>
```

```
    </xsl:if>
  </xsl:template>
```

In this example, `select="current()"` is functionally the same as `select=".".`

Getting the node set count

You can use the `count()` function to get the total number of nodes in the current node set. Its syntax is:

```
number count(nodeset)
```

Anything that appears inside a function's parenthesis is called an *argument*. The `count()` function, for example, has `nodeset` as a single argument.

The following template rule lists the total number of `menu` and `entree` nodes in the source document:

```
<xsl:template match="/">
    menu nodes: <xsl:value-of select="count(//menu)"/>
    entree nodes: <xsl:value-of select="count(//entree)"/>
</xsl:template>
```

The results are:

```
menu nodes: 1
entree nodes: 6
```

Getting a node name

When you add text to your result document, most of the time you are adding the content of the elements or perhaps the values of the attributes. About the only time you think of outputting the elements or attributes themselves is when you are creating an XML output. However, you may have occasions in which you want to treat the name of a node as text. If so, the `name()` function comes to the rescue, which returns a string value of the specified node's name:

```
string name([nodeset])
```

Any parameter that appears in brackets is optional. So, in the case of `name()`, the `nodeset` argument may or may not be defined. If it is not, then the current node is the nodeset being evaluated by the function.

In the template rule that follows, the `name()` function comes in handy in creating the header columns for an HTML table:

```
<xsl:template match="menu">
  <table>
    <tr>
      <th><xsl:value-of select="name( entree/@name
         )"/></th>
      <th><xsl:value-of select="name( //diet )"/></th>
      <th><xsl:value-of select="name( //fatgrams )"/></th>
      <th><xsl:value-of select="name( //features )"/></th>
    </tr>
    <xsl:for-each select="entree">
      <tr>
        <td><xsl:value-of select="@name"/></td>
        <td><xsl:value-of select="diet"/></td>
        <td><xsl:value-of select="fatgrams"/></td>
        <td><xsl:value-of select="features"/></td>
      </tr>
    </xsl:for-each>
  </table>
</xsl:template>
```

The resulting table is as follows:

```
<table>
   <tr>
      <th>name</th>
      <th>diet</th>
      <th>fatgrams</th>
      <th>features</th>
   </tr>
   <tr>
      <td>Sunburnt Chicken</td>
      <td>false</td>
      <td>23</td>
      <td>Salad, Vegetables, Baked Potato, and Dessert</td>
   </tr>
   <tr>
      <td>Filet Mig's None</td>
      <td>true</td>
      <td>0</td>
      <td>Soup, Vegetables, Baked Potato, and Dessert</td>
   </tr>
   <tr>
      <td>Chicken Parmashaun</td>
      <td>false</td>
      <td>20</td>
      <td>Soup, Pasta, Baked Potato, and Dessert</td>
   </tr>
   <tr>
      <td>Eggs Benelux</td>
      <td>false</td>
```

```
        <td>35</td>
        <td>Bacon, Sausage, and Toast</td>
    </tr>
    <tr>
        <td>Jerk Chicken</td>
        <td>true</td>
        <td>5</td>
        <td>Soup, Vegetables, and Dessert</td>
    </tr>
    <tr>
        <td>Gusto Spaghetti</td>
        <td>false</td>
        <td>55</td>
        <td>Soup, Salad, and Dessert</td>
    </tr>
</table>
```

Working with Strings

So much of XSLT is based on pushing text from one place to another and transforming it along the way. Therefore, having functions that can manipulate and transform strings can be a valuable tool for you as an XSLT stylesheet author. This section covers the functions available for string manipulation.

Extracting strings from strings

XPath has three functions that help you extract a string from a larger string: `substring-before()`, `substring-after()`, and `substring()`.

The syntax for the `substring-before()` and `syntax-after()` functions are:

```
string substring-before(source, str)
```

```
string substring-after(source, str)
```

`substring-before()` returns the portion of `source` that comes before the first occurrence of `str`. If `str` is not found, then the result is an empty string. On the other hand, the `substring-after()` function returns the portion of `source` that comes after the first occurrence of `str`. It too returns an empty string if `str` is not found in the `source`.

The following example uses `substring-before()` to test whether or not the `features` child element includes `Soup` before the first comma. If so, then text

is added to the result document. The `substring-after()` function is used
to list everything else that follows the `Soup,` string:

```
<xsl:template match="entree">
  <xsl:if test="substring-before( features, ',') = 'Soup'">
    Soup is offered with <xsl:value-of select="@name"/>
    Also offered are: <xsl:value-of select="substring-
        after( features, 'Soup,')"/>
  </xsl:if>
</xsl:template>
```

The results are :

```
    Soup is offered with Filet Mig's None
    Also offered are:  Vegetables, Baked Potato, and
        Dessert

    Soup is offered with Chicken Parmashaun
    Also offered are:  Pasta, Baked Potato, and Dessert

    Soup is offered with Jerk Chicken
    Also offered are:  Vegetables, and Dessert

    Soup is offered with Gusto Spaghetti
    Also offered are:  Salad, and Dessert
```

You use the `substring()` function to get a string buried inside another
string. The function has the following syntax:

```
string substring( source, start [, length] )
```

The `substring()` function returns the substring of `source` beginning at the
`start` position and having a length of `length`. If `length` is not specified, then it
returns the remainder of the string. The following example extracts a substring
from each description, starting at the position 5 and returning 3 characters:

```
<xsl:template match="entree">
  <xsl:value-of select="substring( description, 5, 3 )"/>
</xsl:template>
```

The result is:

```
ken
mas
awa
att
lic
fam
```

Searching and replacing text

You can use the `translate()` function to search and replace characters within a string. The syntax for the function is:

```
string translate(source, searchstr, replacestr)
```

`searchstr` specifies a string of characters that the `translate()` function looks for inside `source`. When each character is encountered, the character at the same position in `replacestr` replaces the original character.

For example, suppose you want to change all the text of the `entree` name to uppercase. To do so, I can create two variables: `lower` contains an all lower-case alphabet, and `upper` contains uppercase characters of the alphabet. As an `xsl:for-each` instruction runs through each of the entrees, the `translate()` function is used to map all the lowercase characters in the entree's name to the corresponding uppercase character:

```
<xsl:variable
        name="lower">abcdefghijklmnopqrstuvwxzyz</xsl:
        variable>
<xsl:variable name="upper">ABCDEFGHIJKLMNOPQRSTUVWXYZ</xsl:
        variable>

<xsl:template match="menu">
  <xsl:for-each select="entree">
    <xsl:value-of select="translate( @name, $lower, $upper
        )"/><xsl:text>
    </xsl:text>
  </xsl:for-each>
</xsl:template>
```

The result is shown here:

```
SUNBURNT CHICKEN
FILET MIG'S NONE
CHICKEN PARMASHAUN
EGGS BENELUX
JERK CHICKEN
GUSTO SPAGHETTI
```

Remember that the `translate()` function is used to search and replace individual characters, not strings.

Testing strings

You can test the contents of a string to check and see if another string is inside it with the `contains()` and `starts-with()` functions. The syntax for these functions is:

```
boolean contains(source, str)
boolean starts-with(source, str)
```

The contains() function returns true if str is found inside source. If not, then false is returned. starts-with() returns true if str is located at the start of the source string and false if not.

I use the contains() function in the following example to test for the presence of words in the entree's name. Based on the result of these evaluations, I add the entree into the appropriate category name:

```
<xsl:template match="entree">
  <entree>
    <name><xsl:value-of select="@name"/></name>
    <category>
    <xsl:choose>
      <xsl:when test="contains( @name, 'Chicken'
          )">Chicken</xsl:when>
      <xsl:when test="contains( @name, 'Spaghetti'
          )">Italiano</xsl:when>
      <xsl:when test="contains( @name, 'Filet'
          )">Beef</xsl:when>
      <xsl:otherwise>Other</xsl:otherwise>
    </xsl:choose>
    </category>
  </entree>
</xsl:template>
```

The results follow:

```
<entree>
  <name>Sunburnt Chicken</name>
  <category>Chicken</category>
</entree>
<entree>
  <name>Filet Mig's None</name>
  <category>Beef</category>
</entree>
<entree>
  <name>Chicken Parmashaun</name>
  <category>Chicken</category>
</entree>
<entree>
  <name>Eggs Benelux</name>
  <category>Other</category>
</entree>
<entree>
  <name>Jerk Chicken</name>
  <category>Chicken</category>
</entree>
<entree>
  <name>Gusto Spaghetti</name>
```

```
<category>Italiano</category>
</entree>
```

Getting the length of a string

The `string-length()` function returns just what you'd expect from a name like that: the length of a string. It looks like:

```
number string-length([string])
```

The example that follows uses `string-length()` to evaluate the size of the `description` element. If it is over 90 characters in length, it is flagged in the result document as being too long:

```
<xsl:template match="entree">
=============================================
<xsl:value-of select="@name"/>'s description:
=============================================
"<xsl:value-of select="description"/><xsl:text>"
</xsl:text>
<xsl:if test="string-length(description) &gt; 90">
**** Hey there, Tex, this description is too long
        (<xsl:value-of select="string-
        length(description)"/> chars). Please shorten. ***
</xsl:if>
</xsl:template>
```

When the `menu.xml` (refer to Listing 11-1) is applied using this template rule, the output is:

```
=============================================
Sunburnt Chicken's description:
=============================================
"Chicken prepared so hot by our master chef Georgio
        Faucher, you'll need a gallon of soda to wash it
        down. Bring sunscreen!"


=============================================
Filet Mig's None's description:
=============================================
"Our master chef Mig prepares a uniquely no-fat filet
        mignon. You won't believe how great it tastes!"

**** Hey there, Tex, this description is too long (99
        chars). Please shorten. ***


=============================================
Chicken Parmashaun's description:
```

```
============================================
"Our award-winning Chicken Parmesan prepared especially
      for you by our master chef Shaun."


============================================
Eggs Benelux's description:
============================================
"No matter the time of day, enjoy our scrumptious
      breakfast cooked by our famous Belgian and Dutch
      master chefs."

**** Hey there, Tex, this description is too long (110
      chars). Please shorten. ***


============================================
Jerk Chicken's description:
============================================
"A delicious hot Jamaican dish prepared by our most
      obnoxious master chef."


============================================
Gusto Spaghetti's description:
============================================
"Our famous master chef Boyd Ardee prepares a succulent
      dish of spaghetti with zesty gusto!"
```

In this example, two of the descriptions had a string length of over 90 characters and were flagged.

Concatenating a string

To combine several smaller strings into a whopping big string, you can use the concat() function:

```
string concat(string1, string2, [string3,...])
```

This function combines string1 with string2 and as many other strings as you wish and returns them as a single concatenated string.

I use the concat() function in the following template rule to assemble a sentence out of literal text, an attribute value, and the string value of an element:

```
<xsl:template match="entree">
  <xsl:value-of select="concat( 'The ', @name, ' entree has
       ', fatgrams, ' grams of fat.')"/>
</xsl:template>
```

The result is:

```
The Sunburnt Chicken entree has 23 grams of fat.
The Filet Mig's None entree has 0 grams of fat.
The Chicken Parmashaun entree has 20 grams of fat.
The Eggs Benelux entree has 35 grams of fat.
The Jerk Chicken entree has 5 grams of fat.
The Gusto Spaghetti entree has 55 grams of fat.
```

Trimming whitespace from strings

When you work with strings, you may frequently come across a situation in which whitespace is padded onto the beginning or end of a string you are using. The `normalize-space()` function is used to remove these unwanted whitespace areas in your string:

```
string normalize-space([string])
```

The returned string has been stripped of leading and trailing whitespace as well as replacing multiple whitespace characters with a single whitespace character inside of the string.

To demonstrate, the `normalize-space()` function is useful to clean up the `substring-after()` example earlier in the chapter. Note the extra whitespace in the following section from its result document (before `Vegetables`):

```
Soup is offered with Filet Mig's None
Also offered are:  Vegetables, Baked Potato, and
    Dessert
```

Putting a `normalize-space()` inside that template helps clean up the result by removing this extra space:

```
<xsl:template match="entree">
  <xsl:if test="substring-before( features, ',') = 'Soup'">
    Soup is offered with <xsl:value-of select="@name"/>
    Also offered are: <xsl:value-of select="normalize-
        space(substring-after( features, 'Soup,'))"/>
  </xsl:if>
</xsl:template>
```

The trimmed results are:

```
Soup is offered with Filet Mig's None
Also offered are: Vegetables, Baked Potato, and Dessert

Soup is offered with Chicken Parmashaun
Also offered are: Pasta, Baked Potato, and Dessert
```

```
Soup is offered with Jerk Chicken
Also offered are: Vegetables, and Dessert

Soup is offered with Gusto Spaghetti
Also offered are: Salad, and Dessert
```

Converting an object into a string

To convert a node, number, or boolean value to a string, use the string()
function:

```
string string(object)
```

A boolean value of false is converted to the string 'false', while true
becomes 'true'. A number becomes a string representation of the numeric
value. A node returns its string value, while a nodeset returns the string value
of the first node.

For example, the following boolean value

```
He answered: <xsl:value-of select="string( false() )"/>
```

Becomes:

```
He answered: false
```

Numerically Speaking

Although XSLT wasn't designed for number crunching, you can use it to
do some basic manipulation of numbers. Check out the following built-in
functions.

Converting an object into a number

You can use the number() function to convert the specified object into a
number. If the object is a string, then it is converted to the nearest numeric
value specified by the string. A boolean value of false is converted to 0,
while true returns a 1. A node is first converted to a string value and then is
converted as a string. The function's syntax is:

```
number number([object])
```

The following snippet of XSLT converts a string to a number for calculation:

```
<xsl:value-of select="3.34*number('4.5')"/>
```

Results in:

```
15.03
```

Rounding numbers

You can round numbers to the nearest integer number with the `round()` function:

```
number round(number)
```

By applying `round()` to the example in the preceding section:

```
<xsl:value-of select="round( 3.34*number('4.5') )"/>
```

I get a rounded integer value:

```
15
```

Getting highest and lowest integer values

You can obtain the highest and lowest integer values by using the `floor()` and `ceiling()` functions:

```
number floor(number)
number ceiling(number)
```

When called, `floor()` evaluates the specified number value and returns the lowest integer number that is not less than the value. The `ceiling()` function does the converse — returning the highest integer number that is not greater than the value. To see how this works, take a look at the following code snippet:

```
Floor: <xsl:value-of select="floor( 3230.20 )"/>
Ceiling: <xsl:value-of select="ceiling( 3230.20 )"/>
```

The results look like this:

```
Floor: 3230
Ceiling: 3231
```

Summing it all up

The sum() function allows you to get the sum of the number values of the nodes in the specified nodeset:

```
number sum(nodeset)
```

In other words, sum() first converts each node in the nodeset to a number and then tallies up the numbers.

The following template rule uses sum() to add up the numeric values for all the fatgrams elements in the source tree:

```
<xsl:template match="/">
If you eat all of our entrees, you will eat a total of
        <xsl:value-of select="sum( //fatgrams )"/> grams
        of fat.
</xsl:template>
```

The following sentence results from the transformation:

```
If you eat all of our entrees, you will eat a total of 138
        grams of fat.
```

Formatting a number

When numbers are displayed as strings, you'll often want to format them in a specific manner. The format-number() function allows you to take a number and obtain a string version of it in the format you specify. Its syntax is:

```
string format-number(number, formatstring [, decimalformat])
```

When processed, the number argument is converted to a string and is formatted based on formatstring. Table 11-1 shows the symbols you can use to compose the formatstring value.

Table 11-1		formatstring Symbols
Symbol		**Means** **Example (using 1,000 as the number to be formatted)**
0	Any numeric digit	With 00000, 1,000 would display as 01000
#	A digit with zero showing as absent	With #####, 1,000 would display as 1000
.	A decimal point in a number	With #####.00, 1,000 would display as 1000.00

Table 11-1 *(continued)*

Symbol		Means	Example (using 1,000 as the number to be formatted)
,	A thousands grouping symbol		With #,####, 1,000 would display as 1,000
-	Default negative prefix		With -####, 1,000 would display as -1,000
%	Multiply by 100 and show as percentage		With ####%, 1,000 would display as 100000%
$	U.S. currency sign (replaced by appropriate currency symbol)		With $####, 1,000 would display as $1000
X	Any other characters can be used in the prefix or suffix		With ABC-####, 1,000 would display as ABC-1000

The formatstring argument is based on the DecimalFormat class of Java 1.1. For full details, go to java.sun.com/products/jdk/1.1/docs/api/java.text.DecimalFormat.html.

The following template rule shows how the format-number() function can output a variety of numeric formats based on the formatstring argument:

```
<xsl:template match="/">
  <xsl:variable name="constant" select="00433339.03"/>
  <xsl:value-of select="format-number( $constant, '#'
      )"/><xsl:text>
  </xsl:text>
  <xsl:value-of select="format-number( $constant,
      '00000000000' )"/><xsl:text>
  </xsl:text>
  <xsl:value-of select="format-number( $constant, '#.###'
      )"/><xsl:text>
  </xsl:text>
  <xsl:value-of select="format-number( $constant, '#.##'
      )"/><xsl:text>
  </xsl:text>
  <xsl:value-of select="format-number( $constant,
      '$#,###,###.##' )"/><xsl:text>
  </xsl:text>
  <xsl:value-of select="format-number( $constant, '#%'
      )"/><xsl:text>
  </xsl:text>
  <xsl:value-of select="format-number( $constant, 'SE-#-EP'
      )"/><xsl:text>
  </xsl:text>
</xsl:template>
```

The results are shown below:

```
433339
00000433339
433,339
433339.03
$433,339.03
43333903%
SE-433339-EP
```

Booleans: To Be or Not to Be

The final major data type XSLT deals with is boolean, which is a simple binary state (true or false). The four built-in functions for boolean values are: not(), true(), false(), and boolean().

Returning the opposite value

To return a value that's opposite from the one you have, you can use the not() function:

```
boolean not(boolean)
```

The following xsl:if instruction evaluates to true if the myvar variable is not true:

```
<xsl:if test="not( $myvar )">
  This was not true.
</xsl:if>
```

Returning true and false values

To return a true value (no, not the hardware store), use the true() function:

```
boolean true()
```

To return a false value, use the false() function:

```
boolean false()
```

Converting to a boolean

You can convert a value to a boolean with the boolean() function. A string and node returns true when it is not empty, whereas a number is true if it is not equal to 0. The syntax is:

```
boolean boolean(object)
```

General Purpose Functions

In addition to the built-in functions centered around data types, XSLT adds some general purpose functions for specific uses. I discuss these functions in this section.

Generating a unique ID string

You can generate a unique identifier for a node using generate-id(). This becomes useful when you need a unique value for each element in the result document. The XSLT processor generates the identifier during the transformation; the value of the identifier consists of any string of alphabetical or numeric characters, but it must start with an alphabetic character. The syntax for the function is:

```
string generate-id([nodeset])
```

The following example uses generate-id() to assign a value to a new id attribute and declare a new element:

```
<xsl:template match="entree">
  <entree id="{generate-id()}" name="{@name}"><xsl:text>
  </xsl:text><xsl:element name="{generate-
          id()}"/><xsl:text>
</xsl:text></entree>
</xsl:template>
```

The results are:

```
<entree id="d0e3" name="Sunburnt Chicken">
  <d0e3/>
</entree>
<entree id="d0e18" name="Filet Mig's None">
  <d0e18/>
</entree>
<entree id="d0e33" name="Chicken Parmashaun">
  <d0e33/>
</entree>
```

```
<entree id="d0e48" name="Eggs Benelux">
  <d0e48/>
</entree>
<entree id="d0e63" name="Jerk Chicken">
  <d0e63/>
</entree>
<entree id="d0e78" name="Gusto Spaghetti">
  <d0e78/>
</entree>
```

Pay special attention to the fact that, even though generate-id() is used twice in the template rule, the same ID value is generated for each of these times in each entree particular element node. The reason is that generate-id() creates a unique ID for a context node, so as long as the node stays in context, then the same value is returned.

If you run this code more than once, you'll likely get a different set of identifier values each time you run it, because the IDs are generated to be unique for a particular transformation. In fact, if you apply the same stylesheet twice, you will likely get different IDs both times. The important part is not the specific values themselves, but that they are unique within that particular transformation.

Also see Chapter 10 for another example of using generate-id().

Returning system information

You can use the system-property() function to obtain certain system-level information, usually about the processor itself:

```
object system-property(string)
```

Each processor is required to support a minimum of three properties:

- ✔ xsl:version returns a number indicating the version of XSLT that the processor implements. For example, for XSLT processors implementing XSLT 1.0, the number 1.0 is returned.

- ✔ xsl:vendor returns a string that identifies the XSLT processor vendor.

- ✔ xsl:vendor-url returns a string declaring a URL for the vendor of the XSLT processor.

The following stylesheet prints these three properties:

```
<xsl:template match="/">
XSLT Version Supported: <xsl:value-of select="system-
        property( 'xsl:version' )"/><xsl:text>
</xsl:text>
```

```
XSLT Processor: <xsl:value-of select="system-property(
          'xsl:vendor' )"/><xsl:text>
</xsl:text>
For More Info: <xsl:value-of select="system-property(
          'xsl:vendor-url' )"/><xsl:text>
</xsl:text>
</xsl:template>
```

When run against the SAXON 6.4 processor, the following results are generated:

```
XSLT Version Supported: 1
XSLT Processor: SAXON 6.4.4 from Michael Kay
For More Info: http://saxon.sourceforge.net
```

Part IV
eXtreme XSLT

The 5th Wave   By Rich Tennant

"OOPS, I FORGOT TO LOG OFF AGAIN."

In this part . . .

Skydivers, hang gliders, and snowboarders have one thing in common — they like to take their activities to the extreme. If you, too, like to live on the edge, you're ready for this part. You round out your understanding of XSLT by dealing with some of the advanced techniques that you can perform with the markup language. And if those features aren't enough, you can find out how to add your own extensions to the XSLT language.

Chapter 12

Combining XSLT Stylesheets

*A*nyone who rents videos from a local video store has probably seen that little sticker that says, "Be kind; please rewind." As you begin to work with a growing number of XSLT stylesheets, my guess is that you'll quickly find that your motto is "Be kind, please combine."

Managing XSLT code can be challenging, especially when you have common template rules or other instructions that you want to use in more than one context. Isolating sections of XSLT code and placing them into different files can be useful. This practice allows you to mix and match various stylesheets, depending on your current need, without resorting to copying and pasting code from one stylesheet to another.

Combining stylesheets can be a useful organizing tool for XSLT developers. In this chapter, you find out how you can combine XSLT stylesheets and call templates and other instructions from one stylesheet into another.

Comparing xsl:include and xsl:import

XSLT offers two closely related top-level elements for incorporating one stylesheet into another. These are:

  ✔ xsl:include is used to draw the top-level elements of the specified stylesheet into the calling stylesheet. The XSLT processor treats the incoming contents as if you literally inserted them at the point of the xsl:include element. Its required attribute is href, which specifies the file to be included:

```
<xsl:include href="util.xsl"/>
```

✔ `xsl:import` loads the specified stylesheet, but makes it something like an auxiliary resource, extending the top-level elements of the current stylesheet. It has the following syntax:

```
<xsl:import href="util.xsl"/>
```

Both of these elements sound pretty similar, don't they? At first glance, the differences between `xsl:include` and `xsl:import` seem nominal, almost esoteric. But, on closer inspection, you notice some important differences in their usage and behavior. In the following sections, I discuss some of their similarities and differences.

When the XSLT processor encounters an `xsl:include` or `xsl:import` element, the processor takes all the contents of the referenced stylesheet (all the code between the `xsl:stylesheet`'s start and end tags) and processes them based on the rules of the import/include element.

You use `xsl:include` and `xsl:import` to include other XSLT stylesheets, not XML documents. If you want to combine codes from various XML documents, you can use the `document()` function, which I cover in Chapter 14.

Referencing valid stylesheets

Both the `xsl:include` and `xsl:import` elements must reference a valid XSLT stylesheet in their `href` attribute. You can't incorporate a file that has a snippet of XSLT code. Rather, you need to define a `xsl:stylesheet` element in the code and follow normal XSLT stylesheet conventions. Make sure that any stylesheet you want to reference can be called and run by itself, apart from any stylesheet that calls it.

If you've worked with other programming languages before, such as C++ or Java, you're probably familiar with an `include` statement to incorporate source code from one file into another. The `xsl:include` is similar to these uses, except that the included file must be a normal stylesheet, not part of one.

Placing the elements

Both `xsl:include` and `xsl:import` must be added as top-level elements of the calling stylesheet. `xsl:import` has the strictest rules for its placement: It must appear as the *first* child element under an `xsl:stylesheet` element, or you get a processing error. In contrast, `xsl:include` can appear anywhere within the calling stylesheet as long as it's a top-level element. You can't, for example, place an `xsl:include` element inside a template rule.

Resolving conflicts

The most important difference between xsl:include and xsl:import is the different ways they handle conflicts. A conflict occurs when a top-level element from the incoming stylesheet is identical to an element in the calling stylesheet. xsl:import handles any collisions neatly: The element from the calling stylesheet wins because it has greater *import precedence,* discarding the element from the referenced stylesheet. In contrast, xsl:include can't handle conflict well: Any collision causes a processing error and so the transformation fails.

Consider, for example, the case in which a variable defined in the calling stylesheet has the same name as one in the referenced stylesheet. The referenced stylesheet looks like:

```
<!-- referencesheet.xsl -->
<xsl:stylesheet version="1.0"
          xmlns:xsl="http://www.w3.org/1999/XSL/Transform">
  <xsl:variable name="state">pondering</xsl:variable>
</xsl:stylesheet>
```

When another stylesheet uses xsl:import to call this stylesheet and has a conflicting variable name, the one in the calling stylesheet wins. So, in the following case, the state variable has the value of probing.

```
<!-- callingsheet.xsl -->
<xsl:stylesheet version="1.0"
          xmlns:xsl="http://www.w3.org/1999/XSL/Transform">
  <xsl:import href="referencesheet.xsl"/>
  <xsl:variable name="state">probing</xsl:variable>
</xsl:stylesheet>
```

However, if xsl:include is used, you get a processing error because the variables are considered duplicates:

```
<!-- callingsheet.xsl -->
<xsl:stylesheet version="1.0"
          xmlns:xsl="http://www.w3.org/1999/XSL/Transform">
  <xsl:include href="referencesheet.xsl"/>
  <xsl:variable name="state">contemplating</xsl:variable>
</xsl:stylesheet>
```

You have to remove one of these variable declarations before continuing.

REMEMBER

xsl:include can potentially introduce conflict resolution problems that must be corrected before processing can continue. In contrast, a conflict in xsl:import never causes errors because the calling stylesheet always wins.

Handling identical template rules

Two template rules that have the same match pattern aren't considered a conflict per se and don't generate a processing error with xsl:include. I explain in Chapter 4 that XSLT allows this scenario and simply prioritizes template rules based on a system of weighting. So, in the case where a template rule from the calling stylesheet is identical to the template rule of a called stylesheet, the following rules apply:

- ✔ For xsl:import, the template rule in the calling stylesheet always wins.

- ✔ For xsl:include, the template rule that appears last wins. So if the xsl:include element comes before the template rule definition in the calling stylesheet, the calling stylesheet template rule is used. However, if the xsl:include line comes after the calling stylesheet's template rule, the template rule from the called stylesheet wins.

Practical Use of xsl:import

When you fully understand how xsl:include and xsl:import are used and their potential implications, you can use them effectively to make your stylesheet development process more efficient. Following is a fairly basic, yet practical example of how you can use xsl:import. Suppose that a company has an XML document of employees which it uses as the data source for multiple output needs:

- ✔ An HTML summary report of employees

- ✔ A comma-delimited text file which separates each piece of employee data with a comma for importing into an external database

- ✔ A modified XML structure for use in another application

Listing 12-1 shows the XML source file.

Listing 12-1:   company_emp.xml

```
<!-- company_emp.xml -->
<?xml version="1.0"?>
<employees>
  <employee id="101">
    <lastname>Lamotte</lastname>
    <firstname>Mitch</firstname>
    <nickname>The Mitchster</nickname>
    <title>Director of Sales</title>
  </employee>
  <employee id="102">
    <lastname>Williams</lastname>
```

```
      <firstname>Tim</firstname>
      <nickname>Timmy Boy</nickname>
      <title>Director of Quality Assurance</title>
   </employee>
   <employee id="103">
      <lastname>Magruder</lastname>
      <firstname>Randy</firstname>
      <nickname>Randall</nickname>
      <title>Senior Engineer</title>
   </employee>
   <employee id="104">
      <lastname>Drohan</lastname>
      <firstname>Doug</firstname>
      <nickname>Tooltime</nickname>
      <title>Building Director</title>
   </employee>
   <employee id="105">
      <lastname>Burrer</lastname>
      <firstname>Phillip</firstname>
      <nickname>Flip</nickname>
      <title>Resident Physician</title>
   </employee>
</employees>
```

To act on this source document, I have created three stylesheets, each of which generates one of the three outputs I want.

The first stylesheet (shown in Listing 12-2) defines a template rule for outputting the employee elements into an HTML-based list. An xsl:output element is added with method="html" to create an HTML file. A variable named reporttype is declared with a value of 1, which is used in the calling stylesheet I define later.

Listing 12-2:   emp_report_1.xsl

```
<?xml version="1.0"?>
<xsl:stylesheet version="1.0"
          xmlns:xsl="http://www.w3.org/1999/XSL/Transform">

   <!-- Declare HTML output -->
   <xsl:output method="html"/>

   <!-- reporttype definition -->
   <xsl:variable name="reporttype" select="1"/>

   <!-- employee template rule for HTML output-->
   <xsl:template match="employee">
      <p><b><xsl:value-of select="firstname"/><xsl:text>
            </xsl:text><xsl:value-of
            select="lastname"/></b></p><xsl:text>
      </xsl:text>
      <p> * Employee ID: <xsl:value-of select="@id"/></p>
```

```
       <p> * Serves as <xsl:value-of
               select="title"/></p><xsl:text>
       </xsl:text>
       <p> * Likes to be called <i><xsl:value-of
               select="nickname"/></i></p><xsl:text>

       </xsl:text>
       <hr></hr>
   </xsl:template>

</xsl:stylesheet>
```

The second stylesheet is in Listing 12-3 and provides a template rule for creating a comma-delimited text file that lists the values of each child in the employee element. It has an xsl:output element in which the method attribute has a value of text, and its reporttype variable is set to 2.

Listing 12-3:   emp_report_2.xsl

```
<?xml version="1.0"?>
<xsl:stylesheet version="1.0"
           xmlns:xsl="http://www.w3.org/1999/XSL/Transform">

   <!-- Declare Text output -->
   <xsl:output method="text"/>

   <!-- reporttype definition -->
   <xsl:variable name="reporttype" select="2"/>

   <!-- employee template rule for text-only output-->
   <xsl:template match="employee">
   <xsl:value-of select="@id"/>,<xsl:value-of
           select="firstname"/>,<xsl:value-of
           select="lastname"/>,<xsl:value-of
           select="title"/>,<xsl:value-of
           select="nickname"/><xsl:text>
   </xsl:text>
</xsl:template>

</xsl:stylesheet>
```

The third stylesheet (shown in Listing 12-4) creates a template rule that transforms the original XML structure into a derivative XML document. The xsl:output's method is set to xml, while the reporttype variable is declared with a value of 3.

Listing 12-4:   emp_report_3.xsl

```
<?xml version="1.0"?>
```

```
<xsl:stylesheet version="1.0"
          xmlns:xsl="http://www.w3.org/1999/XSL/Transform">

  <!-- Declare XML output -->
  <xsl:output method="xml"/>

  <!-- reporttype definition -->
  <xsl:variable name="reporttype" select="3"/>

  <!-- employee template rule for XML output-->
  <xsl:template match="employee">
  <employee>
    <id><xsl:value-of select="@id"/></id>
    <name><xsl:value-of select="firstname"/><xsl:text>
          </xsl:text><xsl:value-of
          select="lastname"/></name>
    <title><xsl:value-of select="title"/></title>
  </employee>
</xsl:template>

</xsl:stylesheet>
```

Each of these stylesheets can be run independently on the source document to produce the results desired, but it may be more efficient to create a master stylesheet that conditionally runs one of these three stylesheets. This is especially true when you have identical code that needs to be run on each output type.

For example, because I have created these three stylesheets that transform the employee element, I now create a "master" stylesheet that brings everything together:

```
<!-- company_emp.xsl -->
<xsl:stylesheet version="1.0"
          xmlns:xsl="http://www.w3.org/1999/XSL/Transform">

  <!-- Import employee template rule -->
  <xsl:import href="emp_report_1.xsl"/>

  <!-- reportname variable declaration -->
  <xsl:variable name="reportname">Employee
          Summary</xsl:variable>

  <!-- Generate employees report -->
  <xsl:template match="employees">
    <!-- HTML report -->
    <xsl:if test="$reporttype=1">
    <h1><xsl:value-of select="$reportname"/></h1>
    <xsl:apply-templates/>
    </xsl:if>
    <!-- Comma-delimited text report -->
    <xsl:if test="$reporttype=2">
```

```
       <xsl:text>id,name,title,nickname
       </xsl:text>
       <xsl:apply-templates/>
    </xsl:if>
    <!-- XML report -->
    <xsl:if test="$reporttype=3">
       <xsl:text>
</xsl:text><employees_sub1>
    <xsl:apply-templates/>
     </employees_sub1>
    </xsl:if>
  </xsl:template>

</xsl:stylesheet>
```

The xsl:import element is used to specify which of the three reference stylesheets I want to use: emp_report_1.xsl for HTML (Listing 12-2), emp_report_2.xsl for text (Listing 12-3), or emp_report_3.xsl for XML (Listing 12-4). This href value is the only code that needs to be changed, depending on the output type desired.

The xsl:variable defines a reportname variable, which I use to generate a header for each report type in the employees template rule.

The employees template rule tests the value of the reporttype variable (defined in the referenced stylesheets) in the xsl:if statements to determine which of the three output types are desired:

- ✔ For HTML output, the template adds a h1 header.
- ✔ For text output, the field names are listed.
- ✔ Or for XML output, the template adds employees_sub1 as the document element of the new XML file created.

When the company_emp.xsl file is applied to the Listing 12-1 XML file using <xsl:import href="emp_report_1.xsl"/>, the following HTML is generated:

```
<h1>Employee Summary</h1>

<p><b>Mitch Lamotte</b></p>

<p> * Employee ID: 101</p>
<p> * Serves as Director of Sales</p>

<p> * Likes to be called <i>The Mitchster</i></p>


<hr>
```

```
<p><b>Tim Williams</b></p>

<p> * Employee ID: 102</p>
<p> * Serves as Director of Quality Assurance</p>

<p> * Likes to be called <i>Timmy Boy</i></p>


<hr>

<p><b>Randy Magruder</b></p>

<p> * Employee ID: 103</p>
<p> * Serves as Senior Engineer</p>

<p> * Likes to be called <i>Randall</i></p>


<hr>

<p><b>Doug Drohan</b></p>

<p> * Employee ID: 104</p>
<p> * Serves as Building Director</p>

<p> * Likes to be called <i>Tooltime</i></p>


<hr>

<p><b>Phillip Burrer</b></p>

<p> * Employee ID: 105</p>
<p> * Serves as Resident Physician</p>

<p> * Likes to be called <i>Flip</i></p>


<hr>
```

When run with `<xsl:import href="emp_report_2.xsl"/>`, the following text file is produced:

```
 id,name,title,nickname
101,Mitch,Lamotte,Director of Sales,The Mitchster
102,Tim,Williams,Director of Quality Assurance,Timmy Boy
103,Randy,Magruder,Senior Engineer,Randall
104,Doug,Drohan,Building Director,Tooltime
105,Phillip,Burrer,Resident Physician,Flip
```

Finally, when run with `<xsl:import href="emp_report_2.xsl"/>`, the XML result is:

```
<?xml version="1.0" encoding="utf-8"?>
<employees_sub1>
  <employee><id>101</id><name>Mitch
          Lamotte</name><title>Director of
          Sales</title></employee>
  <employee><id>102</id><name>Tim
          Williams</name><title>Director of Quality
          Assurance</title></employee>
  <employee><id>103</id><name>Randy
          Magruder</name><title>Senior
          Engineer</title></employee>
  <employee><id>104</id><name>Doug
          Drohan</name><title>Building
          Director</title></employee>
  <employee><id>105</id><name>Phillip
          Burrer</name><title>Resident
          Physician</title></employee>
</employees_sub1>
```

Chapter 13

"Gimme Some Space" and Other Output Issues

*B*ecause the whole purpose of XSLT is to generate new documents from other documents, the transformation language ought to have considerable flexibility in determining what the resulting document structure looks like. After all, if not, why use it? Fortunately, XSLT does have several ways to tweak the result of your transformation. In Chapter 9, I explain how you can sort and number the content. In this chapter, I discuss some of the more advanced issues concerning XSLT output.

Gimme Some Space

Whitespace is a term used to describe those invisible characters inside a document. You know, all those characters that you never see, but you know they're there, such as spaces, tabs, carriage returns, and line feeds. They're kind of like those creepy microscopic creatures you see on PBS specials that supposedly crawl all over you and me. Yuck! I'm itching all over just thinking about it . . . let me change the subject and talk about something much more pleasant: whitespace.

Whitespace is one of those tricky issues in XSLT, because so many variables that determine what whitespace appears in the result tree are at play. Whitespace has origins in the XML source, the template rules of the XSLT stylesheet, and specific space-related XSLT elements, such as `xsl:strip-space`.

And if that isn't complicated enough, in what must be nothing more than a sick joke, some XSLT processors handle whitespace quite differently from others, which can result in varying outputs.

msxsl3, the 3.0 version of Microsoft's msxsl processor, is particularly problematic in how it deals with whitespace. Unlike other processors, such as Saxon, whitespace is automatically stripped out by default, both from the original XML source document and the XSLT stylesheet. In fact, trying to figure out how to even add whitespace back into it becomes a frustrating exercise. Happily, with version 4.0 of the msxsl processor, this default behavior has been changed to reflect what you'd expected from standard XSLT processors.

Fortunately, in many cases, whitespace in the result document is not that significant of an issue. Nonetheless, when you are trying either to preserve a specific format or to format the result document in a specific manner, then knowing how to work with whitespace becomes important.

Whitespace in XSLT stylesheets

The general rule of thumb is that, inside the XSLT stylesheet, whitespace is stripped out of the template before any transformation occurs. However, you can make sure the processor preserves the whitespace based on how you work with the text nodes and xsl:text instructions.

Whitespace in text nodes

Whitespace in text nodes is normally ignored, but when a text node contains nonwhitespace characters, then whitespace characters are automatically preserved. To demonstrate how this works, take a look at my sample XML source in Listing 13-1.

Listing 13-1:   afifilms.xml

```
<!-- American Film Institute Top 10 Films -->
<!-- afifilms.xml -->
<topfilms createdby="AFI">
  <film place="1" date="1941">Citizen Kane</film>
  <film place="2" date="1942">Casablanca</film>
  <film place="3" date="1972">The Godfather</film>
  <film place="4" date="1939">Gone With The Wind</film>
  <film place="5" date="1962">Lawrence Of Arabia</film>
  <film place="6" date="1939">The Wizard Of Oz</film>
  <film place="7" date="1967">The Graduate</film>
  <film place="8" date="1954">On The Waterfront</film>
  <film place="9" date="1993">Schindler's List</film>
  <film place="10" date="1952">Singin' In The Rain</film>
</topfilms>
```

Suppose I want to use this list of the American Film Institute's top ten films to generate a list of each film and the date it was made. I can create such a result with this code:

```
<xsl:template match="film">
 <xsl:apply-templates/>
 <xsl:value-of select="@date"/>
</xsl:template>
```

The template rule then generates the following result:

```
Citizen Kane1941
Casablanca1942
The Godfather1972
Gone With The Wind1939
Lawrence Of Arabia1962
The Wizard Of Oz1939
The Graduate1967
On The Waterfront1954
Schindler's List1993
Singin' In The Rain1952
```

Although you can easily forget about it, a text node is actually between the `xsl:apply-templates` and `xsl:value-of` instructions. However, because all the characters that the text node contains are whitespace (carriage return, line feed), the text node is ignored in the output. Therefore, the following two ways of expressing the code produce the same output:

```
<xsl:apply-templates/>
<xsl:value-of select="@date"/>
```

and

```
<xsl:apply-templates/><xsl:value-of select="@date"/>
```

To make the output more readable, I can add literal text between these two instructions to make each list item into a sentence. The new template rule looks like:

```
<xsl:template match="film">
 <xsl:apply-templates/> was made in <xsl:value-of
          select="@date"/>
</xsl:template>
```

This revised template produces the following result:

```
Citizen Kane was made in 1941
Casablanca was made in 1942
The Godfather was made in 1972
Gone With The Wind was made in 1939
Lawrence Of Arabia was made in 1962
```

```
The Wizard Of Oz was made in 1939
The Graduate was made in 1967
On The Waterfront was made in 1954
Schindler's List was made in 1993
Singin' In The Rain was made in 1952
```

However, imagine that I alter the text between the xsl:apply-templates and xsl:value-of instructions in the template rule by adding line break between the text node:

```
<xsl:template match="film">
 <xsl:apply-templates/> was
 made in <xsl:value-of select="@date"/>
</xsl:template>
```

The results in this case show the line break:

```
Citizen Kane was
 made in 1941
Casablanca was
 made in 1942
The Godfather was
 made in 1972
Gone With The Wind was
 made in 1939
Lawrence Of Arabia was
 made in 1962
The Wizard Of Oz was
 made in 1939
The Graduate was
 made in 1967
On The Waterfront was
 made in 1954
Schindler's List was
 made in 1993
Singin' In The Rain was
 made in 1952
```

The XSLT processor can't ignore the line break in this template rule because nonwhitespace characters appear in the same text node. The whitespace characters are all preserved along with the adjoining nonwhitespace characters.

Whitespace inside xsl:text

Any whitespace appearing inside the xsl:text element is automatically preserved, making it a good tool to control exactly what whitespace you want to appear in the result document. For example, if I want to add an XML comment to precede each item in the list, I add an xsl:comment instruction to the template. (I discuss the use of xsl:comment later in the chapter.) But if I use the following snippet, the comment appears on the same line as the list entry:

```
<xsl:template match="film">
  <xsl:comment>List entry</xsl:comment>
  <xsl:apply-templates/> was made in <xsl:value-of
         select="@date"/>
</xsl:template>
```

The result is:

```
<!--List entry-->Citizen Kane was made in 1941
<!--List entry-->Casablanca was made in 1942
<!--List entry-->The Godfather was made in 1972
<!--List entry-->Gone With The Wind was made in 1939
<!--List entry-->Lawrence Of Arabia was made in 1962
<!--List entry-->The Wizard Of Oz was made in 1939
<!--List entry-->The Graduate was made in 1967
<!--List entry-->On The Waterfront was made in 1954
<!--List entry-->Schindler's List was made in 1993
<!--List entry-->Singin' In The Rain was made in 1952
```

Just as you found out in the preceding section, whitespace is ignored between `</xsl:comment>` and `<xsl:apply-templates>` tags. Therefore, to add a line break between the comment and line text and after each item, you need to use `xsl:text`:

```
<xsl:template match="film">
<xsl:comment>List entry</xsl:comment><xsl:text>
</xsl:text>
<xsl:apply-templates/> was made in <xsl:value-of
         select="@date"/><xsl:text>
</xsl:text>
</xsl:template>
```

So, even though the `xsl:text` instruction contains nothing but a carriage return, the XSLT processor preserves it because whitespace that falls between the start and end tags of `xsl:text` is considered significant. The text generated is as follows:

```
<!--List entry-->
  Citizen Kane was made in 1941

<!--List entry-->
  Casablanca was made in 1942

<!--List entry-->
  The Godfather was made in 1972

<!--List entry-->
  Gone With The Wind was made in 1939

<!--List entry-->
  Lawrence Of Arabia was made in 1962
```

```
<!--List entry-->
  The Wizard Of Oz was made in 1939

<!--List entry-->
  The Graduate was made in 1967

<!--List entry-->
  On The Waterfront was made in 1954

<!--List entry-->
  Schindler's List was made in 1993

<!--List entry-->
  Singin' In The Rain was made in 1952
```

Whitespace in source XML documents

When creating XML documents, I often want to visually show the hierarchy of the document structure by indenting each level, but I don't want this white-space to actually show up in my result tree. Although this seems logical, it causes problems with the XML processor, because it doesn't know whether or not those whitespace characters are significant. Because preserving infor-mation that could be significant is better than deleting it, the XML processor preserves all whitespace outside the start and end tags of the XML elements. For example, I can change the spacing of the source document I've been using so that it looks like this:

```
<!-- American Film Institute Top 25 Films -->
<topfilms createdby="AFI">
  <film place="1" date="1941">Citizen Kane</film>
        <film place="2" date="1942">Casablanca</film>

  <film place="3" date="1972">The Godfather</film>


            <film place="4" date="1939">Gone With The
        Wind</film><film place="5" date="1962">Lawrence Of
        Arabia</film>
  <film place="6" date="1939">The Wizard Of Oz</film>

   <film place="7" date="1967">The Graduate</film><film
        place="8" date="1954">On The Waterfront</film>

  <film place="9" date="1993">Schindler's List</film>



   <film place="10" date="1952">Singin' In The Rain</film>
</topfilms>
```

To show how this whitespace is carried over to the result document, I create a basic template rule

```
<xsl:template match="film">
  <xsl:apply-templates/>
</xsl:template>
```

After transformation, the output is as follows:

```
Citizen Kane
            Casablanca

The Godfather

                Gone With The WindLawrence Of Arabia
The Wizard Of Oz

  The GraduateOn The Waterfront

Schindler's List



Singin' In The Rain
```

Using xsl:strip-space and xsl:preserve-space

You can use the xsl:strip-space element to get rid of all this extra whitespace in the source document. This element has a single required attribute named elements. You use the elements attribute to list the names of elements containing whitespace that you want to strip. If you want to add more than one element name, separate the names with (ironically enough) whitespace. You can also use * to specify all elements.

For my example, I want to specify the topfilms element, because all the extra whitespace is part of its content:

```
<xsl:strip-space elements="topfilms"/>
```

By adding this as a top-level element to my stylesheet, the transformation now looks quite different:

```
Citizen KaneCasablancaThe GodfatherGone With The WindLawrence
              Of ArabiaThe Wizard Of OzThe GraduateOn The
              WaterfrontSchindler's ListSingin' In The Rain
```

The xsl:strip-space removes whitespace only for the elements specified by the elements attribute and doesn't strip whitespace from the descendents of those elements. In this example, if I want to remove any extra whitespace appearing in film elements, I need to explicitly add it to the elements attribute value: elements="topfilms film".

The `xsl:preserve-space` element preserves whitespace in the source document. By default, XSLT conserves space already, so this element is needed only to offset the use of `xsl:strip-space`. A common example of how developers use this element is when you want to remove the space in all elements except one or two. So if I want to remove all the whitespace in the source document, except for the whitespace inside the `film` elements, I use the following:

```
<xsl:strip-space elements="*"/>
<xsl:preserve-space elements="film"/>
```

The `xsl:strip-space` and `xsl:preserve-space` elements are top-level elements for a stylesheet. If you put them inside a template rule, you get an error.

Preserving with xml:space

A second way of preserving whitespace in the source document is to add a special XML attribute named `xml:space` to one or more of the document elements. The `xml:space` attribute has two possible values:

- `xml:space="preserve"` tells the processor to keep the whitespace for this element intact.
- `xml:space="default"` tells the processor to return to its default setting.

The `xml:space` applies to the element that defines it as well as any of its descendants.

When the XSLT processor encounters an `xml:space`, it remembers the value as text nodes are processed. Text nodes take on the `xml:space` value of their closest ancestor.

Indenting Your Result Document

The `xsl:output` element includes the `indent` attribute, which enables you to specify whether the XSLT processor can indent the result document so that the document displays the hierarchy of the tree.

Indenting your result document can help others read it but doesn't impact how the document is processed. For example, imagine you have a flat-looking XML file that you want to transform into something more readable. Start with the following source:

```
<topfilms createdby="AFI">
<film place="1" date="1941">Citizen Kane</film>
<film place="2" date="1942">Casablanca</film>
<film place="3" date="1972">The Godfather</film>
```

```
<film place="4" date="1939">Gone With The Wind</film>
<film place="5" date="1962">Lawrence Of Arabia</film>
<film place="6" date="1939">The Wizard Of Oz</film>
<film place="7" date="1967">The Graduate</film>
<film place="8" date="1954">On The Waterfront</film>
<film place="9" date="1993">Schindler's List</film>
<film place="10" date="1952">Singin' In The Rain</film>
</topfilms>
```

You can use the following stylesheet to copy all the elements into an indented output:

```
<xsl:output method="xml" indent="yes"/>

<xsl:template match="/">
  <xsl:copy-of select="*"/>
</xsl:template>
```

When the stylesheet is applied to the XML source, the XSLT processor indents each level of the result tree hierarchy, resulting in a much more legible document:

```
<topfilms createdby="AFI">

   <film place="1" date="1941">Citizen Kane</film>

   <film place="2" date="1942">Casablanca</film>

   <film place="3" date="1972">The Godfather</film>

   <film place="4" date="1939">Gone With The Wind</film>

   <film place="5" date="1962">Lawrence Of Arabia</film>

   <film place="6" date="1939">The Wizard Of Oz</film>

   <film place="7" date="1967">The Graduate</film>

   <film place="8" date="1954">On The Waterfront</film>

   <film place="9" date="1993">Schindler's List</film>

   <film place="10" date="1952">Singin' In The Rain</film>

</topfilms>
```

By using the indent="yes" option, you tell the XSLT processor that it can indent to show the document hierarchy. But, that does not necessarily mean that all processors support indenting. Some processors, like Saxon, provide explicit support for indenting, while others (msxsl) do not.

Adding Comments

XSLT includes the `xsl:comment` instruction to create an XML/HTML-like comment and add it to the result document. After transformation, the comment text you provide becomes surrounded by a `<!--` and `-->`. For example, suppose I'd like to output the `afifilms.xml` document (refer to Listing 13-1) as an HTML-based numbered list. However, I'd like to add a comment at the top of the document identifying the list along with comments both before and after the list denoting its start and end. The following stylesheet can be used to do this:

```
<xsl:stylesheet
        xmlns:xsl="http://www.w3.org/1999/XSL/Transform"
        version="1.0">

  <xsl:output method="html"/>

  <!-- Add HTML element, comments -->
  <xsl:template match="/topfilms">
    <html>
    <xsl:comment>List created by <xsl:value-of
        select="@createdby"/></xsl:comment>
    <xsl:comment>***** Start List *****</xsl:comment>
    <ol>
    <xsl:apply-templates/>
    </ol>
    <xsl:comment>***** End List *****</xsl:comment>
    </html>
  </xsl:template>

  <!-- Apply to each film -->
  <xsl:template match="film">
    <li><i><xsl:apply-templates/></i></li>
  </xsl:template>

</xsl:stylesheet>
```

The first template rule demonstrates the use of the `xsl:comment`. Any text placed between the start and end tags of the `xsl:comment` instruction are added as comments in the result tree. As you can see, you can include literal text or anything that evaluates to text, such as `xsl:value-of`. The second template rule adds the HTML code to create an italicized list (the `li` element creates a list item and `i` adds italics). The HTML code that is generated after the transformation is shown here:

```
<html>
   <!--List created by AFI-->
   <!--***** Start List *****-->
   <ol>
```

```
     <li><i>Citizen Kane</i></li>
     <li><i>Casablanca</i></li>
     <li><i>The Godfather</i></li>
     <li><i>Gone With The Wind</i></li>
     <li><i>Lawrence Of Arabia</i></li>
     <li><i>The Wizard Of Oz</i></li>
     <li><i>The Graduate</i></li>
     <li><i>On The Waterfront</i></li>
     <li><i>Schindler's List</i></li>
     <li><i>Singin' In The Rain</i></li>
     </ol>
     <!--***** End List *****-->
</html>
```

Avoid putting -- in your comment text or ending your text with a -. These characters are used to denote an end of comment tag and so could potentially goof up the resulting XML document structure. Some XSLT processors handle this syntax problem by adding a space around the last dash to prevent an error, but other processors may generate a runtime error.

You may have noticed that the XML comments from the original source document weren't copied to the result document. If you read the discussion on built-in templates in Chapter 4, you may recall that XSLT automatically strips out comments. If you want to carry over comments from the source to the result document, you need to add the following template rule to the stylesheet:

```
<xsl:template match="comment()">
  <xsl:copy/>
</xsl:template>
```

The `<!-- American Film Institute Top 25 Films -->` comment is then included in the output.

Adding Processing Instructions

XML processing instructions provide a way for documents to contain instructions for applications that deal with the output document. Although you can use processing instructions for any custom purpose, probably the most common use for a processing instruction today is to attach an XSLT stylesheet with an XML document (see Chapter 10 for more information on this instruction):

```
<?xml-stylesheet href="defaultstyles.css" type="text/css"?>
```

Processing instructions stand apart from other XML elements due to their `<?` prefix and `?>` suffix.

Although it looks like one, XML declarations like `<?xml version="1.0"?>` are technically not processing instructions. Therefore, you cannot use `xsl:processing-instruction` to add an XML declaration to your output document. Instead, use the `xsl:output` instruction with `method="xml"` defined to have the processor automatically add an XML declaration to the top of your result document.

You can create processing instructions and add them to your result document with the handy `xsl:processing-instruction` element. It has two parts:

- ✔ The `name` attribute specifies the name of the processing instruction.
- ✔ The content of the element is used for adding any other name/value pairs that you need.

Suppose, for example, you have an application that's using a processing instruction called `xsl-my_custom_instruction`. To generate the following instruction in the output file:

```
<? my_custom_instruction lang-"en" customid="kimmers"
            type="absolute" ?>
```

You use the following XSLT:

```
<xsl:processing-instruction name="xsl-my_custom_instruction">
   lang="en" customid="kimmers" type="absolute"
</xsl:processing-instruction>
```

Putting `xsl:processing-instruction` into action, I use the instruction to add an `xml-stylesheet` reference to the film list stylesheet I use earlier in this chapter:

```
<xsl:template match="/">
  <html><xsl:text>
  </xsl:text>
  <xsl:processing-instruction name="xml-
          stylesheet">href="liststyle.css"
          type="text/css"</xsl:processing-instruction>
  <xsl:comment>List created by <xsl:value-of
          select="@createdby"/></xsl:comment>
  <xsl:comment>***** Start List *****</xsl:comment>
  <xsl:apply-templates/>
  <xsl:comment>***** End List *****</xsl:comment>
  </html>
</xsl:template>
```

You can't include `?>` as part of your processing instruction definition or you generate a processing error. The symbol `?>` is reserved for the ending of a processing instruction.

By default, all processing instructions contained in the source document are removed during transformation. However, to override this behavior and copy processing instructions from the source directly to the result document, use the following template rule:

```
<xsl:template match="processing-instruction()">
  <xsl:copy/>
</xsl:template>
```

Chapter 14

Keys and Cross-Referencing

I remember the first time I ever heard the term *cross-reference*. I was in school, scouring through the library's card catalogue, trying to find some obscure book on Ancient Greece. With today's technology, cross-referencing has been transformed from the kind of labor-intensive process that I faced in that dusty ol' library into a simple, point-and-click motion on a computer. (Did I also tell you that I had to walk two miles to school each day in a foot of snow in bare feet? Well, I tell my kids that anyway.)

The Web is built on top of this notion of cross-referencing. The reason is obvious: Storing all the information available on the Web in a single gigantic page makes no sense, of course, because such a page would be unusable. Instead, related Web pages are linked together using hypertext.

Relational databases, such as Microsoft Access, are another example of how you can effectively cross-reference related information. For people who need to work with even small amounts of data, storing data across multiple tables is easier to maintain than dumping everything into a single massive table.

In case you're unfamiliar with databases, the basic notion of a relational database is to store the information in the place that makes the most sense. For example, you may store customers' information, orders, and parts into separate databases. And, then, when you want to use this information, you can link the related pieces together for the task you wish to perform.

It follows, then, that for XSLT to be flexible and useable for a variety of purposes, it also needs to offer a similar cross-referencing device. Otherwise, you could never bring together elements from disparate XML structures and integrate them in a result document. Instead, you'd be forced to create huge monolithic XML elements that would contain every possible piece of data in it, including the kitchen sink. In this chapter, you find out about how XSLT uses keys that enable you to cross-reference your source documents.

Keys to the Kingdom

You cross-reference in XSLT by using a key. No, not the kind of key you use to start your car, but something far different; in XSLT, a *key* is a point of access that you can use to connect one data set to another, similar to the way a hypertext link connects two HTML documents.

If you are unfamiliar with the term *key*, then it is helpful to think of it in the same way as a hyperlink in an HTML file. Although the two terms aren't synonymous, the comparison is helpful when you're beginning. The hypertext link provides a point of access that another document references so that people can obtain more information from the target document. So too, an XSLT key gives you a means to access more information from a node set.

The notches in a key

Keys are used in XSLT to cross-reference through a combination of the `xsl:key` element and the `key()` built-in function; `xsl:key` defines the key and `key()` references it.

Looking closer, the `xsl:key` element is used to define a key for a node set. Its syntax is:

```
<xsl:key name="keyname" match="pattern" use="expression"/>
```

This element has three attributes:

- ✔ `name` defines the name of the key. This label is used to reference the key elsewhere in the stylesheet.
- ✔ `match` specifies an XPath pattern, typically returning a node set that contains the key.
- ✔ `use` is an expression that names the value of the key.

If you've worked with relational databases before, you've obviously worked with key fields in a database table. An `xsl:key` element that you define in your stylesheet works in much the same way.

To demonstrate how to use keys, consider the following `states` document:

```
<states region="New England">
  <state id="01">Maine</state>
  <state id="02">New Hampshire</state>
  <state id="03">Vermont</state>
  <state id="04">Massachusetts</state>
  <state id="05">Connecticut</state>
```

```
      <state id="06">Rhode Island</state>
   </states>
```

I'd like to define a key on this document so that, when a state element's id attribute is requested, the content is returned. I can declare this key with the following element:

```
<xsl:key name="StateKey" match="state" use="@id"/>
```

In this statement, the StateKey key returns all the state elements, specifying that the id attribute of the returning nodes in the node set is the key to use.

Linking with the key () function

The xsl:key element is ready, but it can't do anything on its own. You need to use the key() built-in function to actually do something with it. The key() function syntax is:

```
key(KeyName, LookupValue)
```

The key() function has two parameters:

- ✔ KeyName specifies the name of the xsl:key element you wish to use.
- ✔ LookupValue is an expression that provides a value to look up.

Given this syntax, if I want to return the value of Rhode Island, I can use the following code:

```
key('StateKey', '06')
```

Although putting a literal text value can be useful on occasion, what makes the key() function powerful is when the LookupValue of the key() function is the value of another element or attribute. To demonstrate, mull over the following source document:

```
<?xml version="1.0"?>
<customers>
   <states region="New England">
      <state id="01">Maine</state>
      <state id="02">New Hampshire</state>
      <state id="03">Vermont</state>
      <state id="04">Massachusetts</state>
      <state id="05">Connecticut</state>
      <state id="06">Rhode Island</state>
   </states>
   <customer id="C3020" stateid="04">Bridget
         McFarland</customer>
   <customer id="C3021" stateid="04">Cheri Burrer</customer>
```

```
<customer id="C3022" stateid="02">Greg
        Stephenson</customer>
<customer id="C3023" stateid="05">Mark Horine</customer>
<customer id="C3024" stateid="01">Don Shafer</customer>
<customer id="C3025" stateid="04">Leo Minster</customer>
</customers>
```

Rather than cramming state-related information into the customer element, the preceding structure separates this information and places it in the separate states element. However, to provide a link between a customer and the state of residence, each of the customer elements have a stateid that references the id attribute of one of the state elements. For example, Bridget McFarland has a stateid of 04, which refers to the Massachusetts state element.

The xsl:key element is designed to bridge these two worlds, or source documents. The following stylesheet does just that, by using a key to print out the state for each customer:

```
<?xml version="1.0"?>
<xsl:stylesheet version="1.0"
        xmlns:xsl="http://www.w3.org/1999/XSL/Transform">

<xsl:output method="text"/>

<!-- Define key -->
<xsl:key name="StateKey" match="state" use="@id"/>

<!-- Plug in key value -->
<xsl:template match="customer">
  <xsl:apply-templates/> lives in <xsl:value-of
        select="key('StateKey', @stateid)"/>
  <xsl:text>.</xsl:text>
</xsl:template>

<!-- Empty template -->
<xsl:template match="states"/>
</xsl:stylesheet>
```

After defining the xsl:key element, a customer template rule adds the customer name by using xsl:apply-templates and then adds the key() function to return the state name for that customer. Instead of using a string value as the lookup value, key() uses the expression @stateid, so that for each customer node, its stateid attribute is used as the lookup value. Finally, to prevent the states elements from being displayed outside of my purposes, I define an empty template rule. The resulting document is as follows:

```
Bridget McFarland lives in Massachusetts.
Cheri Burrer lives in Massachusetts.
Greg Stephenson lives in New Hampshire.
```

```
Mark Horine lives in Connecticut.
Don Shafer lives in Maine.
Leo Minster lives in Massachusetts.
```

Working with multiple keys

Keys can be used in a multitude of ways to draw together data from a variety
of different XML structures. Check out the orderprocess document, which
contains states, parts, customers, and orders substructures:

```
<?xml version="1.0"?>
<orderprocess>
  <states region="New England">
    <state id="01">Maine</state>
    <state id="02">New Hampshire</state>
    <state id="03">Vermont</state>
    <state id="04">Massachusetts</state>
    <state id="05">Connecticut</state>
    <state id="06">Rhode Island</state>
  </states>
  <customers>
    <customer id="C3020" stateid="04">Bridget
          McFarland</customer>
    <customer id="C3021" stateid="04">Cheri Burrer</customer>
    <customer id="C3022" stateid="02">Greg
          Stephenson</customer>
    <customer id="C3023" stateid="05">Mark Horine</customer>
    <customer id="C3024" stateid="01">Don Shafer</customer>
    <customer id="C3025" stateid="04">Leo Minster</customer>
  </customers>
  <parts>
    <part id="120" price="3.99">Baseball</part>
    <part id="121" price="8.99">Basketball</part>
    <part id="122" price="6.99">Football</part>
    <part id="123" price="7.99">Soccer Ball</part>
    <part id="124" price="960.99">Football Goalpost</part>
    <part id="125" price="340000000">Outdoor Football
          Stadium</part>
    <part id="126" price="160.99">Foosball Table</part>
    <part id="127" price="899.99">Road Bicycle</part>
    <part id="128" price="799.99">ATB Bicycle</part>
    <part id="129" price="12.99">Baseball Bat</part>
    <part id="130" price="19.99">Basketball Goal</part>
  </parts>
  <orders>
    <order custid="C3020" partid="120" quantity="1"/>
    <order custid="C3021" partid="124" quantity="3"/>
    <order custid="C3021" partid="126" quantity="2"/>
    <order custid="C3020" partid="125" quantity="1"/>
    <order custid="C3024" partid="126" quantity="1"/>
    <order custid="C3024" partid="123" quantity="12"/>
```

```
      <order custid="C3022" partid="127" quantity="2"/>
      <order custid="C3022" partid="128" quantity="3"/>
      <order custid="C3022" partid="130" quantity="2"/>
      <order custid="C3021" partid="130" quantity="1"/>
      <order custid="C3021" partid="126" quantity="7"/>
   </orders>
</orderprocess>
```

My objective is to create an order summary report, providing summary information about each order. The order elements bring all the related data together, but its primary task is to reference the other XML structures rather than to contain the actual data. Specifically, for each order, I want to list five pieces of data: customer name, state that the order is shipping to, part ordered, quantity, unit price, and total price.

Because portions of this information are in the other XML structures, I define three keys for the state, customer, and part elements:

```
<xsl:key name="StateKey" match="state" use="@id"/>
<xsl:key name="CustomerKey" match="customer" use="@id"/>
<xsl:key name="PartKey" match="part" use="@id"/>
```

Inside a template rule that uses order as the match pattern, I reference the CustomerKey key by using the custid of the current order in the returning node set to retrieve the customer name:

```
<xsl:template match="order">
  <xsl:value-of select="key('CustomerKey', @custid)"/>
```

Retrieving the customer's state is trickier, because the order element doesn't include any state-related links. Therefore, I need to perform a double look up — first, look up the matching customer element and, second, look up his or her state by using the following instruction:

```
<xsl:value-of select="key('StateKey', key('CustomerKey',
        @custid)/@stateid )"/>
```

The part information is retrieved through a link between the PartKey key and the order element's partid attribute:

```
<xsl:value-of select="key('PartKey', @partid)"/>
```

The quantity and unit price values are actually used twice, because the total cost of the order involves multiplying the quantity by the unit price. Rather than retrieve this information multiple times in my stylesheet, I create two variables that hold these values for me because this is more efficient:

```
<xsl:variable name="qty" select="quantity"/>
<xsl:variable name="unitprice" select="key('PartKey',
        @partid)/@price"/>
```

The qty variable gets the value of the order element's quantity attribute, while the unitprice variable retrieves this pricing data by first getting the part through the PartKey key and then returning the price attribute of the matching node:

```
<xsl:variable name="qty" select="quantity"/>
<xsl:variable name="unitprice" select="key('PartKey',
        @partid)/@price"/>
```

These variables can then be simply plugged in:

```
<xsl:value-of select="number($qty)"/>
<xsl:value-of select="format-number( $unitprice, '#,###.##'
        )"/>
<xsl:value-of select="format-number( $qty*$unitprice,
        '#,###.##' )"/>
```

Here's what the complete XSLT stylesheet looks like:

```
<?xml version="1.0"?>
<xsl:stylesheet version="1.0"
        xmlns:xsl="http://www.w3.org/1999/XSL/Transform">

  <xsl:output method="text"/>

  <!-- Define keys -->
  <xsl:key name="StateKey" match="state" use="@id"/>
  <xsl:key name="CustomerKey" match="customer" use="@id"/>
  <xsl:key name="PartKey" match="part" use="@id"/>

  <!-- Order summary -->
  <xsl:template match="order">
-------------------------------------------------
Order Summary

Customer: <xsl:value-of select="key('CustomerKey',
        @custid)"/>
Ship To: <xsl:value-of select="key('StateKey',
        key('CustomerKey', @custid)/@stateid )"/>

Part: <xsl:value-of select="key('PartKey', @partid)"/>
<xsl:variable name="qty" select="@quantity"/>
<xsl:variable name="unitprice" select="key('PartKey',
        @partid)/@price"/>
Quantity: <xsl:value-of select="number($qty)"/>
Unit Price: $<xsl:value-of select="format-number(
        $unitprice, '#,###.##' )"/>
Total Price: $<xsl:value-of select="format-number(
        $qty*$unitprice, '#,###.##' )"/>
-------------------------------------------------

  </xsl:template>
```

```
<!-- Empty templates -->
<xsl:template match="state"/>
<xsl:template match="states"/>
<xsl:template match="parts"/>
<xsl:template match="customer"/>

</xsl:stylesheet>
```

The result of this transformation is a text output report providing a summary for each order in the orderprocess structure:

```
-----------------------------------------------
Order Summary

Customer: Bridget McFarland
Ship To: Massachusetts

Part: Baseball
Quantity: 1
Unit Price: $3.99
Total Price: $3.99
-----------------------------------------------


-----------------------------------------------
Order Summary

Customer: Cheri Burrer
Ship To: Massachusetts

Part: Football Goalpost
Quantity: 3
Unit Price: $960.99
Total Price: $2,882.97
-----------------------------------------------


-----------------------------------------------
Order Summary

Customer: Cheri Burrer
Ship To: Massachusetts

Part: Foosball Table
Quantity: 2
Unit Price: $160.99
Total Price: $321.98
-----------------------------------------------


-----------------------------------------------
Order Summary
```

```
Customer: Bridget McFarland
Ship To: Massachusetts

Part: Outdoor Football Stadium
Quantity: 1
Unit Price: $340,000,000
Total Price: $340,000,000
----------------------------------------------------


----------------------------------------------------
Order Summary

Customer: Don Shafer
Ship To: Maine

Part: Foosball Table
Quantity: 1
Unit Price: $160.99
Total Price: $160.99
----------------------------------------------------


----------------------------------------------------
Order Summary

Customer: Don Shafer
Ship To: Maine

Part: Soccer Ball
Quantity: 12
Unit Price: $7.99
Total Price: $95.88
----------------------------------------------------


----------------------------------------------------
Order Summary

Customer: Greg Stephenson
Ship To: New Hampshire

Part: Road Bicycle
Quantity: 2
Unit Price: $899.99
Total Price: $1,799.98
----------------------------------------------------


----------------------------------------------------
Order Summary

Customer: Greg Stephenson
Ship To: New Hampshire
```

```
Part: ATB Bicycle
Quantity: 3
Unit Price: $799.99
Total Price: $2,399.97
----------------------------------------------


----------------------------------------------
Order Summary

Customer: Greg Stephenson
Ship To: New Hampshire

Part: Basketball Goal
Quantity: 2
Unit Price: $19.99
Total Price: $39.98
----------------------------------------------


----------------------------------------------
Order Summary

Customer: Cheri Burrer
Ship To: Massachusetts

Part: Basketball Goal
Quantity: 1
Unit Price: $19.99
Total Price: $19.99
----------------------------------------------


----------------------------------------------
Order Summary

Customer: Cheri Burrer
Ship To: Massachusetts

Part: Foosball Table
Quantity: 7
Unit Price: $160.99
Total Price: $1,126.93
----------------------------------------------
```

Using Keys with Multiple Source Documents

The preceding example illustrates how you can use keys to link different XML structures, but it did so within a single XML document. In the real world, you often want to use keys that combine data from various XML files. You can do this by using the document() built-in function. This function allows you to include node sets from external files.

As an example, I separate the state-related elements from the customer elements, giving me two source files, Listing 14-1 and Listing 14-2.

Listing 14-1:   key_state.xml

```
<?xml version="1.0"?>
<!-- key_state.xml -->
<states region="New England">
  <state id="01">Maine</state>
  <state id="02">New Hampshire</state>
  <state id="03">Vermont</state>
  <state id="04">Massachusetts</state>
  <state id="05">Connecticut</state>
  <state id="06">Rhode Island</state>
</states>
```

Listing 14-2:   key_customers.xml

```
<?xml version="1.0"?>
<!-- key_customers.xml -->
<customers>
  <customer id="C3020" stateid="04">Bridget
            McFarland</customer>
  <customer id="C3021" stateid="04">Cheri Burrer</customer>
  <customer id="C3022" stateid="02">Greg
            Stephenson</customer>
  <customer id="C3023" stateid="05">Mark Horine</customer>
  <customer id="C3024" stateid="01">Don Shafer</customer>
  <customer id="C3025" stateid="04">Leo Minster</customer>
</customers>
```

In the result document, suppose I'd like to provide a simple listing of the customer and his or her state as I do in the initial example of the chapter. To do so, in my XSLT stylesheet, I can define a StatesLookup variable to be the returning node set of the document('key_state.xml') function:

```
<xsl:variable name="StatesLookup"
        select="document('key_state.xml')"/>
```

Therefore, when I plug in the States Lookup variable in my stylesheet, it references the states element and its contents.

A key is defined for the state elements from the outside file:

```
<xsl:key name="StateKey" match="state" use="@id"/>
```

To perform the key lookup on these elements from another document, I need to set up an xsl:for-each loop to iterate through each of the state elements, calling key() each time to do the lookup. Because the lookup value for the key is the stateid attribute for the customer element, I package it all in a customer template rule:

```
<xsl:template match="customer">
  <xsl:variable name="custstate" select="@stateid"/>
  <xsl:variable name="custname" select="."/>
  <xsl:for-each select="$StatesLookup">
    <xsl:value-of select="$custname"/> lives in <xsl:value-
        of select="key('StateKey', $custstate)"/>
    <xsl:text>.  </xsl:text>
  </xsl:for-each>
</xsl:template>
```

The entire XSLT stylesheet is as follows:

```
<?xml version="1.0"?>
<xsl:stylesheet version="1.0"
        xmlns:xsl="http://www.w3.org/1999/XSL/Transform">

  <xsl:output method="text"/>

  <!-- Assign contents of key_state.xml to var -->
  <xsl:variable name="StatesLookup"
        select="document('key_state.xml')"/>

  <!-- Define key -->
  <xsl:key name="StateKey" match="state" use="@id"/>

  <!-- Plug in key value -->
  <xsl:template match="customer">
    <xsl:variable name="custstate" select="@stateid"/>
    <xsl:variable name="custname" select="."/>
    <xsl:for-each select="$StatesLookup">
      <xsl:value-of select="$custname"/> lives in <xsl:value-
          of select="key('StateKey', $custstate)"/>
      <xsl:text>.  </xsl:text>
    </xsl:for-each>
  </xsl:template>

</xsl:stylesheet>
```

When the stylesheet is applied to the key customers.xml file (refer to Listing 14-2), the result from the transformation is shown here:

```
Bridget McFarland lives in Massachusetts.
Cheri Burrer lives in Massachusetts.
Greg Stephenson lives in New Hampshire.
Mark Horine lives in Connecticut.
Don Shafer lives in Maine.
Leo Minster lives in Massachusetts.
```

Chapter 15

Namespaces Revisited

XML uses namespaces to distinguish a set of element names from another group. It does so by associating a namespace identifier (or prefix) with a URI. By this time, using the `xsl:` prefix in your stylesheets to designate the `http://www.w3.org/1999/XSL/Transform` namespace is probably second nature for you. That's the basic concept of a namespace.

When your source and result documents use the default namespace, you can ignore namespaces altogether during your transformations. However, XSLT also allows you to add namespaces to your result document or carry them over from the source document. In this chapter, I talk about how you can do this by using XSLT.

Speaking the Namespace Lingo

XML namespaces have their own lingo to describe the parts that make up namespaces and element names. In Chapter 3, I talk about the namespace URI and the associated prefix, but other terms, such as QName, NCName, local name, and expanded name, also come into play when working with namespaces. Knowing the lingo gives you a better understanding of namespaces, but it also comes in handy when your mother-in-law asks you about a problem she's having with her QName.

Consider the following XML snippet:

```
<nfl:teams xmlns:nfl="http://www.nfl.com">
    <nfl:broncos></nfl:broncos>
    <broncos></broncos>
</nfl:teams>
```

I can define several namespace-related terms from this XML code, including the following:

- ✔ **QName:** In this example, `nfl:teams` and `nfl:broncos` are two examples of QNames. A *QName* is a *qualified name* that consists of an optional namespace prefix and colon and a required local part. The `nfl:broncos` QName includes `nfl` as the namespace prefix and `broncos` as its local part. The `broncos` element, which has no defined namespace, has a QName of simply `broncos`.

- ✔ **NCName:** An *NCName* (No-Colon Name) is a generic term used to describe the name of either the element or namespace prefix, minus the colon. An NCName must begin with either an alphabetical character or underscore. In the `nfl:broncos` QName, both `nfl` and `broncos` are considered NCNames.

- ✔ **Local name:** The *local name* or local part is the name of the element minus any namespace prefix. Both `nfl:broncos` and `broncos` have local names of `broncos`.

- ✔ **Expanded-name:** An *expanded-name* consists of a local part name and its companion namespace URI. For example, the expanded name of `nfl:broncos` is considered the combination of the `broncos` element and the `http://www.nfl.com` URI.

Don't confuse the term *expanded-name* with a QName that has both the namespace prefix and local part defined. An expanded name includes the actual namespace URI, not the namespace prefix.

Showing these terms in action, the following stylesheet lists the QName, local name, and namespace URI of the two `broncos` elements in an HTML table. To do so, the stylesheet uses the XPath functions `name()`, `local-name()`, and `namespace-uri()`:

```
<xsl:stylesheet version="1.0"
  xmlns:xsl="http://www.w3.org/1999/XSL/Transform"
  xmlns:nfl="http://www.nfl.com">
<xsl:output method="html"/>

  <xsl:template match="/">
<html>
<body>
<xsl:apply-templates/>
</body>
</html>
  </xsl:template>

<xsl:template match="nfl:broncos|broncos">
  <table border="1">
  <tr>
    <td>QName</td>
    <td><xsl:value-of select="name()"/></td>
```

```
    </tr>
    <tr>
      <td>Local Name</td>
      <td><xsl:value-of select="local-name()"/></td>
    </tr>
    <tr>
      <td>Namespace URI</td>
      <td>
      <xsl:if test="namespace-uri()=''">
      null
      </xsl:if>
      <xsl:if test="namespace-uri()!=''">
      <xsl:value-of select="namespace-uri()"/>
      </xsl:if>
      </td>
    </tr>
    </table>
    </xsl:template>
</xsl:stylesheet>
```

The HTML generated is shown here:

```
<html xmlns:nfl="http://www.nfl.com">
    <body>

        <table border="1">
            <tr>
                <td>QName</td>
                <td>nfl:broncos</td>
            </tr>
            <tr>
                <td>Local Part</td>
                <td>broncos</td>
            </tr>
            <tr>
                <td>Namespace URI</td>
                <td>http://www.nfl.com</td>
            </tr>
        </table>

        <table border="1">
            <tr>
                <td>QName</td>
                <td>broncos</td>
            </tr>
            <tr>
                <td>Local Part</td>
                <td>broncos</td>
            </tr>
            <tr>
                <td>Namespace URI</td>
                <td>
```

```
                null

              </td>
            </tr>
          </table>

      </body>
</html>
```

Adding a Namespace to the Result Document

Now that you talk namespace and you've got your mother-in-law's QName problem solved, it's time to add namespaces to your result documents. You can add namespaces to an output document by performing two steps:

✔ Declaring the result document's namespace in the XSLT stylesheet's stylesheet element.

✔ Adding the namespace prefixes to the associated elements or attributes.

Suppose, for example, that I use the following nations.xml file as the source document, as shown in Listing 15-1.

Listing 15-1: nations.xml

```
<?xml version="1.0"?>
<nationstates>
  <nation>Botswana</nation>
  <nation>Burkina Faso</nation>
  <nation>Cameroon</nation>
  <nation>Canada</nation>
  <nation>France</nation>
  <nation>Netherlands</nation>
  <nation>United Kingdom</nation>
</nationstates>
```

In this illustration, I add a United Nations namespace to this source and generate a new result document, using the namespace URI of http://www. un.org with a prefix of un:. To do so, a stylesheet needs to include this information as a namespace declaration:

```
<xsl:stylesheet version="1.0"
  xmlns:xsl="http://www.w3.org/1999/XSL/Transform"
  xmlns:un="http://www.un.org">
```

In the template rules, I add the `un:` abbreviation onto the `nationstates` and `nation` elements. The complete stylesheet follows:

```
<?xml version="1.0"?>
<xsl:stylesheet version="1.0"
  xmlns:xsl="http://www.w3.org/1999/XSL/Transform"
  xmlns:un="http://www.un.org">

  <xsl:output method="xml" omit-xml-declaration="yes"/>

  <xsl:template match="nationstates">
    <un:nationstates><xsl:apply-templates/></un:nationstates>
  </xsl:template>

  <xsl:template match="nation">
    <un:nation><xsl:value-of select="."/></un:nation>
  </xsl:template>
</xsl:stylesheet>
```

When the XSLT processor transforms the source document (refer to Listing 15-1) based on this stylesheet, the result is:

```
<un:nationstates xmlns:un="http://www.un.org">
  <un:nation>Botswana</un:nation>
  <un:nation>Burkina Faso</un:nation>
  <un:nation>Cameroon</un:nation>
  <un:nation>Canada</un:nation>
  <un:nation>France</un:nation>
  <un:nation>Netherlands</un:nation>
  <un:nation>United Kingdom</un:nation>
</un:nationstates>
```

As you can see, the XSLT processor automatically adds the `xmlns` declaration to the document element of the result document. The `un:` namespace prefixes are now included as a result of the template rules.

If you take a quick glance at the result documents from previous chapters, it appears that I have avoided using namespaces. Actually, when you don't explicitly define a namespace, XSLT uses the default namespace. Although the default (or null) namespace has no visible presence in the document, don't confuse its implicit nature with no namespace at all.

Working with Multiple Namespaces

You can also work with multiple namespaces within the source and result documents. A Microsoft Word 2000 document provides a practical example of how you can use multiple namespaces within a single document. Word 2000 can save documents as HTML so that you can easily view the text in a Web browser. But Microsoft Word 2000 preserves Word-specific information by embedding XML and other proprietary markup text inside the Web document. This technique enables you to view the document as an HTML page but still reopen the document in Word, retaining all the additional formatting and setting information Word needs. Word uses multiple namespaces to handle different parts of the document data:

- ✔ The urn:schemas-microsoft-com:office:office namespace is used for Office-related properties of the document, such as title, author, and revision date.
- ✔ The urn:schemas-microsoft-com:office:word is used for Word-specific properties, such as Zoom Level and View State.
- ✔ The default namespace is used for the text and formatting of the document.

Knowing this, I can create a Word document from an XML structure by using XSLT to transform basic XML code into a format that Word can understand and process. In Listing 15-2, I use the following XML version of a letter as the source document.

Listing 15-2: annchovie.xml

```
<?xml version="1.0"?>
<!-- annchovie.xml -->
<letter xmlns:o="urn:schemas-microsoft-com:office:office"
        xmlns:w="urn:schemas-microsoft-com:office:word">
  <o:properties>
    <o:Author>Ann Chovie</o:Author>
    <o:Revision>2</o:Revision>
    <o:Company>Fisher Brothers</o:Company>
  </o:properties>
  <w:properties>
    <w:View>Print</w:View>
    <w:Zoom>150</w:Zoom>
    <w:DoNotOptimizeForBrowser/>
  </w:properties>
  <lettertext>
    <para style="address">Ann Chovie</para>
    <para style="address">233 Phish Lane</para>
    <para style="address">Guppie Hill, VT 12032</para>
    <para style="default">March 3, 2002</para>
    <para style="default">Dear Editor, </para>
    <para style="default">I am canceling my subscription to
          <italic>Goldfish Monthly</italic>
    due to your recent article on the <bold><span
          style='color:red'>Goldfish of the
    Year</span></bold>. While <span style='font-
          variant:small-caps'>Billy the Georgian
    Goldfish</span> may be worthy of some sort of reward, he
          cannot compete with
    the likes of <span style='font-variant:small-
```

```
                 caps'>Jumping Jack</span> from
   Jacksonville.</para>
   <para style="default">I am concerned that this contest
           was not fair. Specifically,
   in your cover photo, I noticed the pebbles at the bottom
           of the goldfish bowl
   spelled out the word <italic><span style='color:red'>w-a-
           t-e-r-g-a-t-e</span></italic>,
   perhaps alluding to some sort of cover-up at your
           magazine. What's more,
   Billy's fish face has a haunting resemblance to Richard
           Nixon. This whole thing
   is starting to smell fishy to me, so I am demanding a
           full investigation.</para>
   <para style="default">By the way, I did like your recent
           article on gourmet guppy
   food. My fish have not been happier since trying the
           guppuccino!</para>
   <para style="default">Sincerely,</para>
   <para style="default">Ann Chovie</para>
   </lettertext>
</letter>
```

In this source document, the `letter` element defines the `o` and `w` namespaces. These are the same namespaces that Word uses, so I just need to carry them over into the result document. In my XSLT stylesheet, I add the following namespace declarations to my `xsl:stylesheet` instruction:

```
<xsl:stylesheet version="1.0"
        xmlns:xsl="http://www.w3.org/1999/XSL/Transform"
                        xmlns:o="urn:schemas-
        microsoft-com:office:office"
                        xmlns:w="urn:schemas-
        microsoft-com:office:word"

        xmlns="http://www.w3.org/TR/REC-html40">
```

The `o:properties` element contains the Office document properties that Word uses. However, Word looks for a container element named `o:DocumentProperties`, so I need to rename this element during the transformation and add surrounding `xml` tags around the element. For the remaining `o:` namespace elements, I simply need to transfer them over as is. The following two template rules perform these actions:

```
   <!-- Add DocumentProperties container, changing element
           name -->
   <xsl:template match="o:properties">
    <xml>
    <o:DocumentProperties>
       <xsl:apply-templates/>
    </o:DocumentProperties>
```

```
    </xml>
  </xsl:template>

  <!-- Add individual DocumentProperties -->
  <xsl:template match="o:*">
    <xsl:copy>
      <xsl:apply-templates select="@*|node()"/>
    </xsl:copy>
  </xsl:template>
```

You can't create a template rule to match a namespace alone, because you can't use an XPath pattern to match namespace nodes. So, when you wish to search for specific namespaces, you must do it in combination with an element pattern.

Similarly, I need to rename the `w:properties` element to `w:WordDocument`, surrounded by `xml` tags, and copy its child elements over to the result document:

```
  <!-- Add WordDocument container, changing element name -->
  <xsl:template match="w:properties">
   <xml>
   <w:WordDocument>
      <xsl:apply-templates/>
   </w:WordDocument>
   </xml>
  </xsl:template>

  <!-- Add individual WordDocument properties -->
  <xsl:template match="w:*">
    <xsl:copy>
      <xsl:apply-templates select="@*|node()"/>
    </xsl:copy>
  </xsl:template>
```

Before adding the text of the letter, I need to construct the `head` section of the HTML document. The document header contains the `o:` and `w:` XML elements, as well as some style-related information I'm adding on the fly.

To determine the point where I need to insert the `o:` and `w:` XML sections into the result document, I create a template rule for the `letter` element and use `<xsl:apply-templates select="w:*"/>` to apply all the elements within the `w:` namespace, and `<xsl:apply-templates select="o:*"/>` to apply all the elements within the `o:` namespace. After adding style information, I close the `head` element and then use `xsl:apply-templates` on the `lettertext` element:

```
<!-- Letter element, add header information -->
<xsl:template match="letter">
  <head>
    <title>Ann Chovie</title>
    <xsl:apply-templates select="w:*"/>
    <xsl:apply-templates select="o:*"/>
    <style>
      p.MsoNormal, li.MsoNormal, div.MsoNormal
        {mso-style-parent:"";
        margin-top:0in;
        margin-right:0in;
        margin-bottom:12.0pt;
        margin-left:0in;
        mso-pagination:widow-orphan;
        font-size:12.0pt;
        font-family:"Times New Roman";
        mso-fareast-font-family:"Times New Roman";}
      p.Address, li.Address, div.Address
        {mso-style-name:Address;
        margin-top:0in;
        margin-right:0in;
        margin-bottom:12.0pt;
        margin-left:0in;
        mso-pagination:widow-orphan;
        font-size:12.0pt;
        font-family:"Times New Roman";
        mso-fareast-font-family:"Times New Roman";}
      @page Section1
        {size:8.5in 11.0in;
        margin:1.0in 1.25in 1.0in 1.25in;
        mso-header-margin:.5in;
        mso-footer-margin:.5in;
        mso-paper-source:0;}
      div.Section1
        {page:Section1;}
    </style>
  </head>
<xsl:apply-templates select="lettertext"/>
</xsl:template>
```

The `lettertext` element contains the actual body of the letter and so needs to be surrounded by an HTML `body` element, as shown in the following template rule:

```
<!-- Lettertext, convert to body -->
<xsl:template match="lettertext">
  <body lang="EN-US" style='tab-interval:.5in'>
  <div class="Section1">
  <xsl:apply-templates/>
  </div>
  </body>
</xsl:template>
```

The original source includes two types of para elements, differentiated by the style attribute. In the stylesheet, address type paragraphs are converted to p elements, given a class="Address" attribute, and provided with special formatting rules, such as right alignment and no margin spacing. Normal paragraphs are also changed to p elements but given the class="MsoNormal" attribute:

```
<!-- Para, apply style for address and normal -->
<xsl:template match="para">
  <!-- Address -->
  <xsl:if test="@style='address'">
    <p class="Address" align="right" style="margin-
        bottom:0in;margin-bottom:.0001pt;text-
        align:right">
      <xsl:apply-templates/>
    </p>
  </xsl:if>
  <!-- Default -->
  <xsl:if test="@style='default'">
    <p class="MsoNormal">
      <xsl:apply-templates/>
    </p>
  </xsl:if>
</xsl:template>
```

Custom formatting tags like bold and italic are transformed into the HTML-friendly formatting elements used by Word. The span elements, however, are simply carried over as is to the result document:

```
   <!-- Italic, change element name -->
<xsl:template match="italic">
  <i><xsl:apply-templates/></i>
</xsl:template>

<!-- Bold, change element name -->
<xsl:template match="bold">
  <b><xsl:apply-templates/></b>
</xsl:template>

<!-- Span, copy as is -->
<xsl:template match="span">
  <xsl:copy-of select="."/>
</xsl:template>
```

The complete stylesheet is shown here:

```
<!--annchovie.xsl -->
<xsl:stylesheet version="1.0"
        xmlns:xsl="http://www.w3.org/1999/XSL/Transform"
                          xmlns:o="urn:schemas-
        microsoft-com:office:office"
                          xmlns:w="urn:schemas-
```

```
            microsoft-com:office:word"

            xmlns="http://www.w3.org/TR/REC-html40">

<xsl:output method="html"/>

<!-- Add DocumentProperties container, changing element
        name -->
<xsl:template match="o:properties">
 <xml>
 <o:DocumentProperties>
    <xsl:apply-templates/>
  </o:DocumentProperties>
 </xml>
</xsl:template>

<!-- Add individual DocumentProperties -->
<xsl:template match="o:*">
  <xsl:copy>
    <xsl:apply-templates select="@*|node()"/>
  </xsl:copy>
</xsl:template>

<!-- Add WordDocument container, changing element name -->
<xsl:template match="w:properties">
 <xml>
 <w:WordDocument>
    <xsl:apply-templates/>
  </w:WordDocument>
 </xml>
</xsl:template>

<!-- Add individual WordDocument properties -->
<xsl:template match="w:*">
  <xsl:copy>
    <xsl:apply-templates select="@*|node()"/>
  </xsl:copy>
</xsl:template>

<!-- Letter element, add header information -->
<xsl:template match="letter">
  <head>
    <title>Ann Chovie</title>
    <xsl:apply-templates select="w:*"/>
    <xsl:apply-templates select="o:*"/>
    <style>
      p.MsoNormal, li.MsoNormal, div.MsoNormal
        {mso-style-parent:"";
        margin-top:0in;
        margin-right:0in;
        margin-bottom:12.0pt;
        margin-left:0in;
```

```
        mso-pagination:widow-orphan;
        font-size:12.0pt;
        font-family:"Times New Roman";
        mso-fareast-font-family:"Times New Roman";}
      p.Address, li.Address, div.Address
        {mso-style-name:Address;
        margin-top:0in;
        margin-right:0in;
        margin-bottom:12.0pt;
        margin-left:0in;
        mso-pagination:widow-orphan;
        font-size:12.0pt;
        font-family:"Times New Roman";
        mso-fareast-font-family:"Times New Roman";}
      @page Section1
        {size:8.5in 11.0in;
        margin:1.0in 1.25in 1.0in 1.25in;
        mso-header-margin:.5in;
        mso-footer-margin:.5in;
        mso-paper-source:0;}
      div.Section1
        {page:Section1;}
      </style>
  </head>
<xsl:apply-templates select="lettertext"/>
</xsl:template>

<!-- Lettertext, convert to body -->
<xsl:template match="lettertext">
  <body lang="EN-US" style='tab-interval:.5in'>
  <div class="Section1">
  <xsl:apply-templates/>
  </div>
  </body>
</xsl:template>

<!-- Para, apply style for address and normal -->
<xsl:template match="para">
  <!-- Address -->
  <xsl:if test="@style='address'">
    <p class="Address" align="right" style="margin-
        bottom:0in;margin-bottom:.0001pt;text-
        align:right">
      <xsl:apply-templates/>
    </p>
  </xsl:if>
  <!-- Default -->
  <xsl:if test="@style='default'">
    <p class="MsoNormal">
      <xsl:apply-templates/>
    </p>
  </xsl:if>
```

```
    </xsl:template>

    <!-- Italic, change element name -->
    <xsl:template match="italic">
      <i><xsl:apply-templates/></i>
    </xsl:template>

    <!-- Bold, change element name -->
    <xsl:template match="bold">
      <b><xsl:apply-templates/></b>
    </xsl:template>

    <!-- Span, copy as is -->
    <xsl:template match="span">
      <xsl:copy-of select="."/>
    </xsl:template>

    <!-- Add html element at top -->
    <xsl:template match="/">
      <html>
      <xsl:apply-templates/>
      </html>
    </xsl:template>

</xsl:stylesheet>
```

After the stylesheet is applied to the annchovie.xml file (see Listing 15-2), the resulting document is shown here as XML:

```
<html xmlns="http://www.w3.org/TR/REC-html40"
          xmlns:o="urn:schemas-microsoft-com:office:office"
          xmlns:w="urn:schemas-microsoft-com:office:word">
    <head>
      <meta http-equiv="Content-Type" content="text/html;
      charset=utf-8">

      <title>Ann Chovie</title>
      <xml>
        <w:WordDocument>

          <w:View>Print</w:View>

          <w:Zoom>150</w:Zoom>


          <w:DoNotOptimizeForBrowser></w:DoNotOptimizeForBro
          wser>
        </w:WordDocument>
      </xml>
      <xml>
        <o:DocumentProperties>
```

```
                <o:Author>Ann Chovie</o:Author>

                <o:Revision>2</o:Revision>

                <o:Company>Fisher Brothers</o:Company>

            </o:DocumentProperties>
        </xml><style>
         p.MsoNormal, li.MsoNormal, div.MsoNormal
           {mso-style-parent:"";
           margin-top:0in;
           margin-right:0in;
           margin-bottom:12.0pt;
           margin-left:0in;
           mso-pagination:widow-orphan;
           font-size:12.0pt;
           font-family:"Times New Roman";
           mso-fareast-font-family:"Times New Roman";}
         p.Address, li.Address, div.Address
           {mso-style-name:Address;
           margin-top:0in;
           margin-right:0in;
           margin-bottom:12.0pt;
           margin-left:0in;
           mso-pagination:widow-orphan;
           font-size:12.0pt;
           font-family:"Times New Roman";
           mso-fareast-font-family:"Times New Roman";}
         @page Section1
           {size:8.5in 11.0in;
           margin:1.0in 1.25in 1.0in 1.25in;
           mso-header-margin:.5in;
           mso-footer-margin:.5in;
           mso-paper-source:0;}
         div.Section1
           {page:Section1;}
         </style></head>
<body lang="EN-US" style="tab-interval:.5in">
    <div class="Section1">

        <p class="Address" align="right" style="margin-
           bottom:0in;margin-bottom:.0001pt;text-
           align:right">Ann Chovie</p>

        <p class="Address" align="right" style="margin-
           bottom:0in;margin-bottom:.0001pt;text-
           align:right">233 Phish Lane</p>

        <p class="Address" align="right" style="margin-
           bottom:0in;margin-bottom:.0001pt;text-
           align:right">Guppie Hill, VT 12032</p>
```

```
        <p class="MsoNormal">March 3, 2002</p>

        <p class="MsoNormal">Dear Editor, </p>

        <p class="MsoNormal">I am canceling my subscription
          to <i>Goldfish Monthly</i>
                due to your recent article on the <b><span
          xmlns="" style="color:red">Goldfish of the
                    Year</span></b>. While <span xmlns=""
          style="font-variant:small-caps">Billy the Georgian
                Goldfish</span> may be worthy of some sort
          of reward, he cannot compete with
                the likes of <span xmlns="" style="font-
          variant:small-caps">Jumping Jack</span> from
                Jacksonville.
        </p>

        <p class="MsoNormal">I am concerned that this
          contest was not fair. Specifically,
                in your cover photo, I noticed the pebbles at
          the bottom of the goldfish bowl
                spelled out the word <i><span xmlns=""
          style="color:red">w-a-t-e-r-g-a-t-e</span></i>,
                perhaps alluding to some sort of cover-up at
          your magazine. What's more,
                Billy's fish face has a haunting resemblance
          to Richard Nixon. This whole thing
                is starting to smell fishy to me, so I am
          demanding a full investigation.
        </p>

        <p class="MsoNormal">By the way, I did like your
          recent article on gourmet guppy
                food. My fish have not been happier since
          trying the guppuccino!
        </p>

        <p class="MsoNormal">Sincerely,</p>

        <p class="MsoNormal">Ann Chovie</p>

      </div>
    </body>
</html>
```

Chapter 16

Extending XSLT

. . . .

. . . .

*Y*ou know how it is. You get a shiny, new digital gizmo that does 1,001 things for you, but not two weeks go by before you discover the 1,002nd task you really need this gizmo to do, really want it to do, but lo and behold, it cannot do this task. This same Murphy's Law of Gizmos applies to XSLT: The language does 1,001 kinds of transformations, but sooner or later, you encounter a need that XSLT doesn't provide a solution for as part of its basic language. Perhaps you need to use a while loop inside your template rule. Or maybe you need to compare nodes from two different node sets and are throwing up your arms trying to do it with XSLT alone. Before you X out XSLT, read on.

As with any new technology, there are gaps in what comes "in the box" with XSLT. Fortunately, you don't have to wait on future versions of the language to solve the problem. Instead, XSLT supports extensions that allow you to expand the scope of what you can do inside an XSLT stylesheet.

In this chapter, you find out how you can broaden your XSLT horizons through extensions.

Going Beyond the Basics

Extensions are modules that the XSLT processor implements and that support additional functionality. They can surface in XSLT as an element, attribute, or function, such as in the following code snippet:

```
<xsl:template match="coffees" grd:guard="true">
  <grd:guardian select="@bean">
  <xsl:apply-templates select="grd:guardnodes(coffee)"/>
</xsl:template>
```

The `grd:guard="true"` gives an example of what an extension attribute might look like, the `grd:guardian` element demonstrates an extension element, and `grd:guardnodes()` represents an extension function.

If an XSLT processor doesn't understand the extension, you *cannot* use it during your transformations.

By their very nature, extensions give you functionality that is outside standard XSLT, meaning their support is closely tied to the XSLT processor you use. In most cases, extensions are proprietary to a given processor and are useless when you attempt to transform the stylesheet with another vendor's processing engine. However, a new community-led effort called EXSLT (Extensions for XSLT) seeks to provide a common set of XSLT extensions that can be supported across multiple XSLT processors. The obvious advantage in using EXSLT extensions is that, if EXSLT catches on, you'll be able to use them on any processing engine that implements EXSLT support. SAXON is perhaps the best example of an XSLT processor that has started adding support for EXSLT functions. For the latest information on EXSLT extensions, go to the community-supported Web site (`www.exslt.org`).

When you are evaluating XSLT processors, take a close look at the extensions that are provided. Even if you don't need extensions now, extension support may be important for you in the future as your needs grow.

Microsoft's approach to extensions with msxsl is slightly different than the other XSLT processor vendors. Rather than supporting a rich library of extension elements and functions, msxsl has a single extension element called `msxsl:script` that serves as their gateway for adding scripting (JavaScript or VBScript) into your stylesheets. In effect, this feature of msxsl enables you to write your own extensions by using a script.

Using an Extension Element

Extension elements expand the `xsl:` built-in element set by providing new instructions inside your stylesheet. Take, for example, SAXON's `while` extension. I can use this element to add true conditional looping inside a stylesheet.

Before using an extension element like the while extension in my stylesheet, I must first declare the extension namespace in the xsl:stylesheet element. All SAXON extensions use the following namespace declaration:

```
xmlns:saxon="http://icl.com/saxon"
```

Although you can use any prefix, I recommend you stick with saxon to conform to the standards of the processor vendor and to minimize any possible confusion.

Second, add the extension-element-prefixes attribute to the xsl:stylesheet element, using saxon as the attribute value. This attribute tells the processing engine what namespace prefixes are reserved for extensions:

```
<xsl:stylesheet version="1.0"
   xmlns:xsl="http://www.w3.org/1999/XSL/Transform"
   xmlns:saxon="http://icl.com/saxon"
   extension-element-prefixes="saxon">
```

Inside a template rule, the saxon:while element executes a series of instructions so long as the test pattern returns true. In this simple example, I have test evaluate the value of a variable. However, because the value of an XSLT variable normally doesn't change, I use a second SAXON extension element, saxon:assign, that allows me to assign a new value to this variable. The template rule is shown here:

```
<xsl:template match="/">
   <xsl:variable name="idx" saxon:assignable="yes"
         select="1"/>
   <saxon:while test="$idx &lt; 11">
      Value of idx is <xsl:value-of select="$idx"/>
      <saxon:assign name="idx" select="$idx+1"/>
   </saxon:while>
</xsl:template>
```

In the xsl:variable instruction, notice the saxon:assignable extension attribute. The SAXON processor requires that this attribute be added to any xsl:variable that you intend to change by using saxon:assign.

The output of my looping is as follows:

```
The value of idx is 1
The value of idx is 2
The value of idx is 3
The value of idx is 4
The value of idx is 5
The value of idx is 6
The value of idx is 7
The value of idx is 8
The value of idx is 9
The value of idx is 10
```

For more information on `saxon:while`, `saxon:assign`, and other SAXON
extensions, visit the SAXON Web site at `saxon.sourceforge.net`.

Using an Extension Function

You can also add extension functions to your stylesheet expressions and use
the functions in the same way you use XPath and XSLT built-in functions. To
demonstrate, suppose I have two node sets and my objective is to produce a
report comparing the like and unlike nodes between them. Rather than going
through a series of hoops using XSLT alone to do this, EXSLT supports two
functions called `set:intersection()` and `set:difference()` that make
this task a breeze. For this exercise, I create two reports by using the following XML document, Listing 16-1.

Listing 16-1: afifilms.xml

```
<?xml version="1.0"?>
<!-- American Film Institute Top 25 Films -->
<topfilms createdby="AFI">
  <film place="1" date="1941" genre="Drama">Citizen
          Kane</film>
  <film place="2" date="1942" genre="Romantic
          Drama">Casablanca</film>
  <film place="3" date="1972" genre="Crime Drama">The
          Godfather</film>
  <film place="4" date="1939" genre="Epic Drama">Gone With
          The Wind</film>
  <film place="5" date="1962" genre="War">Lawrence Of
          Arabia</film>
  <film place="6" date="1939" genre="Fantasy">The Wizard Of
          Oz</film>
  <film place="7" date="1967" genre="Drama">The
          Graduate</film>
  <film place="8" date="1954" genre="Crime Drama">On The
          Waterfront</film>
  <film place="9" date="1993" genre="Epic">Schindler's
          List</film>
  <film place="10" date="1952" genre="Musical">Singin' In The
          Rain</film>
  <film place="11" date="1946" genre="Drama">It's A Wonderful
          Life</film>
  <film place="12" date="1950" genre="Drama">Sunset
          Boulevard</film>
  <film place="13" date="1957" genre="War">The Bridge On The
          River Kwai</film>
  <film place="14" date="1959" genre="Drama">Some Like It
          Hot</film>
  <film place="15" date="1977" genre="Epic Fantasy">Star
```

```
Wars</film>
  <film place="16" date="1950" genre="Drama">All About
         Eve</film>
  <film place="17" date="1951" genre="Romantic Comedy">The
         African Queen</film>
  <film place="18" date="1960" genre="Thriller">Psycho</film>
  <film place="19" date="1974"
         genre="Thriller">Chinatown</film>
  <film place="20" date="1975" genre="Drama">One Flew Over
         The Cuckoo's Nest</film>
  <film place="21" date="1940" genre="Drama">The Grapes Of
         Wrath</film>
  <film place="22" date="1968" genre="Space">2001: A Space
         Odyssey</film>
  <film place="23" date="1941" genre="Crime Drama">The
         Maltese Falcon</film>
  <film place="24" date="1980" genre="Ouch">Raging
         Bull</film>
  <film place="25" date="1982" genre="Fantasy">E.T, The
         Extra-Terrestrial</film>
</topfilms>
```

In the first report, my objective is to list these films by decade. To create this listing of films, I rely on EXSLT extensions to do much of the work for me. So, in an XSLT stylesheet, my first step is to add the appropriate extension namespace to the xsl:stylesheet element:

```
<xsl:stylesheet version="1.0"
  xmlns:xsl="http://www.w3.org/1999/XSL/Transform"
  xmlns:set="http://exslt.org/sets"
  extension-element-prefixes="set">
```

Because I'm working with multiple node sets, I create several variables, each of which has a node set assigned to it:

```
<xsl:variable name="Post1940"
        select="//film[1940&lt;=date]"/>
<xsl:variable name="Post1950"
        select="//film[1950&lt;=date]"/>
<xsl:variable name="Post1960"
        select="//film[1960&lt;=date]"/>
<xsl:variable name="Post1970"
        select="//film[1970&lt;=date]"/>
<xsl:variable name="Post1980"
        select="//film[1980&lt;=date]"/>
<xsl:variable name="Post1990"
        select="//film[1990&lt;=date]"/>

<xsl:variable name="Pre1940"
        select="//film[date&lt;=1939]"/>
<xsl:variable name="Pre1950"
```

```
                select="//film[date&lt;=1949]"/>
  <xsl:variable name="Pre1960"
                select="//film[date&lt;=1959]"/>
  <xsl:variable name="Pre1970"
                select="//film[date&lt;=1969]"/>
  <xsl:variable name="Pre1980"
                select="//film[date&lt;=1979]"/>
  <xsl:variable name="Pre1990"
                select="//film[date&lt;=1989]"/>
  <xsl:variable name="Pre2000"
                select="//film[date&lt;=1999]"/>
```

Each of these variables represents a node set based on the film element's date attribute.

Assigning a node set to a variable can simplify the way you work with the node set in your stylesheet.

In the stylesheet's template rule, these variables are used to group the films by decade. One way to create this listing is to use the EXSLT set:intersection(nodeset1, nodeset2) function. This function returns the nodes that are common to both node sets provided as the function parameters.

A xsl:for-each instruction loops through each of the nodes returned by its select attribute and performs the instructions contained between its start and end tags. I can use set:intersection() as the value of the select attribute, so that the for-each loop iterates through each of the common nodes and uses xsl:value-of to print out the film element's content:

```
- - - - - - - - - - - - - - - - - - - - - - - - - - - - - -
1940's Films:
  <xsl:for-each select="set:intersection($Post1940,
        $Pre1950)">
  * <xsl:value-of select="."/>
  </xsl:for-each>
```

I create a similar xsl:for-each loop for each of the remaining decades.

The entire stylesheet is shown here:

```
<xsl:stylesheet version="1.0"
  xmlns:xsl="http://www.w3.org/1999/XSL/Transform"
  xmlns:set="http://exslt.org/sets"
  extension-element-prefixes="set">

  <xsl:output method="text"/>

  <xsl:variable name="Post1940"
                select="//film[1940&lt;=date]"/>
  <xsl:variable name="Post1950"
```

```
              select="//film[1950&lt;=date]"/>
<xsl:variable name="Post1960"
              select="//film[1960&lt;=date]"/>
<xsl:variable name="Post1970"
              select="//film[1970&lt;=date]"/>
<xsl:variable name="Post1980"
              select="//film[1980&lt;=date]"/>
<xsl:variable name="Post1990"
              select="//film[1990&lt;=date]"/>

<xsl:variable name="Pre1940"
              select="//film[date&lt;=1939]"/>
<xsl:variable name="Pre1950"
              select="//film[date&lt;=1949]"/>
<xsl:variable name="Pre1960"
              select="//film[date&lt;=1959]"/>
<xsl:variable name="Pre1970"
              select="//film[date&lt;=1969]"/>
<xsl:variable name="Pre1980"
              select="//film[date&lt;=1979]"/>
<xsl:variable name="Pre1990"
              select="//film[date&lt;=1989]"/>
<xsl:variable name="Pre2000"
              select="//film[date&lt;=1999]"/>

<xsl:template match="/">
-------------------------------
1930's Films:
 <xsl:for-each select="$Pre1940">
  * <xsl:value-of select="."/>
 </xsl:for-each>


-------------------------------
1940's Films:
 <xsl:for-each select="set:intersection($Post1940,
         $Pre1950)">
  * <xsl:value-of select="."/>
 </xsl:for-each>


-------------------------------
1950's Films:
 <xsl:for-each select="set:intersection($Post1950,
         $Pre1960)">
  * <xsl:value-of select="."/>
 </xsl:for-each>


-------------------------------
1960's Films:
 <xsl:for-each select="set:intersection($Post1960,
         $Pre1970)">
  * <xsl:value-of select="."/>
 </xsl:for-each>
```

```
----------------------------------------
1970's Films:
 <xsl:for-each select="set:intersection($Post1970,
         $Pre1980)">
  * <xsl:value-of select="."/>
 </xsl:for-each>


----------------------------------------
1980's Films:
 <xsl:for-each select="set:intersection($Post1980,
         $Pre1990)">
  * <xsl:value-of select="."/>
 </xsl:for-each>


----------------------------------------
1990's Films:
 <xsl:for-each select="set:intersection($Post1990,
         $Pre2000)">
  * <xsl:value-of select="."/>
 </xsl:for-each>

</xsl:template>

<xsl:template match="film"/>

</xsl:stylesheet>
```

The stylesheet is applied to afifilms.xml, shown in Listing 16-1. When this transformation is done by a processor, such as SAXON, that supports `set:intersection()`, the result is as follows:

```
----------------------------------------
1930's Films:

   * Gone With The Wind
   * The Wizard Of Oz


----------------------------------------
1940's Films:

   * Citizen Kane
   * Casablanca
   * It's A Wonderful Life
   * The Grapes Of Wrath
   * The Maltese Falcon


----------------------------------------
1950's Films:

   * On The Waterfront
   * Singin' In The Rain
   * Sunset Boulevard
   * The Bridge On The River Kwai
```

```
        * Some Like It Hot
        * All About Eve
        * The African Queen

    ----------------------------------
    1960's Films:

        * Lawrence Of Arabia
        * The Graduate
        * Psycho
        * 2001: A Space Odyssey

    ----------------------------------
    1970's Films:

        * The Godfather
        * Star Wars
        * Chinatown
        * One Flew Over The Cuckoo's Nest

    ----------------------------------
    1980's Films:

        * Raging Bull
        * E.T. The Extra-Terrestrial

    ----------------------------------
    1990's Films:

        * Schindler's List
```

Now I want to create a second report based on the XML source document —
a list of films organized into categories: epic dramas, dramas that are not
epics, epics that are not dramas, and dramas that are not romantic. To do so,
I define three variables that return node sets based on the value of the genre
attribute:

```
<xsl:variable name="DramaFilms"
        select="//film[contains(@genre, 'Drama')]"/>
<xsl:variable name="EpicFilms"
        select="//film[contains(@genre, 'Epic')]"/>
<xsl:variable name="RomanticFilms"
        select="//film[contains(@genre, 'Romantic')]"/>
```

DramaFilms returns all the film elements that contain the word Drama in
their genre attributes. The other two variables use similar logic for their
node sets.

Now that I have these three subsets of films, I can use set:intersection()
and set:difference() to create the desired lists. The stylesheet is as
follows:

```xslt
<xsl:stylesheet version="1.0"
  xmlns:xsl="http://www.w3.org/1999/XSL/Transform"
  xmlns:set="http://exslt.org/sets"
  extension-element-prefixes="set">

  <xsl:output method="text"/>

  <xsl:variable name="DramaFilms"
          select="//film[contains(@genre, 'Drama')]"/>
  <xsl:variable name="EpicFilms"
          select="//film[contains(@genre, 'Epic')]"/>
  <xsl:variable name="RomanticFilms"
          select="//film[contains(@genre, 'Romantic')]"/>

  <xsl:template match="/">
  --------------------------------
  Epic Dramas:
   <xsl:for-each select="set:intersection($DramaFilms,
          $EpicFilms)">
    * <xsl:value-of select="."/>
   </xsl:for-each>

  --------------------------------
  Non-Epic Dramas:
   <xsl:for-each select="set:difference($DramaFilms,
          $EpicFilms)">
    * <xsl:value-of select="."/>
   </xsl:for-each>

  --------------------------------
  Non-Drama Epics:
   <xsl:for-each
          select="set:difference($EpicFilms,$DramaFilms)">
    * <xsl:value-of select="."/>
   </xsl:for-each>

  --------------------------------
  Non-Romantic Dramas:
   <xsl:for-each select="set:difference($DramaFilms,
          $RomanticFilms)">
    * <xsl:value-of select="."/>
   </xsl:for-each>

  </xsl:template>

  <xsl:template match="film"/>

</xsl:stylesheet>
```

Looking closer at the extension functions that are used, the first xsl:for-each loop uses a set:intersection() function to return all the common nodes that have Drama and Epic strings as part of their genre value. However, the next xsl:for-each instruction uses the set:difference() function to return the nodes from the DramaFilms node set that are *not* part of the EpicFilms node set. The remaining xsl:for-each loops follow the same pattern to return the nodes desired.

When transformed by a processor that supports these extensions, the result is:

```
---------------------------------
Epic Dramas:

   * Gone With The Wind


---------------------------------
Non-Epic Dramas:

   * Citizen Kane
   * Casablanca
   * The Godfather
   * The Graduate
   * On The Waterfront
   * It's A Wonderful Life
   * Sunset Boulevard
   * Some Like It Hot
   * All About Eve
   * One Flew Over The Cuckoo's Nest
   * The Grapes Of Wrath
   * The Maltese Falcon


---------------------------------
Non-Drama Epics:

   * Schindler's List
   * Star Wars


---------------------------------
Non-Romantic Dramas:

   * Citizen Kane
   * The Godfather
   * Gone With The Wind
   * The Graduate
   * On The Waterfront
   * It's A Wonderful Life
   * Sunset Boulevard
   * Some Like It Hot
   * All About Eve
   * One Flew Over The Cuckoo's Nest
   * The Grapes Of Wrath
   * The Maltese Falcon
```

TIP

More extension functions are available than elements or attributes. Take a close look at the function set offered by EXSLT and processor vendors; these many extension functions can save you a considerable amount of time and effort when authoring stylesheets.

Ensuring Portability of Your Stylesheets

As I said from the get-go, because extension elements or functions are not part of the XSLT standard, their support depends entirely on the XSLT processor vendor. The obvious problem that can then surface is that, when you try to run your extension-laden stylesheet, the XSLT processor you're using may not support the extensions you're using. For example, if you try to run the `saxon:while` example earlier in the chapter using msxsl, you get a processing error saying that `saxon:while` is an unrecognized element.

Rather than allowing this error to occur, you need a fallback strategy, in the event that the stylesheet is run by a processor that doesn't support the extension. As I discuss in the following sections, you can add a fallback plan to your stylesheet and test for the support of extension elements or functions before they are processed as part of the stylesheet.

Testing extension elements

For extension elements, the first way in which you can handle unsupportive processors is to use the `xsl:fallback` element, which you can embed inside the extension element you're using. If the processor runs the extension successfully, then the `xsl:fallback` instruction is simply ignored. But suppose all heck breaks loose and the processing engine doesn't recognize the extension. When this event occurs, the processor executes the instructions provided inside `xsl:fallback`. If you add `xsl:fallback` to the `saxon:while` stylesheet shown earlier in this chapter, the stylesheet looks like this:

```
<xsl:stylesheet version="1.0"
  xmlns:xsl="http://www.w3.org/1999/XSL/Transform"
  xmlns:saxon="http://icl.com/saxon"
  extension-element-prefixes="saxon">

<xsl:template match="/">
  <xsl:variable name="idx" saxon:assignable="yes"
       select="1"/>
  <saxon:while test="$idx &lt; 11">
    The value of idx is <xsl:value-of select="$idx"/>
    <saxon:assign name="idx" select="$idx+1"/>
    <xsl:fallback>
```

```
        <xsl:message terminate="yes">XSLT processor does not
            support saxon:while extension.</xsl:message>
        </xsl:fallback>
    </saxon:while>

  </xsl:template>

</xsl:stylesheet>
```

In this case, if the processor doesn't support `saxon:while`, then an
`xsl:message` instruction is nestled inside `xsl:fallback`. When encountered, the `xsl:message` instruction sends its contents as a template to the
processor and its `terminate` attribute specifies whether or not the processor should stop processing. It is up to the processor to determine how it
wants to handle the `xsl:message` template; some may output it in the result
document, while others display a message box with the template contents.
Therefore, if the `xsl:fallback` instruction is executed, you know the processor does not support the extension.

A second way to determine whether or not an element is supported is by
using the `element-available()` built-in function. This function allows you
to test an extension element so that you can determine whether or not it is
supported before you try to call it. The typical scenario is to test it inside an
`xsl:choose` instruction, as shown here:

```
<xsl:stylesheet version="1.0"
  xmlns:xsl="http://www.w3.org/1999/XSL/Transform"
  xmlns:saxon="http://icl.com/saxon"
  extension-element-prefixes="saxon">

  <xsl:template match="/">
    <xsl:variable name="idx" saxon:assignable="yes"
        select="1"/>
    <xsl:choose>
      <xsl:when test="element-available('saxon:while')">
        <saxon:while test="$idx &lt; 11">
          The value of idx is <xsl:value-of select="$idx"/>
          <saxon:assign name="idx" select="$idx+1"/>
        </saxon:while>
      </xsl:when>
      <xsl:otherwise>
        Sorry, Charlie. No support here for while looping.
      </xsl:otherwise>
    </xsl:choose>
  </xsl:template>

</xsl:stylesheet>
```

In this example, `xsl:when` tests to determine whether `saxon:while` is an element that the processor can use. If so, then the processor executes the contents of `saxon:while`. If not, the `xsl:otherwise` element is used instead, adding the "Sorry, Charlie" literal text to the result document.

For most purposes, the choice of using `xsl:fallback` versus `element-available()` is personal preference. However, the one case in which `element-available()` is the more powerful option is when you want to test for multiple extension elements and, depending on which element is available, add a different result to the output.

For example, I can add an extra `xsl:when` to the preceding stylesheet to test to see if `msxsl:script` is available if `saxon:while` is not. The `xsl:choose` instruction would be changed to:

```
<xsl:choose>
  <xsl:when test="element-available('saxon:while')">
    <saxon:while test="$idx &lt; 11">
      The value of idx is <xsl:value-of select="$idx"/>
      <saxon:assign name="idx" select="$idx+1"/>
    </saxon:while>
  </xsl:when>
  <xsl:when test="element-available('msxsl:script')">
    <!-- run a script -->
  </xsl:when>
  <xsl:otherwise>
    Sorry, Charlie. No support here for while looping.
  </xsl:otherwise>
</xsl:choose>
```

When this stylesheet is applied, the XSLT processor first tests to see whether `saxon:while` is available. If not, then `msxsl:script` is tested. And if it is not available too, then `xsl:otherwise` is chosen.

Testing extension functions

Extension functions can be evaluated in a way eerily similar to the `element-available()` function described in the preceding section. The `function-available()` built-in function tests whether the processor supports a function. For example:

```
<xsl:stylesheet version="1.0"
  xmlns:xsl="http://www.w3.org/1999/XSL/Transform"
  xmlns:date="http://exslt.org/dates-and-times"
  extension-element-prefixes="date">

<xsl:template match="/">

  <xsl:choose>
```

```
    <xsl:when test="function-available( 'date:time' )">
       <xsl:value-of select="date:time()"/>
    </xsl:when>
    <xsl:otherwise>
       What do you think I am? A Timex?
    </xsl:otherwise>
   </xsl:choose>

 </xsl:template>

</xsl:stylesheet>
```

In this example, the xsl:when instruction checks to see if the date:time()
function is available. If the test returns true, then the function is run. But if
not, then the XSLT processor uses the xsl:otherwise element and outputs
its contents to the result document.

Even if you use a single XSLT processor, it is good programming practice to
add fallback code if you use extension elements in your stylesheets. Doing so
helps ensure that your stylesheets produce exactly the results you intend.

Chapter 17

Debugging XSLT Transformations

I have a confession to make: Yes, it may be hard to believe, but I *have* had bugs appear in my XSLT stylesheets before. Perhaps you have never had that happen before, and if so, then feel free to skip this chapter. But, if you're a mere mortal like me, read on. Knowing how to debug in XSLT is an important part of the stylesheet authoring process.

Debugging is one of those necessary evils of programming. It's not much fun, but it sure is necessary. Unfortunately, XSLT is not a language that lends itself to easy debugging. Besides the `xsl:message` element, there is little in the language that provides debugging support. Most of the time, debugging becomes a trial and error process consisting of modifying the stylesheet and then running the transformation. If the results aren't what you expect, then modify the XSLT and try again and again until everything works.

However, as you find out in this chapter, some XSLT debugging techniques are valuable tools that can help you track down problems.

 Got that deer in the headlights look? You may have if you've programmed in a traditional language and are trying to figure out how to debug XSLT. Debugging in a language like C, Java, or Visual Basic is relatively straightforward because you can intuitively see a program being executed line by line as you check the code. But exactly how XSLT is processed is far more opaque, often resembling the "man behind the curtain." But, as you begin to think in XSLT, this new process becomes second nature.

Conditionally Halting Execution

A debugging technique that can be worthwhile is to halt execution of your transformation when certain conditions occur at the time of processing. If those conditions occur, the processor can flag you with an `xsl:message` instruction and you can optionally decide whether or not to terminate processing.

Consider the `coffee.xml` source code in Listing 17-1.

Listing 17-1:   coffee.xml

```
<?xml version="1.0"?>
<coffees>
 <region name="Latin America">
  <coffee name="Guatemalan Express" origin="Guatemala">
    <taste>Mild and Bland</taste>
    <price>11.99</price>
    <availability>Year-round</availability>
    <bestwith>Breakfast</bestwith>
  </coffee>
  <coffee name="Costa Rican Deacon" origin="Costa Rica">
    <taste>Exotic and Untamed</taste>
    <price>12.99</price>
    <availability>Year-round</availability>
    <bestwith>Dessert</bestwith>
  </coffee>
 </region>
 <region name="Africa">
  <coffee name="Ethiopian Sunset Supremo" origin="Ethiopia">
    <taste>Exotic and Untamed</taste>
    <price>14.99</price>
    <availability>Limited</availability>
    <bestwith>Chocolate</bestwith>
  </coffee>
  <coffee name="Kenyan Elephantismo" origin="Kenya">
    <taste>Solid yet Understated</taste>
    <price>3.99</price>
    <availability>Year-round</availability>
    <bestwith>Elephant Ears</bestwith>
  </coffee>
 </region>
</coffees>
```

When I transform this source document, I want to check the price of each `coffee` element to be sure that the price is valid. If the price is below $6, then I want to stop the transformation, because a data error must have occurred. To set this up, I create a template rule for the `coffee` element:

```
<!-- Check price of coffee before continuing -->
<xsl:template match="coffee">
  <xsl:if test="price &lt; 6">
    <xsl:message terminate="yes">
      ERROR: Hold on there Tex. Price should never be under
         $6.00. Price for <xsl:value-of select="@name"/> is
         <xsl:value-of select="price"/>.
```

```
      </xsl:message>
    </xsl:if>
    <xsl:apply-templates select="price"/>
  </xsl:template>
```

Inside this template rule, I use an xsl:if instruction to test the price of coffee. If it is less than $6, then xsl:message gives the error text and stops the execution of the process.

The entire XSLT stylesheet is shown here:

```
    <xsl:stylesheet
         xmlns:xsl="http://www.w3.org/1999/XSL/Transform"
         version="1.0">

<!-- Check price of coffee before continuing -->
<xsl:template match="coffee">
  <xsl:if test="price &lt; 6">
    <xsl:message terminate="yes">
      ERROR: Hold on there Tex. Price should never be under
         $6.00. Price for <xsl:value-of select="@name"/> is
         <xsl:value-of select="price"/>.
    </xsl:message>
  </xsl:if>
  <xsl:apply-templates select="price"/>
</xsl:template>

<!-- Add new element -->
<xsl:template match="price">
  Today's price for <xsl:value-of select="../@name"/> is
       <xsl:value-of select="."/>
</xsl:template>

</xsl:stylesheet>
```

When this stylesheet is applied to the coffee.xml file (refer to Listing 17-1), the Kenyan Elephantismo coffee causes the xsl:if instruction to trigger, so the XSLT processor halts and reports the following error:

```
    ERROR: Hold on there Tex. Price should never be under
         $6.00. Price for Kenyan Elephantismo is 3.99.
```

Adding a Conditional Debug Mode

Many programming languages have a way to run a program in debug mode, which is typically used as a way to obtain additional information about run-time conditions (conditions at the time the transformation occurs). You can add this kind of debug code to your stylesheet, but before you can use it for production, you have to either remove the debug instructions or else comment them out, both of which are inefficient and may lead to the introduction of other, unexpected bugs.

However, you can add a debug mode to your stylesheets and have the debug code conditionally execute without modifying the stylesheet itself. An xsl:param element is the element of choice for this task, because XSLT allows you to specify its value outside the stylesheet at the time you're performing the transformation.

To do so, set up your stylesheet by defining a parameter named debug that is given the value of off:

```
<xsl:param name="debug">off</xsl:param>
```

xsl:choose is a good instruction to add to your stylesheet for testing the value of the debug parameter. If it has the value of 'on', then perform the debug instructions in xsl:when, if not, then execute the regular xsl:otherwise instructions:

```
<xsl:choose>
  <xsl:when test="$debug = 'on'">
    <!-- If debug is on, do this -->
  </xsl:when>
  <xsl:otherwise>
    <!-- Otherwise, do this -->
  </xsl:otherwise>
</xsl:choose>
```

Consider the following use of a conditional debug mode. When debug mode is on, I output a lot of extra debugging information to the result document. Specifically, I add a debugdata element prior to the rest of the result. I stuff this element with debugging information. I also nest the whole result document in a debugmode element and nest the normal results inside a document element. Further, I add a conditional test to ensure that the processedby parameter is specified. The stylesheet is provided here:

```
<xsl:stylesheet
    xmlns:xsl="http://www.w3.org/1999/XSL/Transform"
    version="1.0">

<xsl:param name="debug">off</xsl:param>
<xsl:param name="processedby">none</xsl:param>

<!-- Test for Debug mode -->
<xsl:template match="/">

  <!-- Force a processedby param to be specified -->
  <xsl:if test="$processedby = 'none'">
    <xsl:message terminate="yes">No processedby parameter
        specified. Unable to continue.</xsl:message>
  </xsl:if>
```

```
      <xsl:choose>
        <!-- If debug is on, then add extra debug info -->
        <xsl:when test="$debug = 'on'">
          <debugmode>
            <xsl:comment>*** Debug Mode - For Testing Purposes
            Only ***</xsl:comment>
            <debugdata>
              <processedby><xsl:value-of
              select="$processedby"/></processedby>
              <namespace-uri><xsl:value-of select="namespace-
              uri()"/></namespace-uri>
              <regioncount><xsl:value-of
              select="count(//region)"/></regioncount>
              <coffeecount><xsl:value-of
              select="count(//coffee)"/></coffeecount>
            </debugdata>
            <document>
            <xsl:apply-templates/>
            </document>
          </debugmode>
        </xsl:when>
        <!-- If debug is off, process as normal -->
        <xsl:otherwise>
          <xsl:apply-templates/>
        </xsl:otherwise>
      </xsl:choose>
    </xsl:template>

    <!-- Copy everything else over -->
    <xsl:template match="@*|node()">
      <xsl:copy>
        <xsl:apply-templates select="@*|node()"/>
      </xsl:copy>
    </xsl:template>

    <!-- Add new element -->
    <xsl:template match="coffee">
      <coffee>
        <xsl:apply-templates/>
        <discountprice><xsl:value-of select="format-number(
            price*.8, '##.##' )"/></discountprice>
      </coffee>
    </xsl:template>

</xsl:stylesheet>
```

When I specify the debug parameter to be on at process time (see Chapter 8 to find out about how to do this), I get the following result:

```
<?xml version="1.0" encoding="utf-8"?>
<debugmode>
  <!--*** Debug Mode - For Testing Purposes Only ***-->
```

```
    <debugdata>
      <processedby>$processedby</processedby>
      <namespace-uri/>
      <regioncount>2</regioncount>
      <coffeecount>4</coffeecount>
    </debugdata>
    <document>
<coffees>
  <region name="Latin America">
  <coffee>
    <taste>Mild and Bland</taste>
    <price>11.99</price>
    <availability>Year-round</availability>
    <bestwith>Breakfast</bestwith>
  <discountprice>9.59</discountprice></coffee>
  <coffee>
    <taste>Exotic and Untamed</taste>
    <price>12.99</price>
    <availability>Year-round</availability>
    <bestwith>Dessert</bestwith>
  <discountprice>10.39</discountprice></coffee>
  </region>
  <region name="Africa">
  <coffee>
    <taste>Exotic and Untamed</taste>
    <price>14.99</price>
    <availability>Limited</availability>
    <bestwith>Chocolate</bestwith>
  <discountprice>11.99</discountprice></coffee>
  <coffee>
    <taste>Solid yet Understated</taste>
    <price>3.99</price>
    <availability>Year-round</availability>
    <bestwith>Elephant Ears</bestwith>
  <discountprice>3.19</discountprice></coffee>
  </region>
</coffees>
        </document>
</debugmode>
```

Tracing through Your Code

Outside a full-scale debugger, the best way to obtain detailed information about how the XSLT processor is transforming your XML document is to trace through each of the transformation steps. *Tracing* is a debugging technique that gives you a step-by-step account of the transformation taking place. XSLT itself has no support for stepping through your stylesheet like this, but many XSLT processors add tracing as a feature. Take, for example, the SAXON processor. It has a specific option that you can turn on to output

tracing information. So, suppose I apply the following stylesheet to the
`coffee.xml` document shown in Listing 17-1:

```
<xsl:stylesheet
        xmlns:xsl="http://www.w3.org/1999/XSL/Transform"
        version="1.0">
<xsl:template match="coffees">
  <coffees>
    <xsl:apply-templates/>
  </coffees>
</xsl:template>

<!-- Add new element -->
<xsl:template match="coffee">
  <coffee>
    <xsl:apply-templates/>
    <discountprice><xsl:value-of select="format-number(
        price*.8, '##.##' )"/></discountprice>
  </coffee>
</xsl:template>
</xsl:stylesheet>
```

When I run the SAXON processor from a command line, I can turn trace support on by specifying the `-T` option:

```
saxon -T -o c:\output.txt coffee.xml coffee_tracer.xsl
```

In addition to generating the normal result document, the processor also
spits out the following tracing information to the command line. Notice that
the information is captured in an XML structure, so you can analyze it by
using your XML and XSLT tools if you want:

```
<trace>
<Top-level element="xsl:template" line="3"
           file="file:/C:/Xslt/coffee_tracer.xsl"
           precedence="0"/>
<Top-level element="xsl:template" line="10"
           file="file:/C:/Xslt/coffee_tracer.xsl"
           precedence="0"/>
<Source node="/coffees[1]" line="2" mode="*default*">
 <Instruction element="xsl:template" line="3">
  <Instruction element="coffees" line="4">
   <Instruction element="xsl:apply-templates" line="5">
    <Source node="/coffees[1]/region[1]/coffee[1]" line="4"
           mode="*default*">
     <Instruction element="xsl:template" line="10">
      <Instruction element="coffee" line="11">
       <Instruction element="xsl:apply-templates" line="12">
       </Instruction> <!-- xsl:apply-templates -->
       <Instruction element="discountprice" line="13">
        <Instruction element="xsl:value-of" line="13">
        </Instruction> <!-- xsl:value-of -->
```

```
      </Instruction> <!-- discountprice -->
     </Instruction> <!-- coffee -->
    </Instruction> <!-- xsl:template -->
   </Source><!-- /coffees[1]/region[1]/coffee[1] -->
   <Source node="/coffees[1]/region[1]/coffee[2]" line="10"
          mode="*default*">
   <Instruction element="xsl:template" line="10">
    <Instruction element="coffee" line="11">
     <Instruction element="xsl:apply-templates" line="12">
     </Instruction> <!-- xsl:apply-templates -->
     <Instruction element="discountprice" line="13">
      <Instruction element="xsl:value-of" line="13">
      </Instruction> <!-- xsl:value-of -->
     </Instruction> <!-- discountprice -->
    </Instruction> <!-- coffee -->
   </Instruction> <!-- xsl:template -->
   </Source><!-- /coffees[1]/region[1]/coffee[2] -->
   <Source node="/coffees[1]/region[2]/coffee[1]" line="18"
          mode="*default*">
   <Instruction element="xsl:template" line="10">
    <Instruction element="coffee" line="11">
     <Instruction element="xsl:apply-templates" line="12">
     </Instruction> <!-- xsl:apply-templates -->
     <Instruction element="discountprice" line="13">
      <Instruction element="xsl:value-of" line="13">
      </Instruction> <!-- xsl:value-of -->
     </Instruction> <!-- discountprice -->
    </Instruction> <!-- coffee -->
   </Instruction> <!-- xsl:template -->
   </Source><!-- /coffees[1]/region[2]/coffee[1] -->
   <Source node="/coffees[1]/region[2]/coffee[2]" line="24"
          mode="*default*">
   <Instruction element="xsl:template" line="10">
    <Instruction element="coffee" line="11">
     <Instruction element="xsl:apply-templates" line="12">
     </Instruction> <!-- xsl:apply-templates -->
     <Instruction element="discountprice" line="13">
      <Instruction element="xsl:value-of" line="13">
      </Instruction> <!-- xsl:value-of -->
     </Instruction> <!-- discountprice -->
    </Instruction> <!-- coffee -->
   </Instruction> <!-- xsl:template -->
   </Source><!-- /coffees[1]/region[2]/coffee[2] -->
   </Instruction> <!-- xsl:apply-templates -->
  </Instruction> <!-- coffees -->
 </Instruction> <!-- xsl:template -->
</Source><!-- /coffees[1] -->
</trace>
```

More Powerful Debugging

If you are having a particular problem in which nothing else you have tried works, then you may want to consider getting a full-scale XSLT debugger. You can find debuggers with:

- ✔ Full visual step-through capabilities to allow you to see and perform a transformation one step at a time.
- ✔ Breakpoint support to stop the transformation at a specific point so you can check its status.
- ✔ Parameter and variable "watches" to find out their current value during the processing of a document.

Two of particular note are commercial software tools, though they have trial versions that you can download:

- ✔ **MarrowSoft Xselerator:** `www.marrowsoft.com/Products.htm`
- ✔ **eXcelon Stylus:** `www.exceloncorp.com/products/ excelon_stylus.html`

For more tool information, one good Web site to check out is `www.xslt.com/xslt_tools_editors.html`.

Part V
The Part of Tens

In this part . . .

David Letterman has his Top Ten List and Agatha Christie has her *Ten Little Indians*. But *For Dummies* books have The Part of Tens. In this part, you get tips and resources that will make your life easier as you work with XSLT. Get the lowdown on ten confusing things about XSLT. I also include the ten best XSLT resources and processors available on the Web.

Chapter 18

Ten Most Confusing Things About XSLT

XSLT may be logically structured, but it sure does have some peculiarities that can leave you scratching your head if you don't consider them as you create your stylesheets.

Built-In Template: The Man Behind the Screen

A built-in template rule is like the man behind the screen in the *Wizard of Oz* — it takes action, but if you don't realize it, you'll be confused about what happened and why.

The XSLT processor uses built-in template rules to process any node that is not matched with a template rule you explicitly define in your stylesheet. Each node type has different built-in template rules that are applied to it:

- ✔ Element nodes have a built-in template that changes child nodes everywhere (children of both the current and root nodes) by removing their tags but preserving their content.

- ✔ Text and attribute nodes have a built-in template rule that copies their text straight into the result tree.

- ✔ Processing instructions, comments, and namespaces have a built-in template rule that strips them from the result document.

See Chapter 4 for more information on built-in templates.

Thar's Trees in Them Documents

Always keep in mind that an XSLT processor doesn't read an XML document sequentially — one tag at a time — as you or I do; instead, the processor treats the source like a tree-like structure of hierarchical information. Within that tree, relationships among the various parts dictate how the processor reads and navigates the document during the transformation process.

Each XML document has a main document element that contains all the other elements inside its open and close tags. An `xsl:stylesheet` element, for example, contains template rules and all other parts of an XSLT stylesheet, so it acts as the document element of an XSLT stylesheet. Child elements of the document element are the equivalent of the first-level branches of a tree. These child elements may also have children, much like smaller branches. The XSLT processor works its way through the entire tree until it retrieves each leaf and branch and assembles it based on this hierarchy.

Each leaf and branch in the document tree is called a node. Elements are the most common type of node that you work with, but there are actually seven different node types: element, attribute, namespace, processing instruction, comment, and text. With that in mind, an element node has children not only when it contains other elements, but also when it contains attributes and text.

If you want more information on document trees, check out Chapter 3.

Getting to the Root of the Issue

At first glance, you may naturally look at the following XML snippet and conclude that `animals` is the root node of this document tree:

```
<animals>
  <cats>
    <tigers/>
    <lions/>
    <tabby/>
  </cats>
  <dogs>
    <collie/>
    <doberman/>
  </dogs>
</animals>
```

Although animals is the highest level element (known as the *document element*), it is not the root node. The root node is a "built-in" node and automatically serves as the ancestor of all nodes in the document tree. You never actually see the root node show up in your document — it's just there; a given. Therefore, in the preceding example, animals is a child of the root node.

To demonstrate, the following template rule uses / to retrieve the root node:

```
<xsl:template match="/">
<!-- Do something -->
</xsl:template>
```

When run on the preceding XML snippet, the animals element is not returned, but the root above it in the tree hierarchy.

Why the Selected Node Is Not the Same as the Current Node

The *current node* (or *context node*) of a document tree is the node that the XSLT processor is "on" during its walk through the tree. However, don't confuse the current node with the selected node or nodes. The current node is the starting point for the XSLT processor for a given location step (an XPath expression used to retrieve nodes from a source tree), but it is the location step that actually determines what node or set of nodes is actually selected.

Those //@.3* Abbreviations

XPath allows you to use abbreviations to write the axis part of a location step. These shortcuts enable you to write XPath expressions more quickly, but they can also be confusing until you learn the clipped syntax. The ones to memorize appear in Table 18-1.

Table 18-1	XPath Abbreviations
Axis	*Abbreviation*
`child::`	Doesn't need to be explicitly defined, so you can leave it off.
`attribute::`	`@`
`self::node()`	`.` (single period)
`parent::node()`	`..` (double period)
`/descendant-or-self::node()/`	`//`

For more information on axes, see Chapter 5.

To Apply or Copy, That Is the Question

When you create result trees, you may not be sure when to use `xsl:apply-templates`, `xsl:copy`, `xsl:copy-of`, `xsl:value-of`, and other XSLT instructions inside your template rules. The following guidelines can help you decide what to do:

- Use `xsl:apply-templates` when you want to return the content and text nodes of the current element and its children, but not the surrounding element tags.

- Use `xsl:copy` to preserve the current node's start and end tags during processing, but not its children or attributes. Content inside the tags is included only if you add an `xsl:apply-templates` instruction inside the `xsl:copy` element.

- Use `xsl:copy-of` when you want to copy the whole kit 'n caboodle — the current node's tags, content, attributes, and children. This instruction copies all the nodes returned from its required `select` attribute.

- Use `xsl:value-of` when you want to convert the result to text. The conversion process removes all tags and elements. If the result is a single node, its content is converted to text. If the result is a node set, the first node in the set is used in the conversion.

I explain these instructions fully in Chapter 4.

Walk This Way

When the XSLT processor walk the tree to select nodes, the axis part of the location step specifies the direction in which the processor walks. Each of the following axes goes top-to-bottom, left-to-right, much like you read a page in this book: `child`, `self`, `parent`, `descendant`, `following-sibling`, `following`, and `descendant-or-self`. The remaining axes — `ancestor`, `ancestor-or-self`, `preceding`, and `preceding-sibling` — travel in reverse order. Finally, when working with `attribute` and `namespace` axes, the nodes are always unordered.

Chapter 5 gives you more information on axis values.

Expressions, Paths, and Steps

XPath is used to create expressions, but some types of expressions are more important to XSLT than others. In a generic sense, an *expression* is a string of XPath instructions that the XSLT processor evaluates to produce a result, which may be a number, string, Boolean value, or a node set. However, XSLT is most interested in a particular kind of expression called a *location path*, which is a set of instructions that specify what nodes to bring back to the XSLT stylesheet. The location path then consists of a series of smaller parts called location steps. A *location step* consists of an axis, a node test, and an optional predicate and takes the following form: `axis::nodetest[predicate]`.

Check out Chapter 5 for more details on XPath expressions.

Those Cute Little Curly Braces

Curly braces are used in attribute value templates to tell the XSLT processor to evaluate what's inside each of them as an expression, rather than as normal text. In the output tree, the curly braces and expression are replaced with a resulting string. However, keep in mind that curly braces only evaluate expressions inside attribute values, not outside them.

Consider the following XML snippet:

```
<film name="Henry V">
    <director>Kenneth Branagh</director>
    <runtime>137</runtime>
</film>
```

Suppose I want to transform the preceding source by using the following XSLT code:

```
<xsl:template match="film">

  <!-- Curly braces work inside of attributes -->
  <movie director="{director}" length="{runtime}"/>
  <movie newlength="{100+60}"/>

  <!-- Curly braces do not work here -->
  The director is {director} and length is {runtime} and
        newlength is {100+60}

  <!-- Instead, use xsl:value-of outside of attributes -->
  The director is <xsl:value-of select="director"/> and
        length is <xsl:value-of select="runtime"/> and
        newlength is <xsl:value-of select="100+60"/>
  <xsl:apply-templates/>
</xsl:template>

<xsl:template match="director"/>
<xsl:template match="runtime"/>
```

The result is:

```
<movie director="Kenneth Branagh" length="137" /><movie
        newlength="160" />
  The director is {director} and length is {runtime}
  The director is Kenneth Branagh and length is 137 and
        newlength is 160
```

In looking at the transformation, notice that the first part of the template surrounds the element name with curly braces to return the value of the director and runtime elements inside attribute values. In this context, XPath then evaluates director and runtime as element names rather than as plain text. Similarly, XPath evaluates 100+60 as an expression.

The second part of the template shows what happens when you try to use curly braces outside attribute values. These are simply treated as literal text in the output document.

The final part of the template illustrates how you use xsl:value-of to evaluate the same XPath expressions outside attribute values.

See Chapter 4 for more information on attribute value templates.

Whitespace, the Final Frontier

You need to think about several factors as you consider whitespace in your result document, because whitespace has origins in both your XSLT stylesheet and the underlying XML source document.

Inside the XSLT stylesheet, whitespace is usually stripped out of the template before any transformation occurs. However, whitespace is preserved in the following cases:

- ✓ Text nodes that contain nonwhitespace characters.
- ✓ Any whitespace text appearing inside a xsl:text element.
- ✓ When the closest ancestor of a text node has an xml:space attribute with the value of preserve.

Whitespace inside the source XML document follows similar rules, except that you can declare default whitespace rules by using the xsl:preserve-space or xsl:strip-space instructions. Therefore, any text node that occurs inside the range of xsl:preserve-space is preserved.

See Chapter 13 for more details on whitespace.

Chapter 19

Ten All-Pro XSLT Resources on the Web

*W*eb sites are constantly coming and going, but the ten listed here are considered staples for the budding XSLT developer.

Xslt.com

www.xslt.com

This site is perhaps the best all-around site for XSLT. It is a great place to go to get information about the latest XSLT engines, editors, and various utilities. The site also has links to several Web-based tutorials covering all aspects of learning XSLT. Further, you can get information on XSLT-related jobs and events.

W3C XSLT Recommendation

www.w3.org/TR/xslt

This site is the official XSLT standard. Everything in XSLT Land must conform to this document. You'll find a lot of techno-speak, but this site can be helpful as a reference for the nitty-gritty details of XSLT.

W3C XPath Recommendation

www.w3.org/TR/xpath

This site is the official XPath standard. Like the XSLT recommendation, this document has a lot of techno-speak, but you may find it helpful as a reference.

Dave Pawson's XSLT FAQ

www.dpawson.co.uk

In addition to its FAQs, this site also has sections on Things XSLT Can't Do, Special Characters, XSLT Terminology, Where to Start, FO Questions, External Issues, and Extension Issues. Be aware that this site is suited more for XSLT geeks, but you can glean some useful information here.

W3School's XSL School

www.w3schools.com/xsl/default.asp

The W3School's Web site gives you an easy-to-understand online introduction to XSLT and language reference. You will want to bookmark this Web site when you need quick access to an online XSLT language reference.

MSDN's XML Center

```
http://msdn.microsoft.com/xml
```

Although Microsoft-centric, the XML Center, which is part of the Microsoft Developer Network, contains good resources and articles for using XSLT, typically in combination with Microsoft technologies. Go to the XML Center and navigate to the XSLT-related resources.

Xml101.com

```
www.xml101.com/xsl/
```

XML101's XSLT Tutorial offers useful examples of how to use XSLT for practical solutions. Its tutorials on using XSLT on the client and on the server are especially noteworthy.

Jeni's XSLT Pages

```
www.jenitennison.com/xslt/index.html
```

This site is geared for advanced XSLT developers, with a lot of useful information in the form of mail archives. But if you sift through the correspondence, you can find extremely useful tips and techniques.

TopXML: XSLT Reference

```
www.vbxml.com/xsl/xsltref.asp
```

The most interesting and useful part of this site is a chart of XSLT elements and their support in the W3C XSLT Recommendation versions, MSXML versions, and more.

Nic Miloslav's XSLT Tutorial

zvon.org/xxl/XSLTutorial/Books/Book1/index.html

This online XSLT tutorial has interesting examples scattered throughout. The tutorial is more of a survey-like format, but it does provide a good overview of XSLT functionality.

Chapter 20

Ten XSLT Processors
Available Online

*A*n XSLT processor is the engine that applies an XSLT stylesheet to a source XML document to produce a result document. You can purchase commercial versions of XSLT processors, but many free versions, which are available on the Web, can serve common uses you need. I highlight ten of the most popular in this chapter and note those that are easily downloadable as a Windows executable (.exe file).

Saxon

saxon.sourceforge.net

One of the most popular and easy-to-use processors available, Saxon is a W3C-compliant processor that comes in two forms: Full Saxon and Instant Saxon. Full Saxon includes Java source code, API documentation, and related resources. Instant Saxon is a Windows executable version (without source code) and is the one you'll generally want to use.

Saxon includes a wealth of extension functions and elements to supplement the core XSLT language. (See Chapter 16 for more information on extensions.)

Saxon is an Open Source project, which means that its source code is freely available for anyone that conforms to its license agreement.

Available as a Windows executable.

msxsl

```
msdn.microsoft.com/downloads/default.asp?url=/downloads/
          sample.asp?url=/msdn-files/027/001/766/
                msdncompositedoc.xml
```

msxsl does not provide support for extensions at this time. However, because Microsoft is a strong supporter of XML and XSLT technologies, I suspect you will see strong support for msxsl by Microsoft as well as see continued improvements in its capabilities in the future.

Available as a Windows executable.

Sablotron

```
www.gingerall.com/charlie/ga/xml/p_sab.xml
```

Sablotron is a W3C-compliant processor that runs on multiple platforms, including Windows, Linux, FreeBSD, and more. Sablotron has a rich library of XSLT extensions.

Available as a Windows executable.

Sablotron is available as an Open Source project as well, so you have the option of downloading its C++ source code.

Xalan-C++

xml.apache.org/xalan-c/

Xalan-C++ is a W3C compliant XSLT processor written in C++. It runs on multiple platforms, including Windows, Linux, and Solaris. Xalan provides a rich library of extensions.

Along with many of the others, Xalan is Open Source and includes source code.

Available as a Windows executable.

Xalan-Java

xml.apache.org/xalan-j/

Xalan-Java is a Java-based W3C compliant XSLT processor. You can use it from the command line, in an applet or a servlet, or as a module in another program. As with the C++ version, Xalan-Java has a library of extensions.

LotusXSL

www.alphaworks.ibm.com/tech/LotusXSL

This is a Java-based W3C compliant XSLT processor brought to you by the folks from IBM/Lotus.

XT

www.jclark.com/xml/xt.html

This Java-based XSLT processor can be run as a Java application, or you can also download it as a Windows executable (.exe) for easier running on Windows systems.

Available as a Windows executable.

jd.xslt

www.aztecrider.com/xslt

Another Java-based XSLT processor. Open Source.

XML::XSLT

sourceforge.net/projects/perl-xslt

An XSLT processor, written in Perl, that fully implements the W3C XSLT recommendation.

libxslt

xmlsoft.org/XSLT/intro.html

An XSLT processor written in C that works under Linux, Unix, and Windows.

Glossary

· ·

attribute value template: Refers to the use of an XPath expression as the value of an attribute in a result tree. This expression is located inside a template and surrounded by curly braces ({}). For example, in the following code snippet, {saleprice} is the attribute value template:

```
<xsl:template match="book">
  <book price="{saleprice}"
  <xsl:apply-templates/>
</xsl:template>
```

axis: Part of an XPath location step, the axis specifies the relationship of the selected node to the context node. For example, parent is the axis in the following location step: parent::book. The 13 possible axes are as follows: child, descendant, parent, ancestor, following-sibling, preceding-sibling, following-sibling, following, preceding, attribute, namespace, descendant-or-self, and ancestor-or-self.

built-in template rules: Used to process any node that is not matched with an explicitly defined template rule in your stylesheet. Each of the node types has a specific built-in template rule that is applied to it.

context node: The node in the source tree that the XSLT processor is handling. For example, in a template rule, the context node is typically the node that is returned by the pattern. You can think of the context node as the selected node, except when you are using an axis value (other than self) that redirects the selection elsewhere.

current node: See *context node*.

document tree: See *tree*.

element: XSLT elements are the core building blocks of the XSLT language. There are 35 built-in elements, such as xsl:template and xsl:apply-templates.

expression: An XSLT statement that represents a value or is used to calculate a value. The result of an expression can be a number, string, Boolean value, or a set of nodes. The following are valid expressions: 8-5, 'Text', and round(5.129).

extension: An element or function that you include in your XSLT stylesheet but that is not part of the standard XSLT language specification. Extensions come in handy when you need XSLT to do something that the language doesn't already support.

HTML: The publishing language of the Web and the format of Web pages.

instantiate: A techno-term that means to add an instance of a template to the result tree.

instruction: A term for an XSLT element that is used within a template rule for creating parts of the result tree.

key: You use a key to implicitly cross-reference documents. The `xsl:key` element declares a key.

leaf: A node that has no children (nodes underneath it) in a tree structure.

literal result element: Within a template, any elements that are not part of its namespace (`xsl:`) are treated as literal text when added to the result tree. The XSLT processor takes no action on the element and so it comes through unchanged. For example, `<h1>` is considered a literal result element in the following snippet:

```
<xsl:template match="book">
  <h1>
  <xsl:apply-templates/>
  </h1>
</xsl:template>
```

location path: An XPath expression that is composed of one or more location steps separated by slashes. For example, `child:book/sibling:chapter` is a location path with two location steps (`child:book` and `sibling:chapter`).

location step: The basic building block for XPath patterns. It is an XPath expression used by XSLT to tell the processor what node set to bring back from a source tree. Each location step consists of an axis, a node test, and an optional predicate and takes the following form: `axis::nodetest[predicate]`.

markup language: A language, such as HTML, XML, or XSLT, that uses labels enclosed in angle brackets to describe elements of a document.

match pattern: An XPath expression that declares the conditions that a node must meet in order for an action to take place on it. A match pattern always returns a node set. By far, the most common use of patterns is in an `xsl:template`, in which the value of its match attribute is a pattern. For example, in `<xsl:template match="child:book">`, the `child:book` expression inside of the quotes is the pattern. In an XSLT template rule, a pattern contains a location path.

named template: An xsl:template element that has a name attribute declared. Template rules normally have a match attribute declared so that when the XSLT processor encounters them, they are processed immediately based on this match pattern. In contrast, a named template does not have a match attribute in it, and so another template or instruction using xsl:call-template must explicitly call a named template.

namespace: A unique label that you assign a group of elements. This label is then associated with a particular URI, and an XML or XSLT processor uses the label to identify this collection of elements. For example, XSLT stylesheets use the URI http://www.w3.org/1999/XSL/Transform and, by convention, assign this URI to an xsl: namespace.

name-value pair: A term used to describe an attribute and its corresponding value. For example, in <book id="1020">, id is the attribute name and 1020 is its value. Together, they form a name-value pair.

node: A single point on a document tree. A node can be one of six types: element node, attribute node, text node, processing instruction node, comment node, or namespace node.

node set: An unsorted collection of unique nodes.

node test: Part of a location step, a node test identifies the nodes in the axis that meet the conditions of the test. For example, in the location step parent:book, book is the node test.

parameter: Like a variable, a parameter is an XSLT element that can represent a value. However, unlike variables, parameters have the added flexibility of being able to change their values when the XSLT stylesheet is processed. A parameter is defined with the xsl:parameter element. See also *variable*.

pattern: See *match pattern*.

predicate: An optional filter for a location step. If used, it is the final part of a location step that filters out some of the nodes returned by the axis and node test parts. For example, in the location step "book[@date="1956"]", the book node test returns all the nodes with the value of book. The predicate [@date="1956"] then filters out all nodes except those with date attributes that equal 1956. Predicates are always enclosed in square brackets.

processor directive: Information in an XML or XSLT structure that instructs the processor. For example, the xsl:strip-space element tells the processor what to do with whitespace when processing an XSLT document.

QName: A *qualified name* that consists of an optional namespace and a required local part. For example, in xsl:variable, the xsl: is the namespace prefix and variable is the local part. Together they compose a QName.

result document: The product of an XSL transformation that is written out as a file. See also *result tree.*

result tree: The product or output of an XSL transformation represented in a tree-like structure. A result tree is then usually written to a file, the result document.

result tree fragment: Represents a subsection of the result tree.

root node: The mother of all nodes, the root node is the ancestor of all nodes in a document tree. Note that this is not the same node as the highest level element of your document, such as an `xsl:stylesheet` element. Instead, the highest level element of your document tree is always the child of the root node.

stylesheet: A document that contains transformation instructions. By convention, an XSLT stylesheet has an .xsl extension.

template: The part of a template rule that defines how the returning node set is output to a result tree. See also *template rule.*

template rule: The major component of an XSLT stylesheet and is defined with the `xsl:template` element. It provides both input and output instructions. For input, its `match` attribute provides a pattern that specifies what node set to use. For output, it contains instructions on how to add a node and its contents to a result tree. People often confuse the terms *template* and *template rule*, but a template rule is the entire `xsl:template` element, while the template is the contents of the element (in other words, what's inside the start and end tags).

top-level element: Any element that is a child of the document element. For example, in an XSLT template, any element directly under `xsl:stylesheet` is considered a top-level element. The nine top-level XSLT elements are: `xsl:import, xsl:include, xsl:strip-space, xsl:preserve-space, xsl:output, xsl:key, xsl:decimal-format, xsl:namespace-alias, xsl:attribute-set, xsl:variable, xsl:param,` and `xsl:template`.

tree: XSLT views an XML document as a hierarchical tree, much like you may think of an ancestral family tree as a way of representing a family lineage. A tree is composed of nodes, each of which may or may not contain additional nodes. To describe relationships between nodes, XSLT uses family terminology, such as *parent, child,* and *sibling.*

URI: The way in which resources on the Web are named. The most common URIs are Web addresses (`http://www.dummies.com`), which are also known as URLs.

variable: An XSLT element that can represent a value and is defined with the `xsl:variable` element. For example, the variable `<xsl:variable name="myname">Rich</xsl:variable>` is named `myname` and has the string value of `Rich`.

W3C: The primary international body that governs Internet standards.

well-formed: A well-formed document is one that is syntactically correct; in other words, every begin tag has a matching end tag. For example:

```
<book id="10101">War and Peace</book>
```

XML: A markup language that enables you to define elements that describe the data they contain.

XPath: The language used by XSLT to describe how to locate nodes in a source XML document. Think of XPath as the spy or commando who is charged with going into an XML document and picking out the requested information for XSLT.

XSL: The markup language charged with styling, laying out, or transforming XML documents into a form that makes sense to its intended audience. XSL is composed of two independent parts: XSLT for transforming XML from one structure to another; and XSL Formatting Objects and Formatting Properties for formatting XML documents.

XSLT: A language used to transform XML documents into other XML documents or formats.

XSLT processor: Software that applies an XSLT stylesheet to a source XML document to produce a result document.

Index

Notes

Notes